FOR ORGANS, PIANOS & ELECTRONIC KEYBOARDS

98

FLOWER POWER

ISBN 978-1-4768-7165-3

7777 W. BLUEMOUND RD. P.O. BOX 13819 MILWAUKEE, WI 53213

Visit Hal Leonard Online at
www.halleonard.com

CONTENTS

4 Abraham, Martin and John

8 All You Need Is Love

11 Aquarius

14 Bad, Bad Leroy Brown

20 (It's a) Beautiful Morning

24 Blowin' in the Wind

17 Born to Be Wild

26 Both Sides Now

28 Brand New Key

31 Brown Eyed Girl

34 Bus Stop

37 California Dreamin'

40 California Girls

43 Carrie-Anne

46 Cat's in the Cradle

51 Daydream

54 Daydream Believer

57 Everyday People

60 The 59th Street Bridge Song (Feelin' Groovy)

62 Gimme Some Lovin'

65 Good Morning Starshine

68 Good Vibrations

71 Groovin'

74 Hang On Sloopy

80 Happy Together

77 He Ain't Heavy, He's My Brother

82 How Can I Be Sure

90 I'd Like to Teach the World to Sing

87 Imagine

92 Incense and Peppermints

96 It Never Rains in Southern California

99 Joy to the World

102 Leaving on a Jet Plane

108 Lucy in the Sky with Diamonds

105 Magic Carpet Ride

112 Me and You and a Dog Named Boo

118 Mellow Yellow

122 Mr. Tambourine Man

124 Monday, Monday

126 Morning Has Broken

115 New World Coming

130 The Night They Drove Old Dixie Down

133 Oh Happy Day

138 One Toke Over the Line

144 People Got to Be Free

146 Pleasant Valley Sunday

150 San Francisco (Be Sure to Wear
Some Flowers in Your Hair)

141 (Sittin' on) The Dock of the Bay

152 Stoned Soul Picnic (Picnic, a Green City)

156 Summer Breeze

160 Summer in the City

162 Sunshine Superman

165 Teach Your Children

168 Those Were the Days

170 Time in a Bottle

172 Turn! Turn! Turn! (To Everything
There Is a Season)

174 Up, Up and Away

180 Where Have All the Flowers Gone?

177 A Whiter Shade of Pale

182 Wild Thing

184 REGISTRATION GUIDE

Abraham, Martin and John

Registration 8
Rhythm: Pops or Rock

Words and Music by
Richard Holler

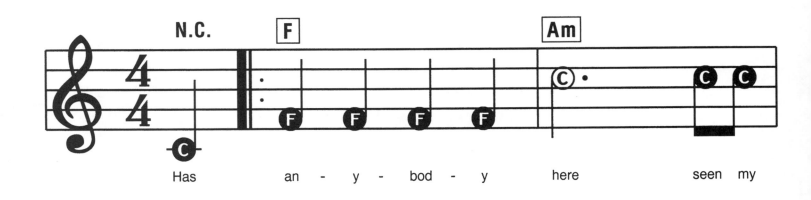

Has an-y-bod-y here seen my

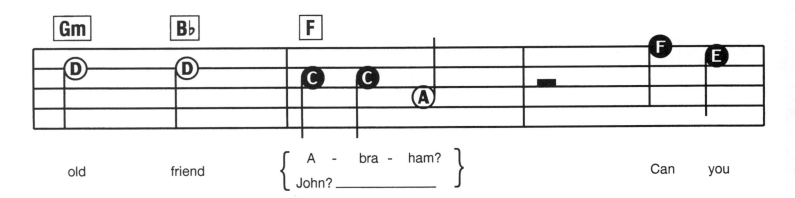

old friend { A - bra - ham? / John? } Can you

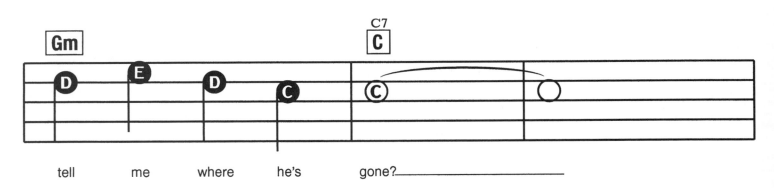

tell me where he's gone?

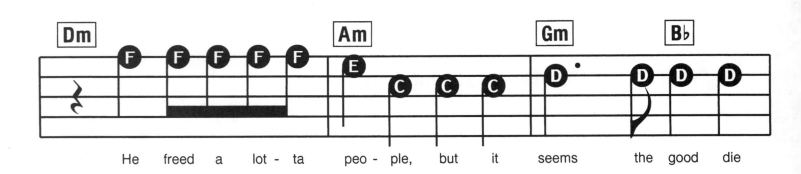

He freed a lot-ta peo-ple, but it seems the good die

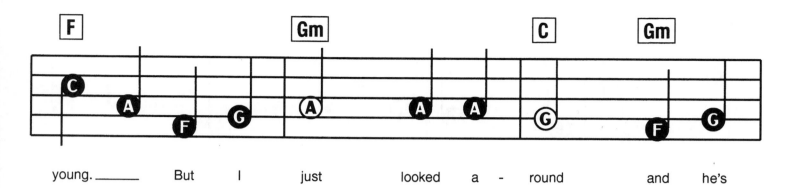

young. _____ But I just looked a - round and he's

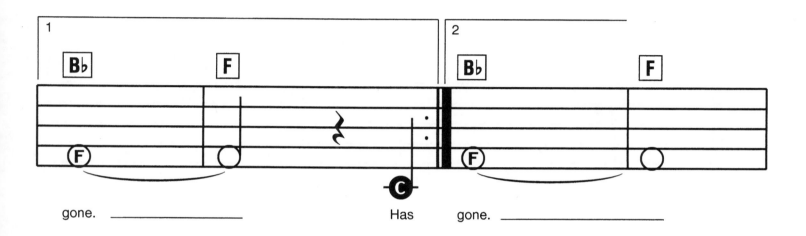

gone. _____ Has gone. _____

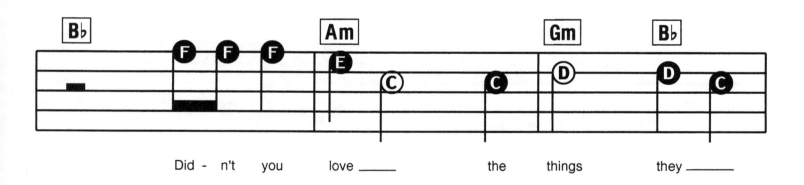

Did - n't you love _____ the things they _____

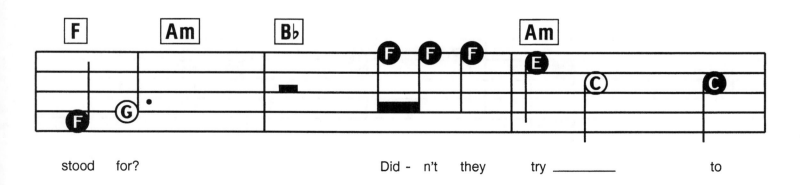

stood for? Did - n't they try _____ to

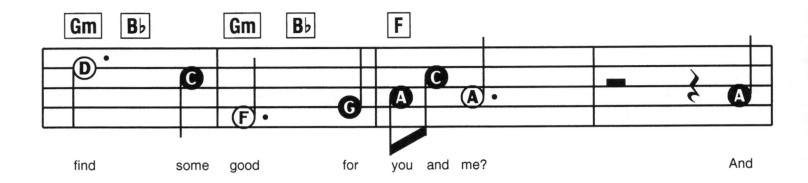

find   some   good   for   you   and   me?   And

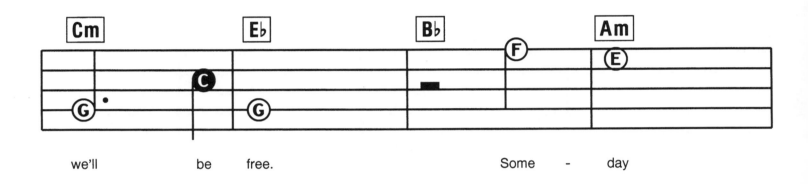

we'll   be   free.   Some - day

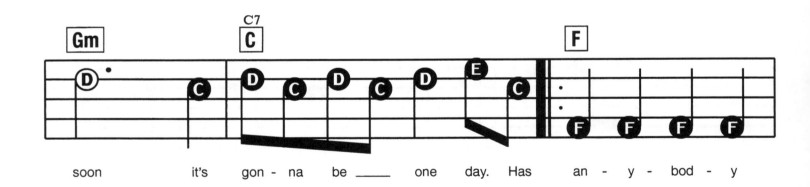

soon   it's   gon - na   be _____ one   day. Has   an - y - bod - y

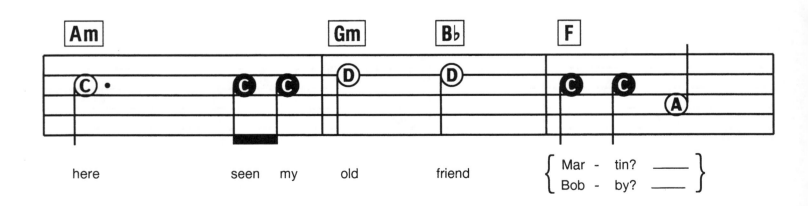

here   seen   my   old   friend   Mar - tin? _____ / Bob - by? _____

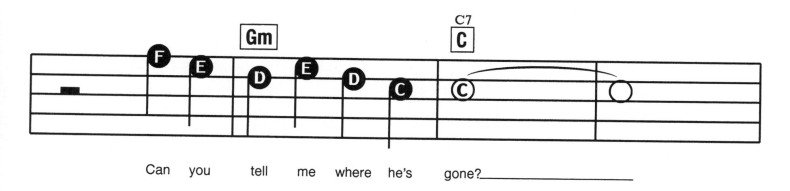

Can you tell me where he's gone?_____

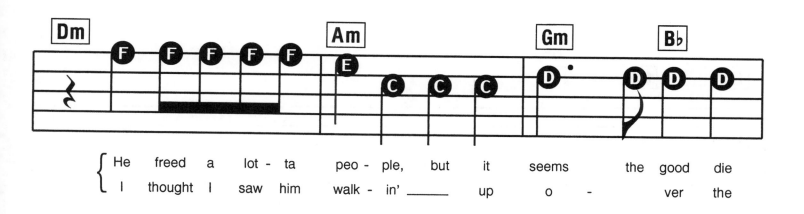

He freed a lot-ta peo-ple, but it seems the good die
I thought I saw him walk-in' _____ up o - ver the

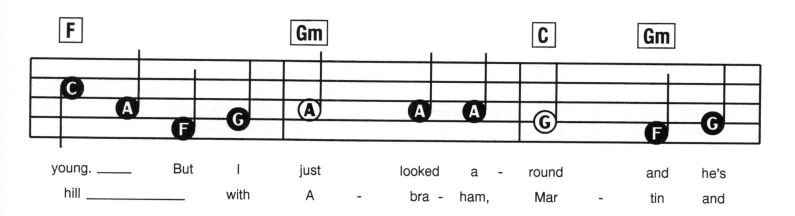

young. _____ But I just looked a - round and he's
hill _____ with A - bra - ham, Mar - tin and

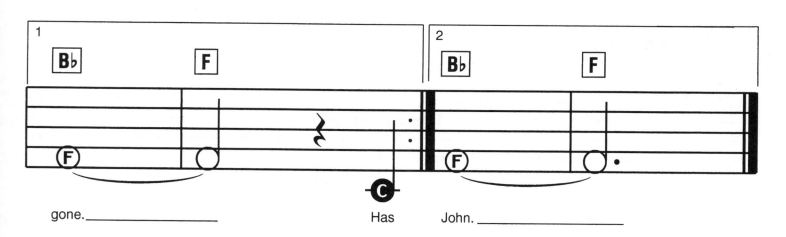

gone._____   Has John._____

All You Need Is Love

Registration 5
Rhythm: Shuffle or Swing

Words and Music by John Lennon
and Paul McCartney

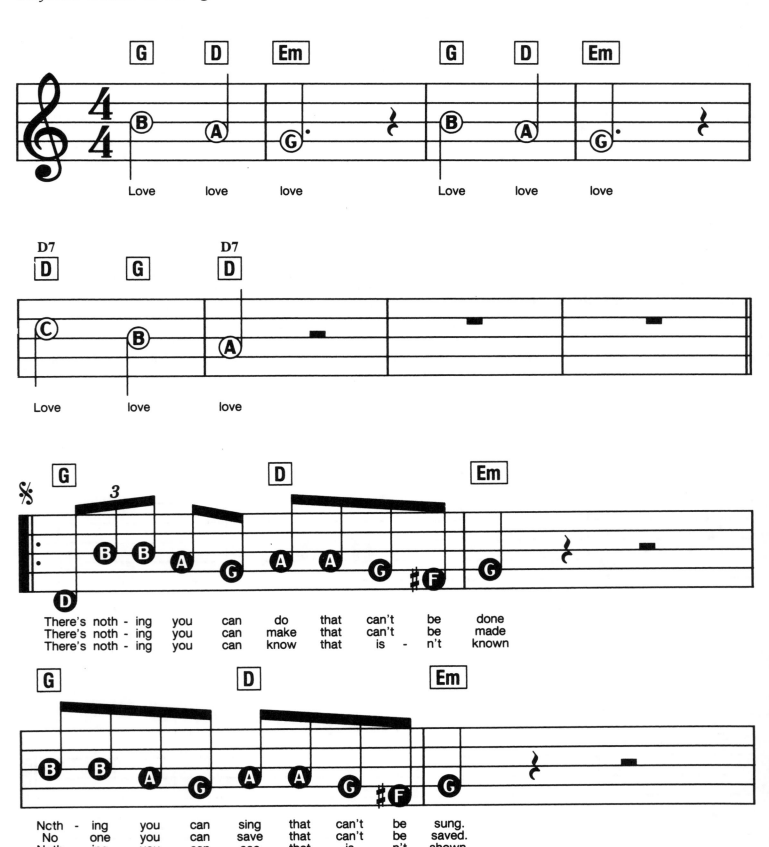

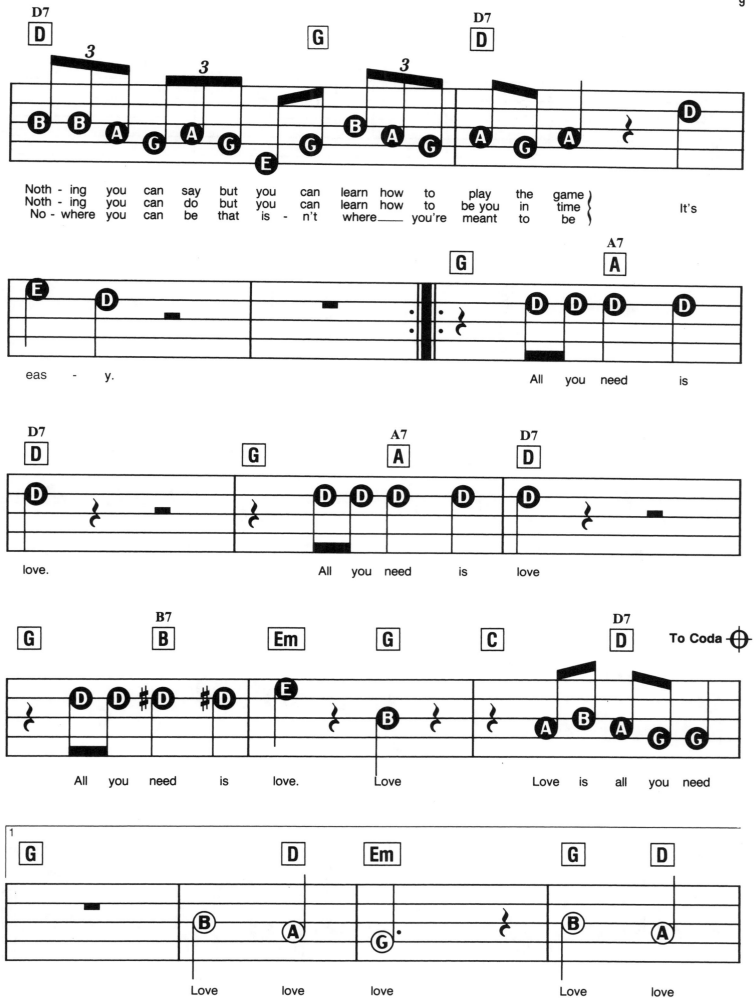

Noth - ing you can say but you can learn how to play the game
Noth - ing you can do but you can learn how to be you in time
No - where you can be that is - n't where you're meant to be

It's eas - y.

All you need is love.

All you need is love

All you need is love. Love

Love is all you need

Love love love

Love love

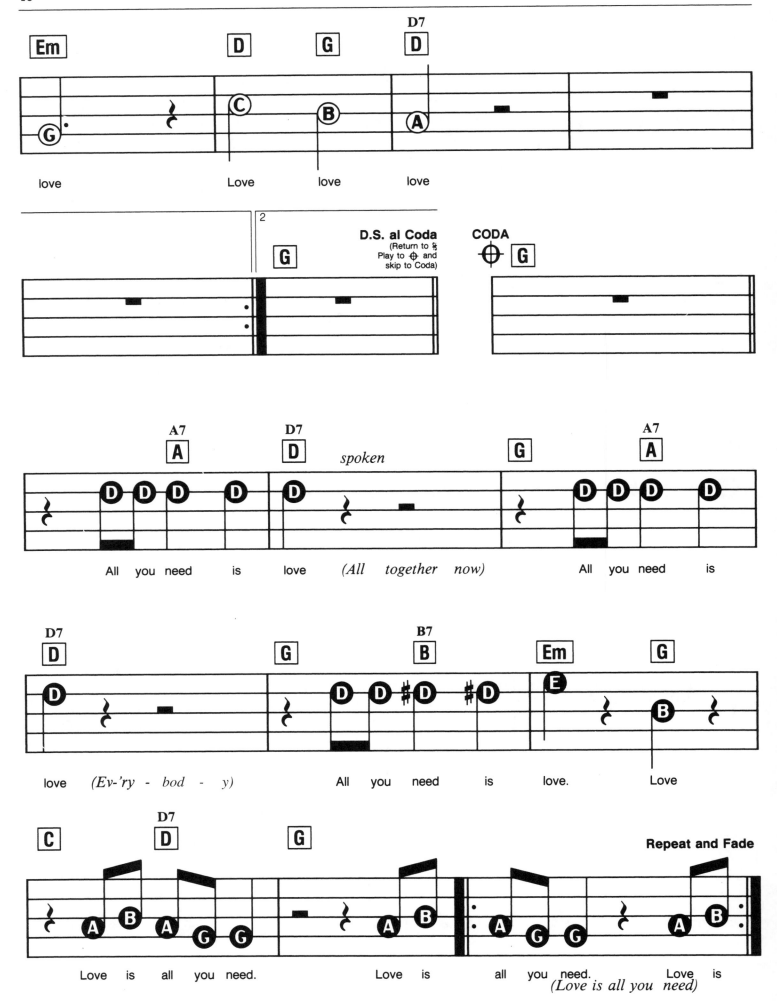

Aquarius
from the Broadway Musical Production HAIR

Registration 5
Rhythm: Rock

Words by James Rado and Gerome Ragni
Music by Galt MacDermot

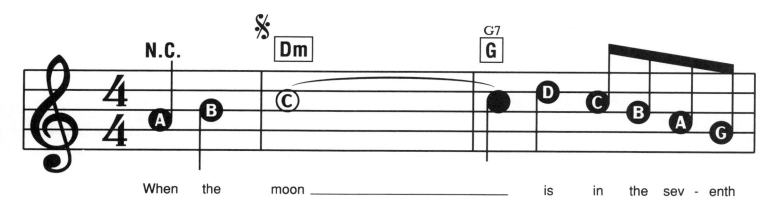

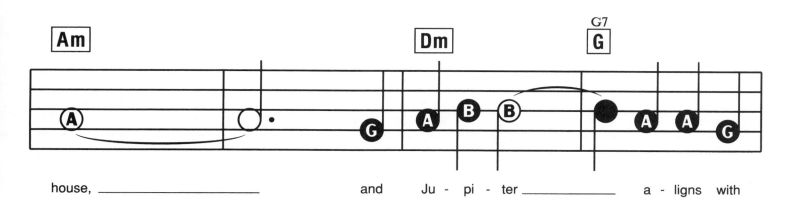

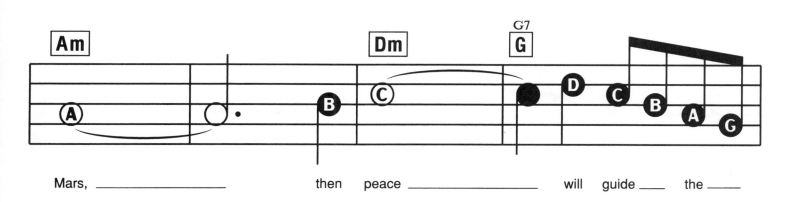

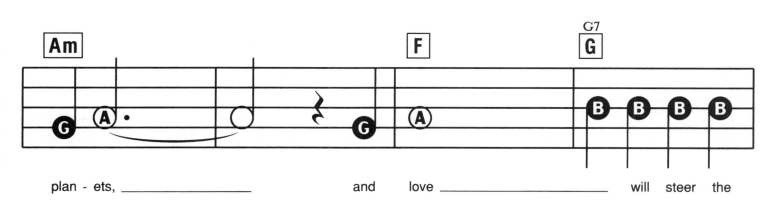

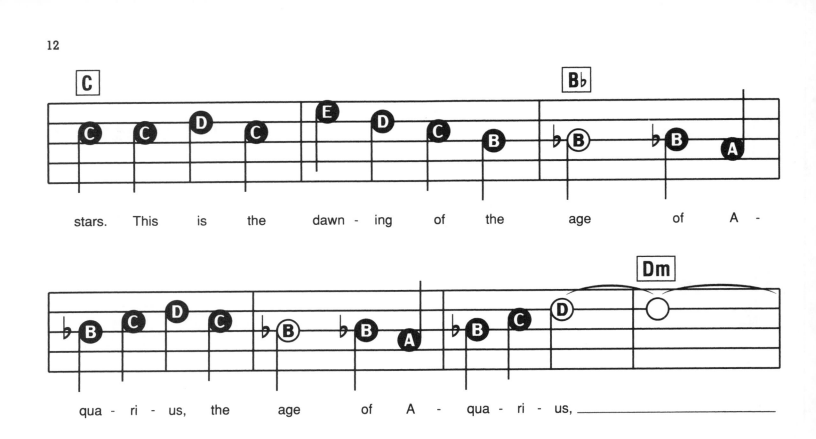

stars. This is the dawn - ing of the age of A -

qua - ri - us, the age of A - qua - ri - us, ____

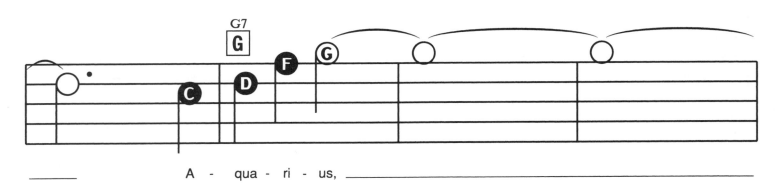

____ A - qua - ri - us, ____

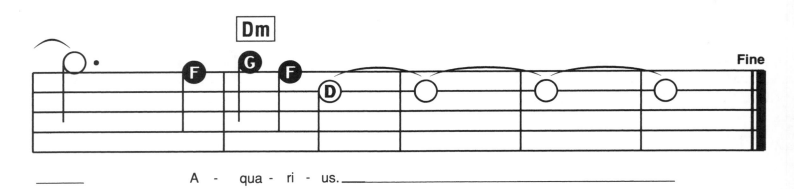

____ A - qua - ri - us. ____

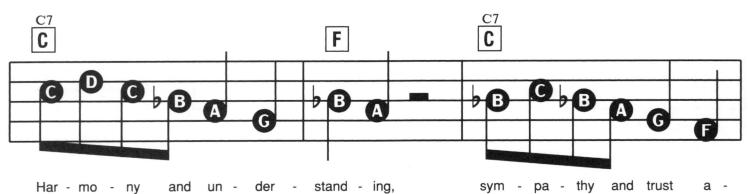

Har - mo - ny and un - der - stand - ing, sym - pa - thy and trust a -

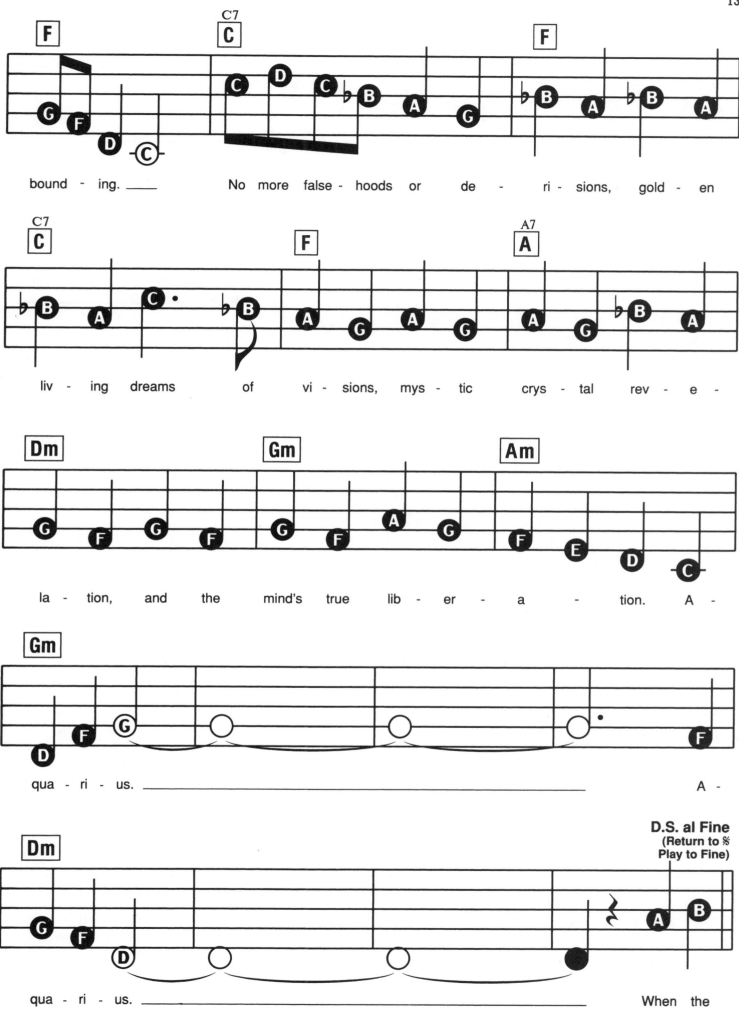

Bad, Bad Leroy Brown

Registration 7
Rhythm: Rock

Words and Music by
Jim Croce

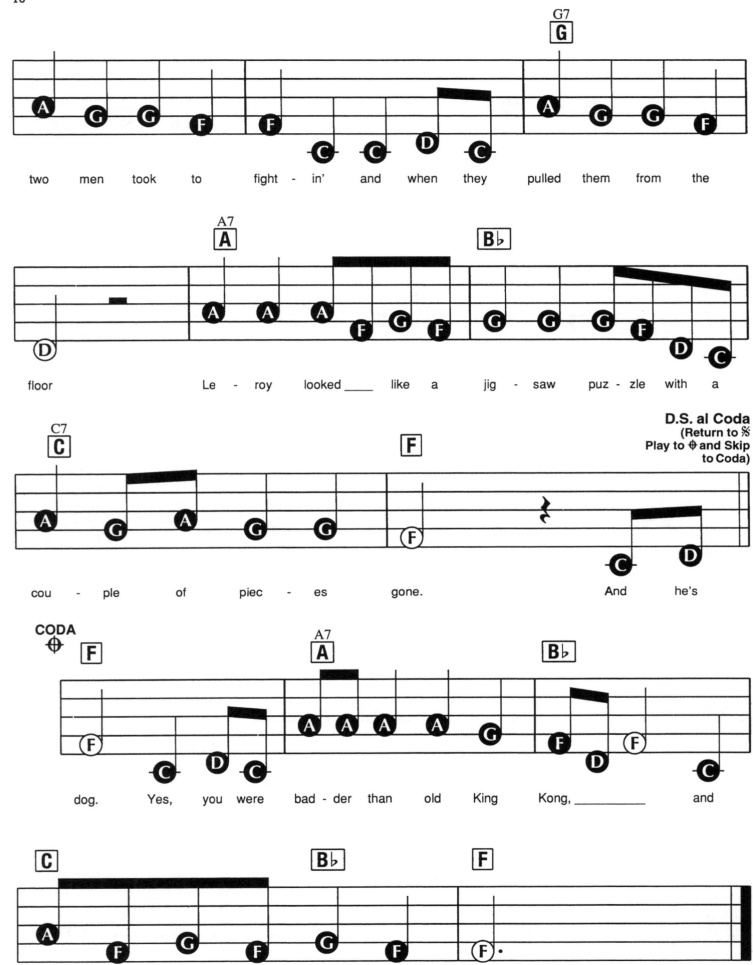

two men took to fight - in' and when they pulled them from the

floor Le - roy looked ____ like a jig - saw puz - zle with a

D.S. al Coda
(Return to ℅
Play to ⊕ and Skip
to Coda)

cou - ple of piec - es gone. And he's

CODA

dog. Yes, you were bad - der than old King Kong, _____ and

mean - er than a junk - yard dog.

Born to Be Wild

Registration 5
Rhythm: Rock

Words and Music by
Mars Bonfire

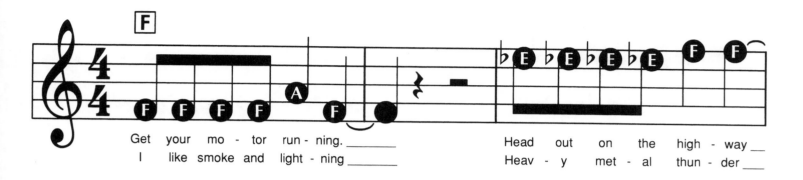

Get your mo - tor run - ning. _____ Head out on the high - way __
I like smoke and light - ning _____ Heav - y met - al thun - der __

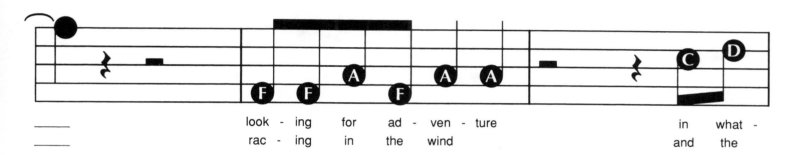

_____ look - ing for ad - ven - ture in what -
_____ rac - ing in the wind and the

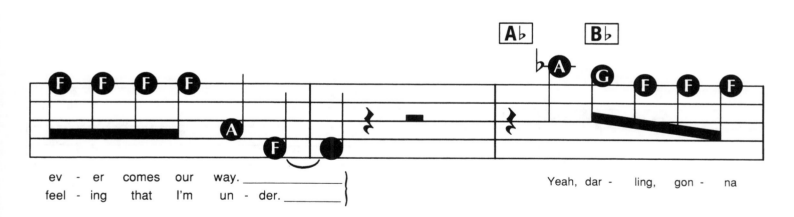

ev - er comes our way. _____ Yeah, dar - ling, gon - na
feel - ing that I'm un - der. _____

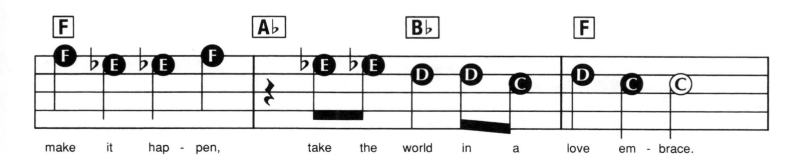

make it hap - pen, take the world in a love em - brace.

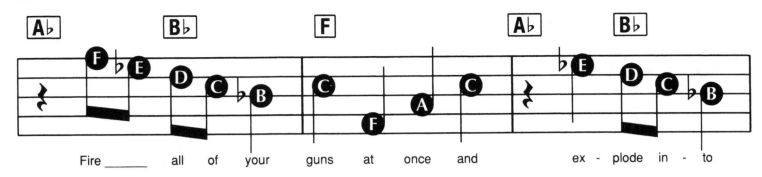

Fire _____ all of your guns at once and ex - plode in - to

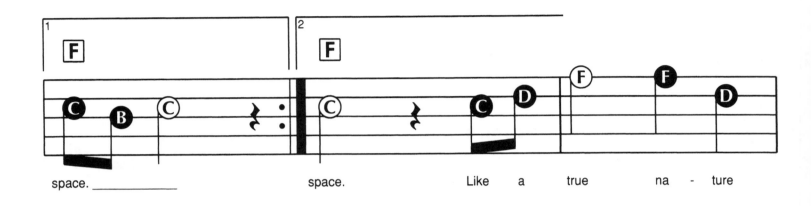

space. _____ space. Like a true na - ture

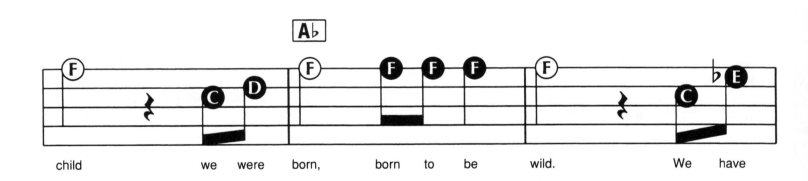

child we were born, born to be wild. We have

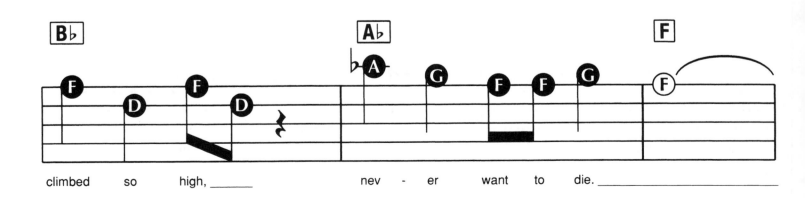

climbed so high, _____ nev - er want to die. _____

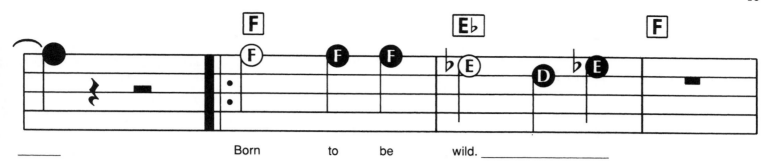

Born to be wild. _____

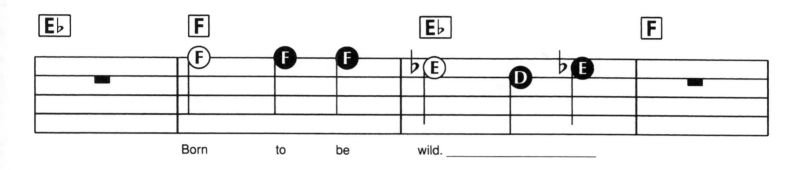

Born to be wild. _____

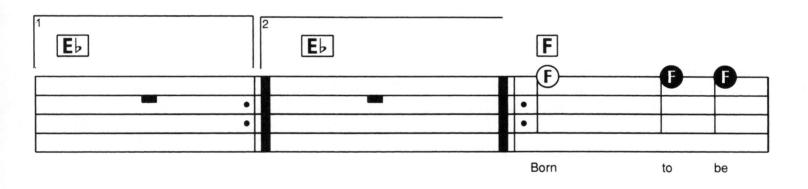

Born to be

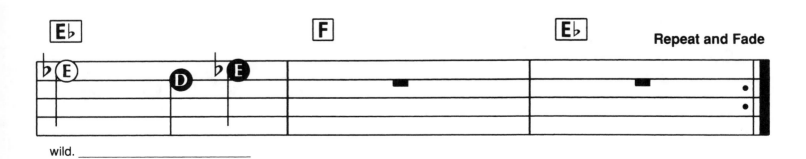

wild. _____

(It's a) Beautiful Morning

Registration 2
Rhythm: Shuffle or Swing

Words and Music by Felix Cavaliere
and Edward Brigati, Jr.

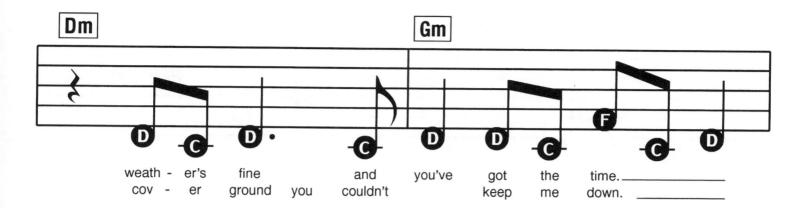

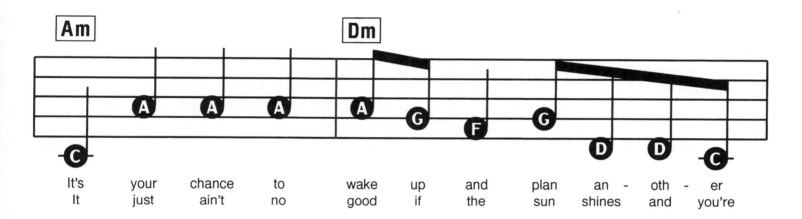

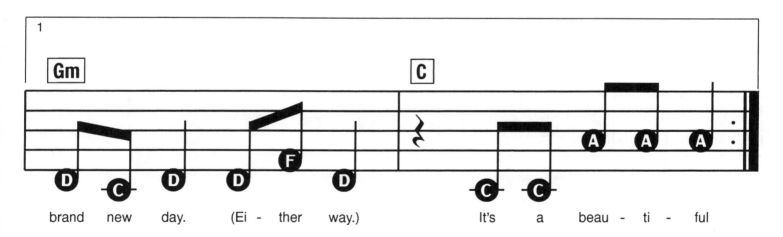

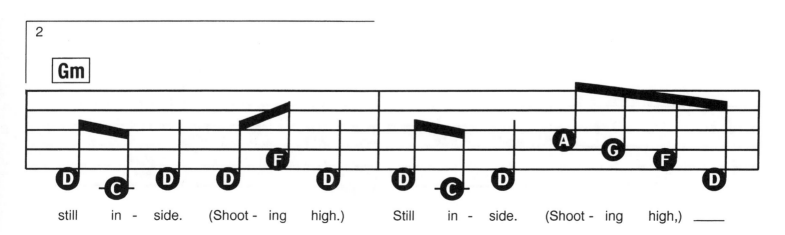

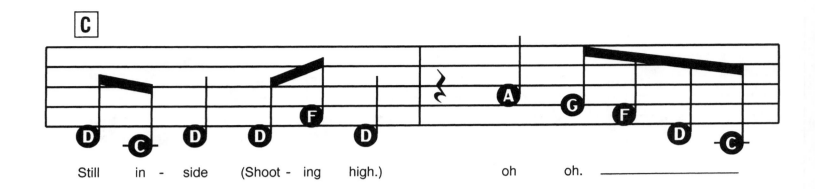

Still in - side (Shoot - ing high.) oh oh. _____

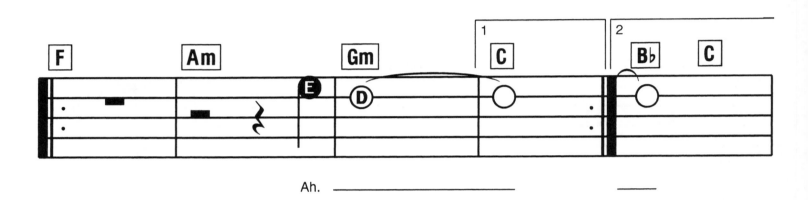

Ah. _____ _____

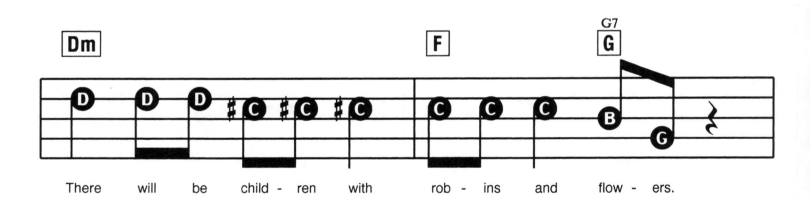

There will be child - ren with rob - ins and flow - ers.

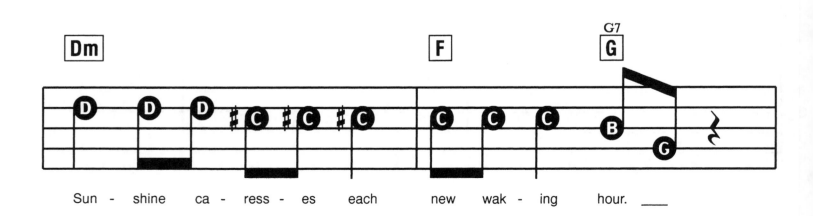

Sun - shine ca - ress - es each new wak - ing hour. ___

23

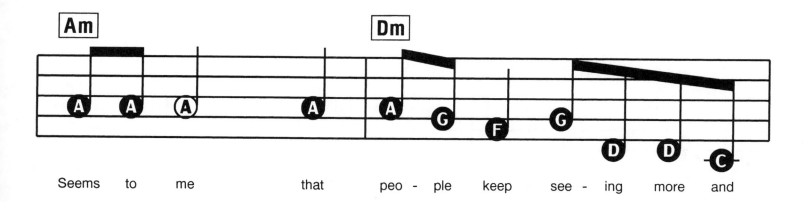

Seems to me that peo - ple keep see - ing more and

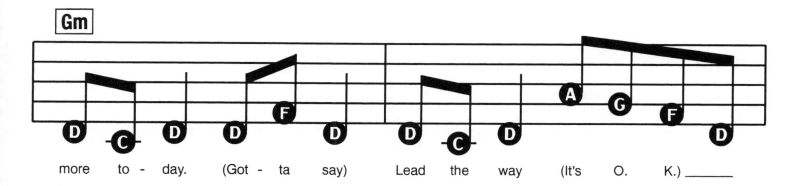

more to - day. (Got - ta say) Lead the way (It's O. K.) _____

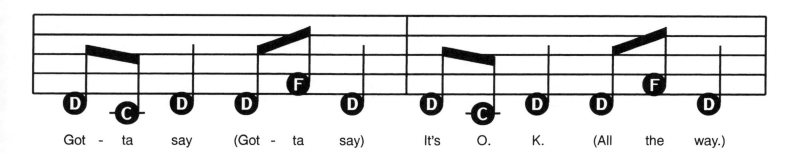

Got - ta say (Got - ta say) It's O. K. (All the way.)

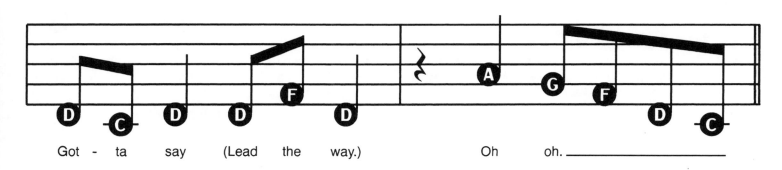

Got - ta say (Lead the way.) Oh oh. _____

Repeat and Fade

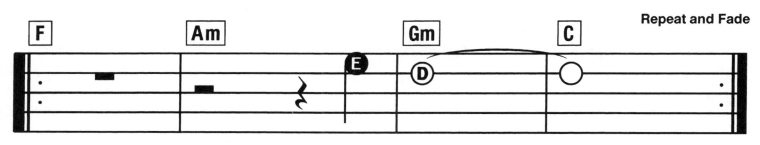

Ah. _____

Blowin' in the Wind

Registration 4
Rhythm: Ballad or Fox Trot

Words and Music by
Bob Dylan

C   F   G   C

G   G G   A   A G   G   E C   E

How man-y roads must a man walk down be-
how man-y years can a moun-tain ex - ist be-
how man-y times must a man look up be-

F   C

G   G   A   G F   G   G G

fore you call him a man?
fore it is washed to the sea? Yes, and
fore he can see _____ the sky? Yes, and

F   G   C

G   G G   A   A G   G   E   C   C

How man-y seas must a white dove sail be-
how man-y years can some peo - ple ex - ist be-
how man-y ears _____ must one man have be-

F   G

G   E   F   E E   D   G G

fore she sleeps in the sand? Yes, and
fore they're al - lowed to be free? Yes, and
fore he can hear peo - ple cry? Yes, and

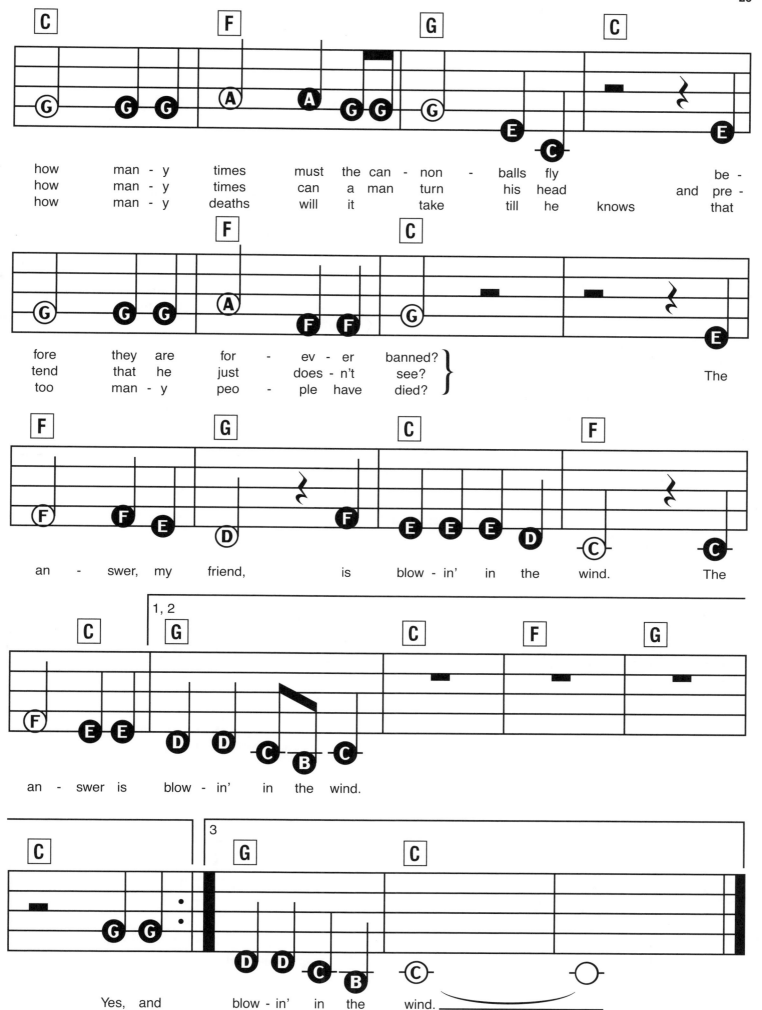

Both Sides Now

Registration 4
Rhythm: Pops or 8-Beat

Words and Music by
Joni Mitchell

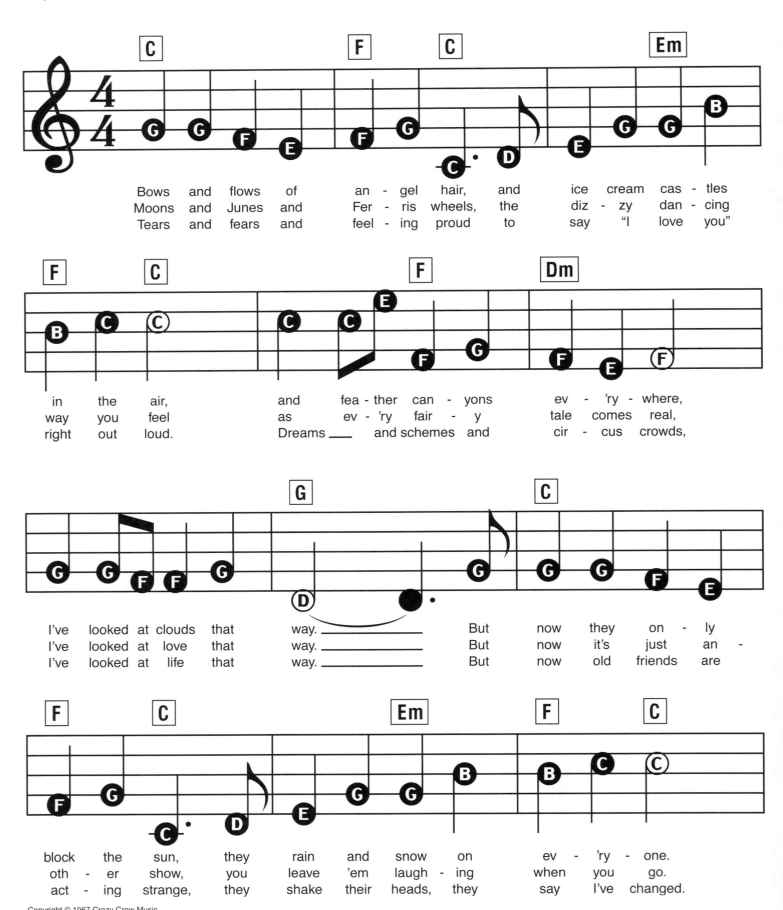

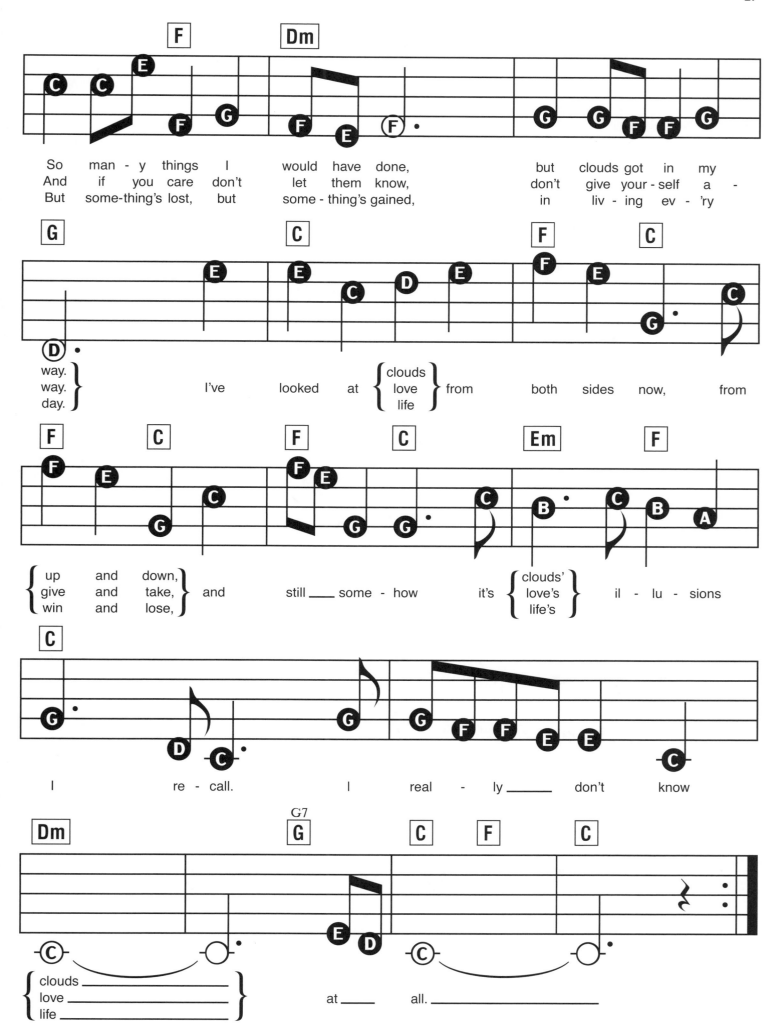

Brand New Key

Registration 5
Rhythm: Rock

Words and Music by
Melanie Safka

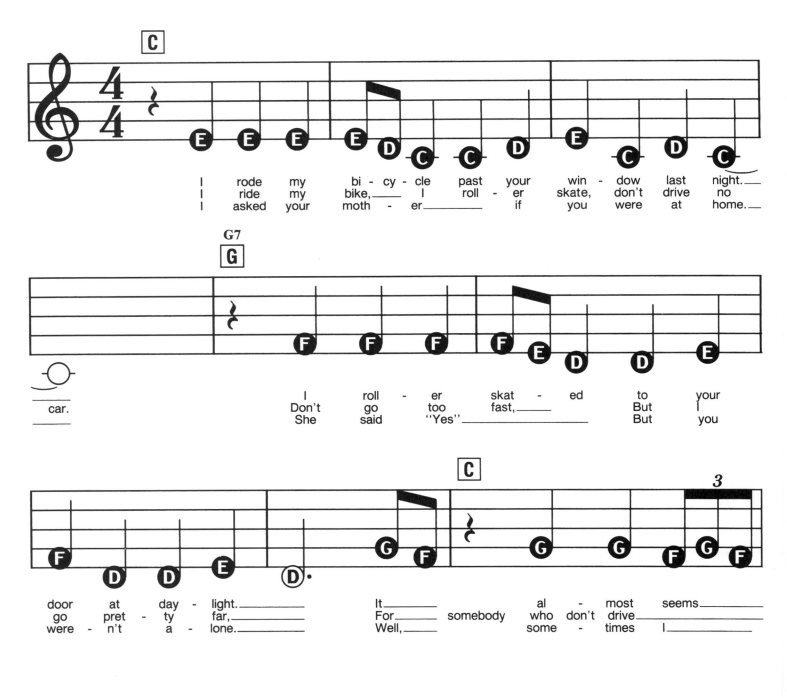

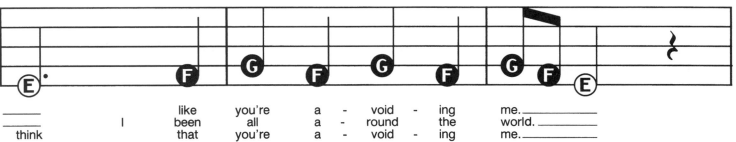

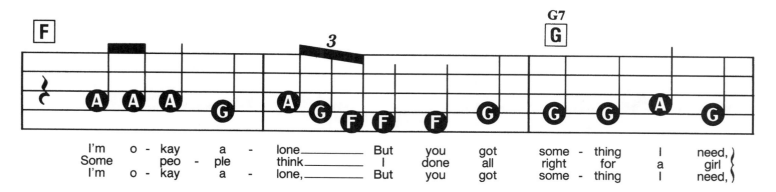

I'm o - kay a - lone_____ But you got some - thing I need,
Some peo - ple think_____ I done all right for a girl
I'm o - kay a - lone,_____ But you got some - thing I need,

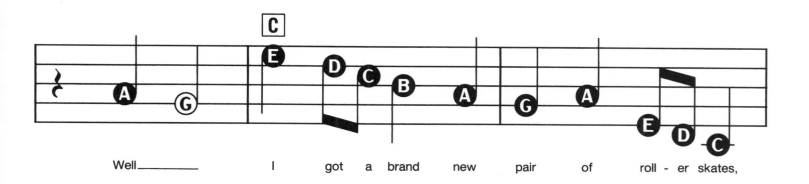

Well_____ I got a brand new pair of roll - er skates,

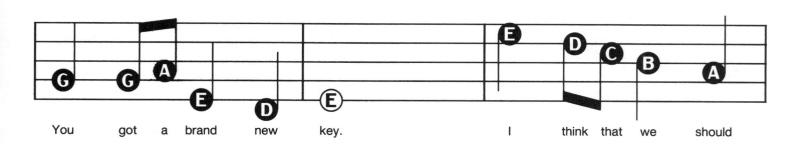

You got a brand new key. I think that we should

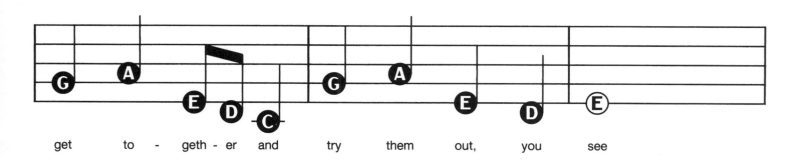

get to - geth - er and try them out, you see

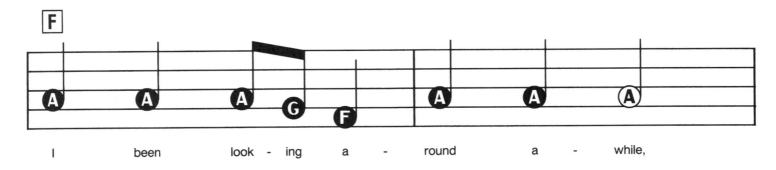

I been look-ing a - round a - while,

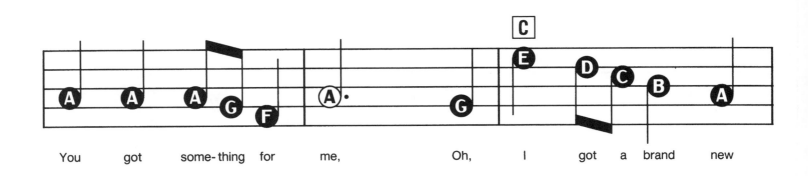

You got some-thing for me, Oh, I got a brand new

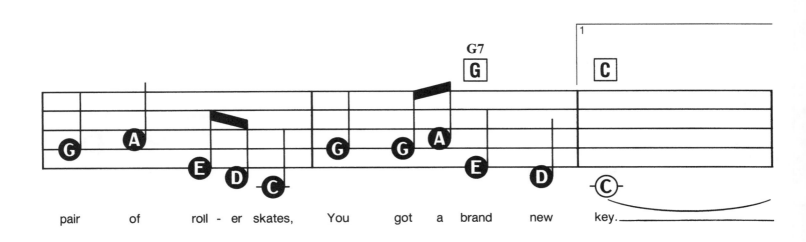

pair of roll - er skates, You got a brand new key._____

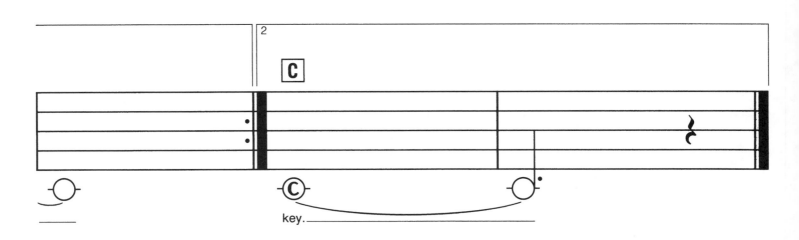

key._____

Brown Eyed Girl

Registration 1
Rhythm: 8-Beat or Rock

Words and Music by
Van Morrison

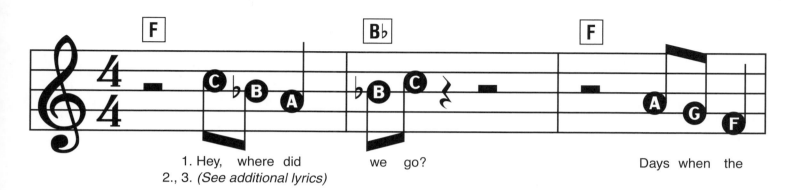

1. Hey, where did we go? Days when the
2., 3. *(See additional lyrics)*

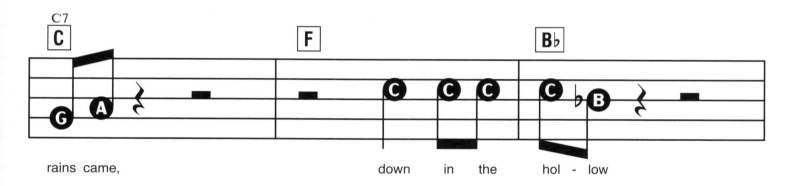

rains came, down in the hol - low

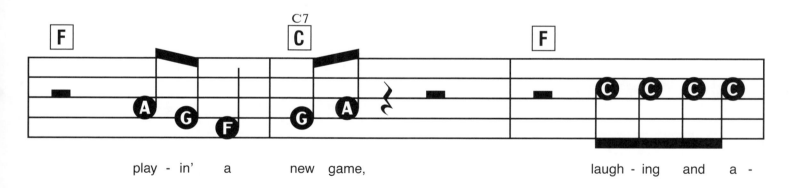

play - in' a new game, laugh - ing and a -

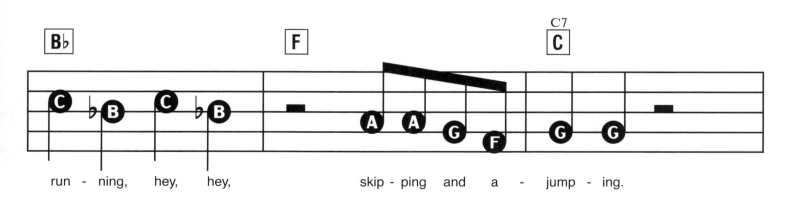

run - ning, hey, hey, skip - ping and a - jump - ing.

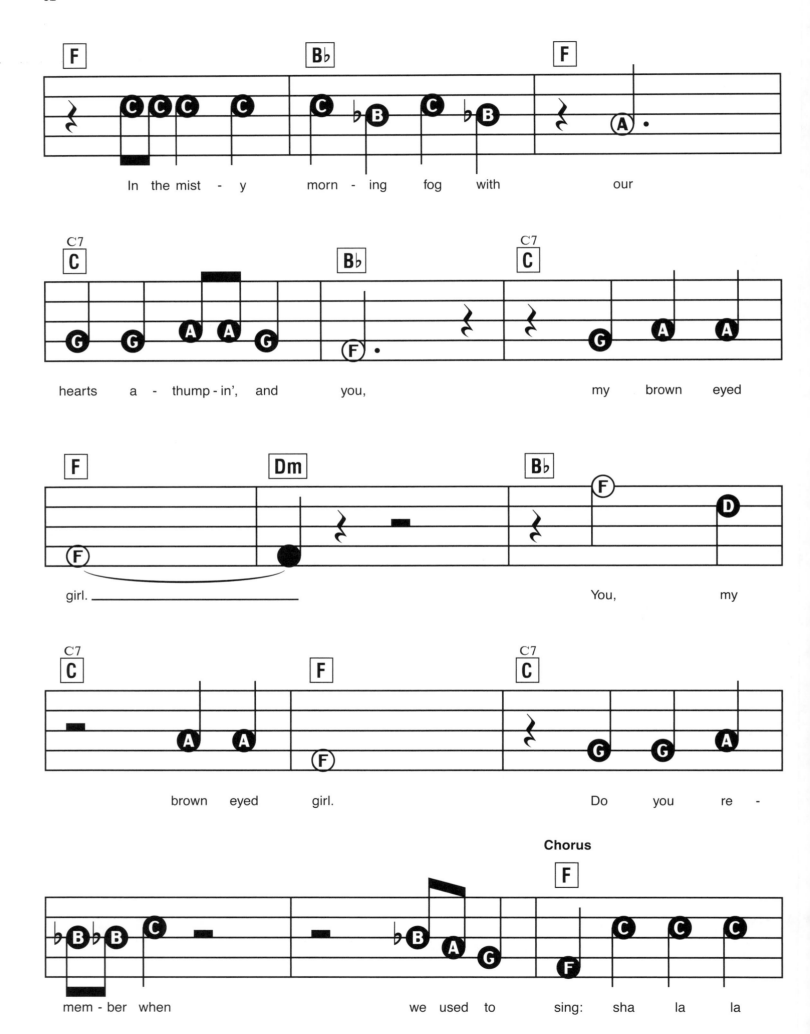

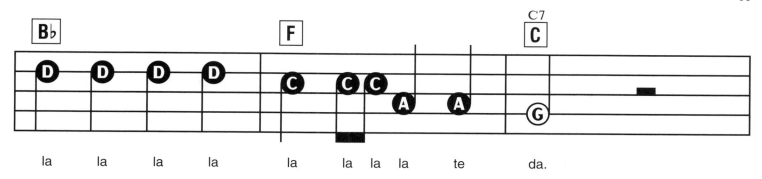

la   la   la   la   la   la   la   la   te   da.

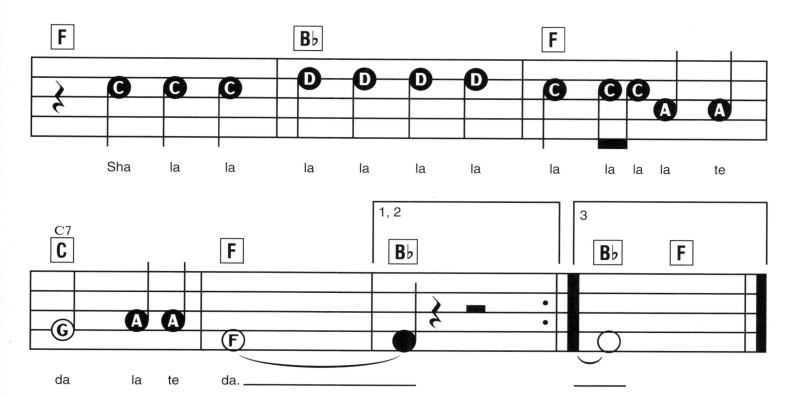

Sha   la   la   la   la   la   la   la   la la la   te

da   la   te   da.

Additional Lyrics

2. Whatever happened to Tuesday and so slow
   Going down the old mine with a transistor radio,
   Standing in the sunlight laughing,
   Hiding behind a rainbow's wall,
   Slipping and a-sliding
   All along the waterfall
   With you, my brown eyed girl.
   You, my brown eyed girl.
   Do you remember when we used to sing:
   Chorus

3. So hard to find my way, now that I'm all on my own.
   I saw you just the other day. My, how you have grown.
   Cast my memory back there, Lord
   Sometime I'm overcome thinking 'bout
   Making love in the green grass
   Behind the stadium
   With you, my brown eyed girl
   With you, my brown eyed girl.
   Do you remember when we used to sing:
   Chorus

Bus Stop

Registration 4
Rhythm: 8-Beat or Rock

Words and Music by
Graham Gouldman

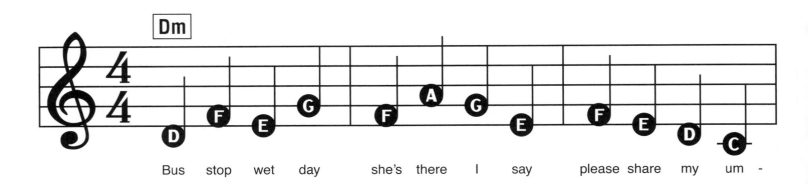

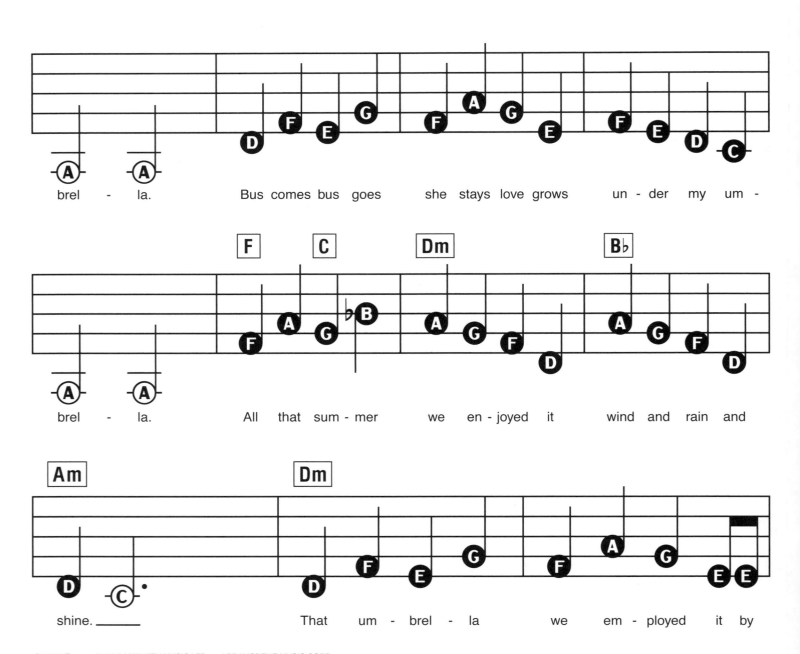

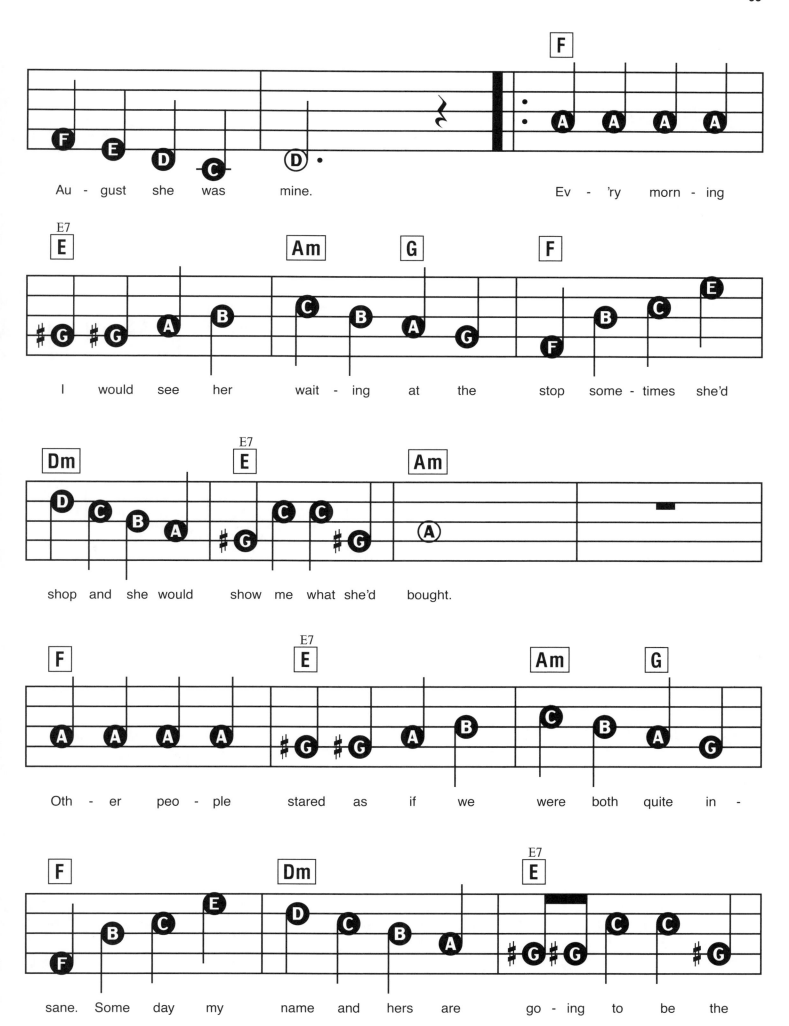

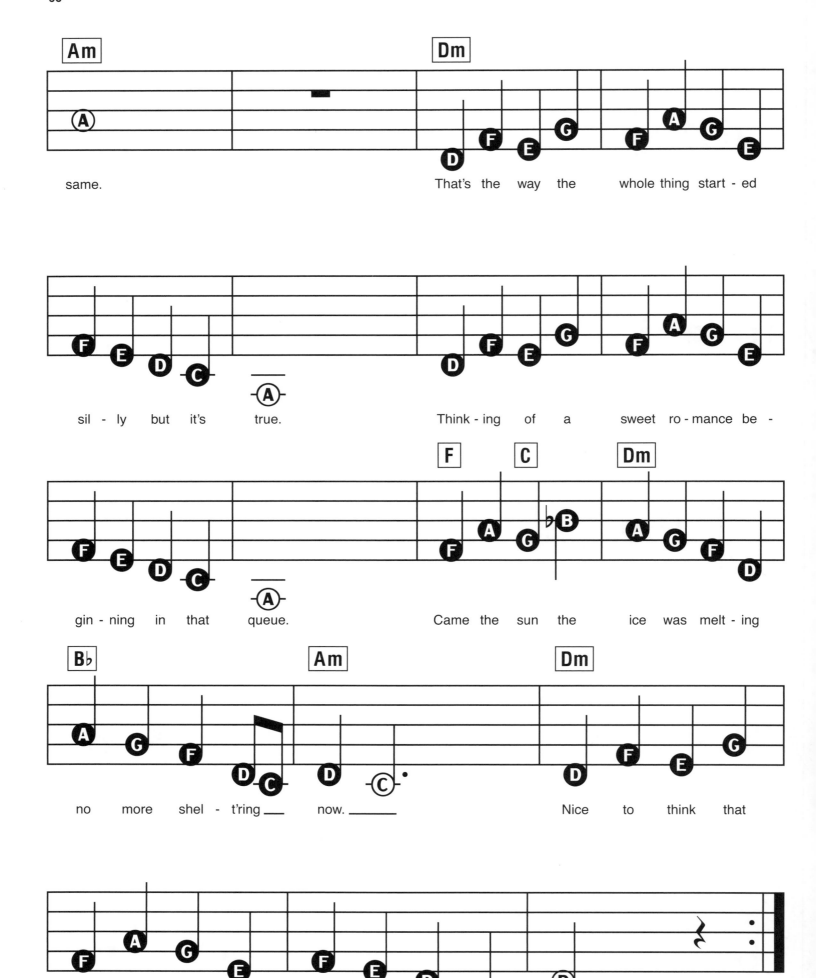

California Dreamin'

Registration 5
Rhythm: Rock

Words and Music by John Phillips
and Michelle Phillips

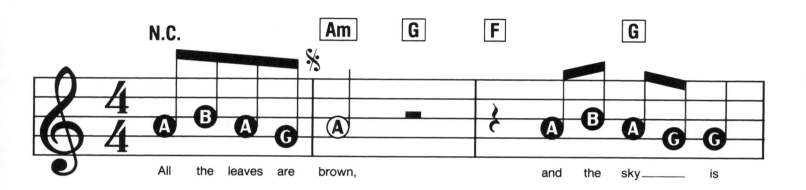

All the leaves are brown, and the sky_____ is

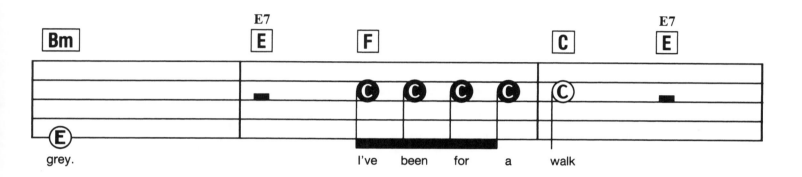

grey. I've been for a walk

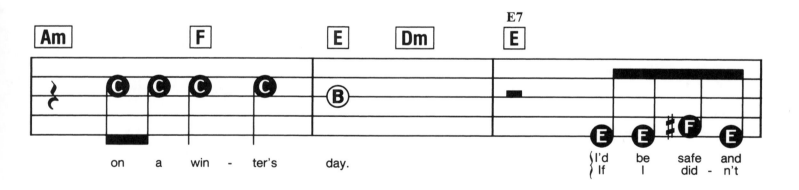

on a win-ter's day.
I'd be safe and
If I did-n't

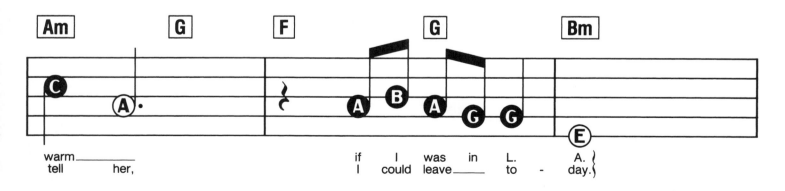

warm_____ tell her,
if I was in L. A.
I could leave_____ to - day

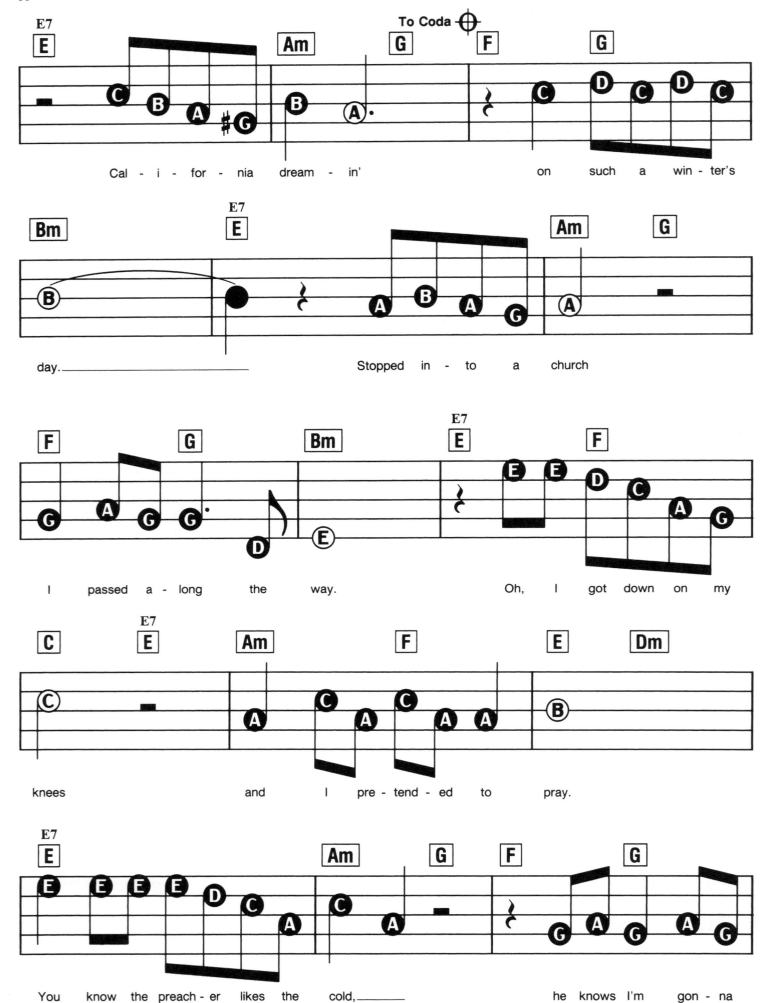

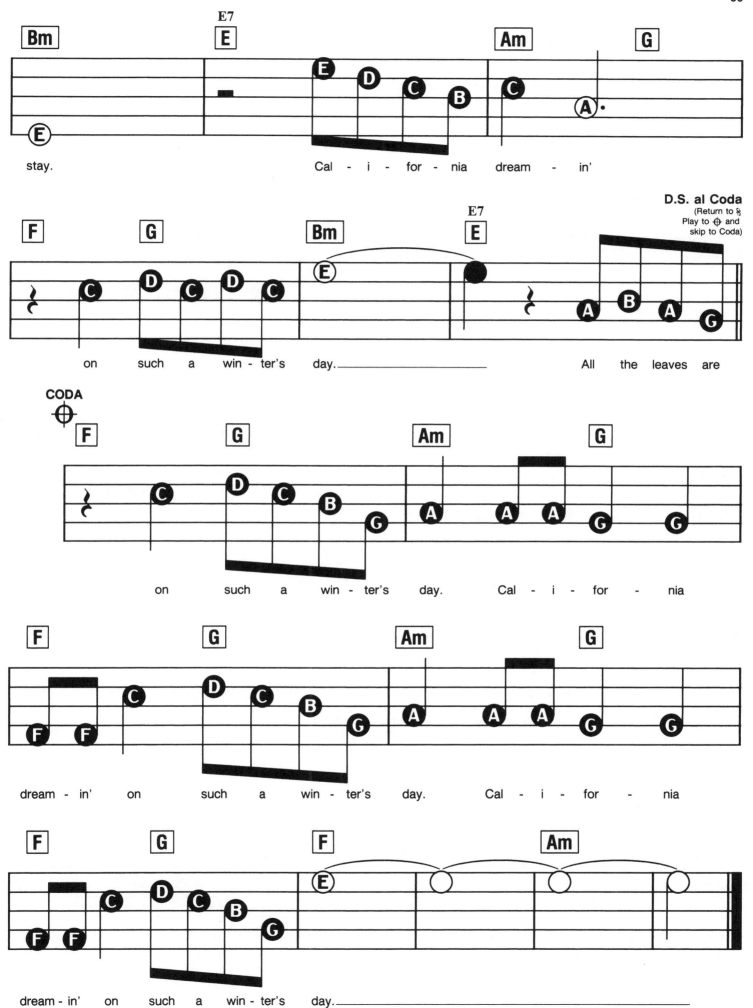

California Girls

Registration 7
Rhythm: Rock

Words and Music by Brian Wilson
and Mike Love

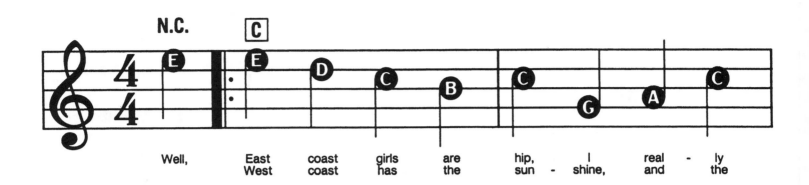

Well, East coast girls are hip, I real - ly
West coast has the sun - shine, and the

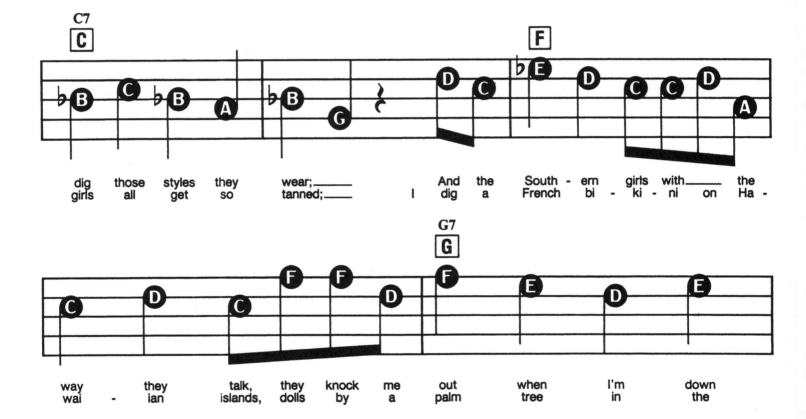

dig those styles they wear;_____ And the South - ern girls with_____ the
girls all get so tanned;_____ I dig a French bi - ki - ni on Ha -

way they talk, they knock me out when I'm down
wai - ian islands, dolls by a palm tree in the

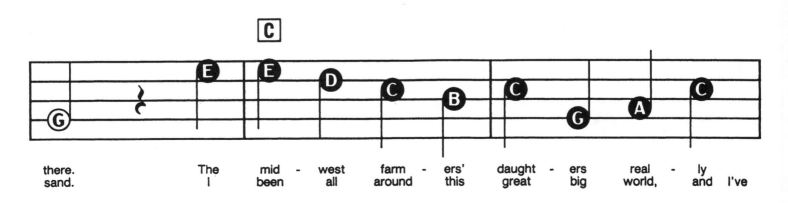

there. The mid - west farm - ers' daught - ers real - ly
sand. I been all around this great big world, and I've

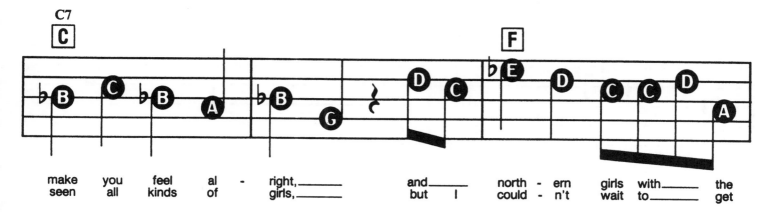

make you feel al - right,_____ and_____ north - ern girls with_____ the
seen all kinds of - girls,_____ but I could - n't wait to_____ get

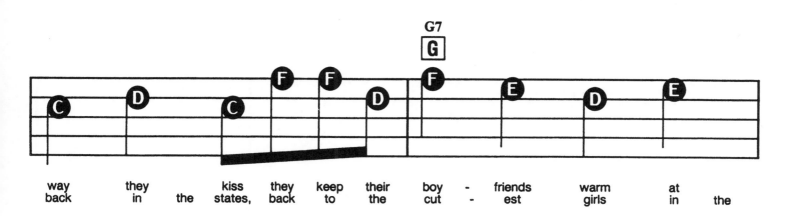

way they the kiss, they keep their boy - friends warm at the
back in the states, back to the cut - est girls in the

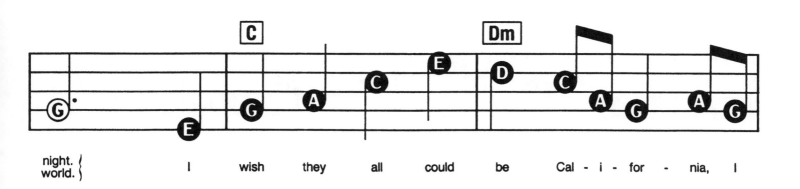

night. I wish they all could be Cal - i - for - nia, I
world.

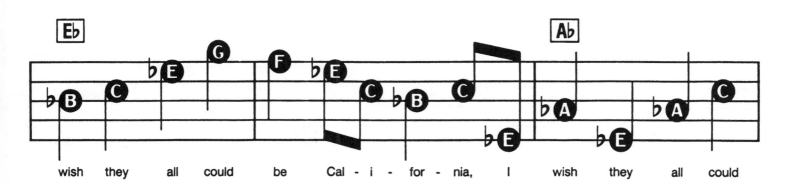

wish they all could be Cal - i - for - nia, I wish they all could

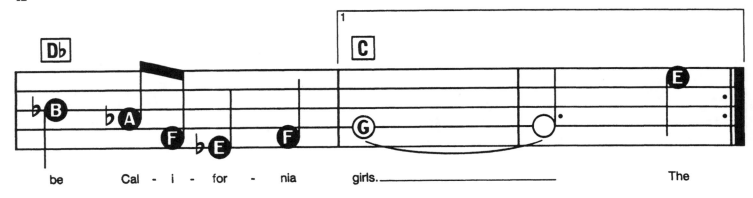

be Cal - i - for - nia girls._____ The

girls._____ I

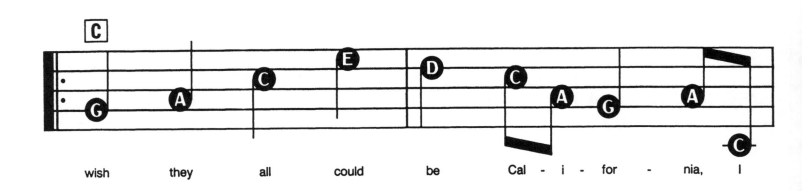

wish they all could be Cal - i - for - nia, I

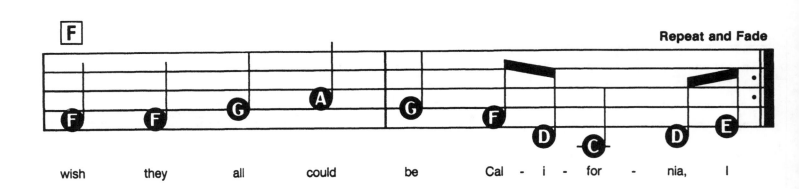

wish they all could be Cal - i - for - nia, I

Carrie-Anne

Registration 2
Rhythm: Rock or Slow Rock

Words and Music by Allan Clarke,
Tony Hicks and Graham Nash

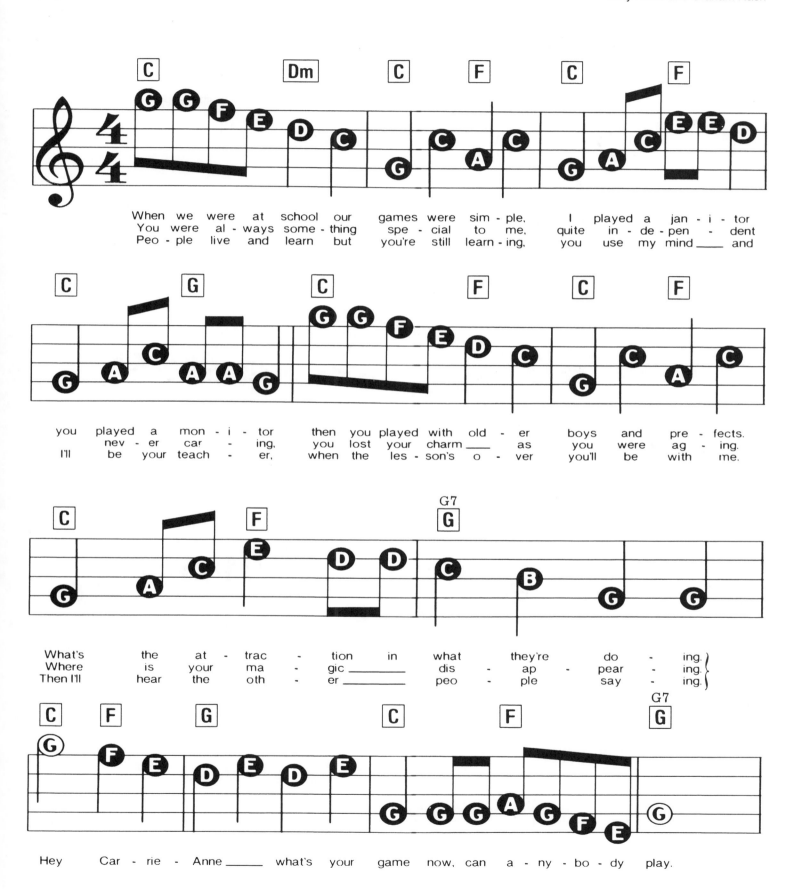

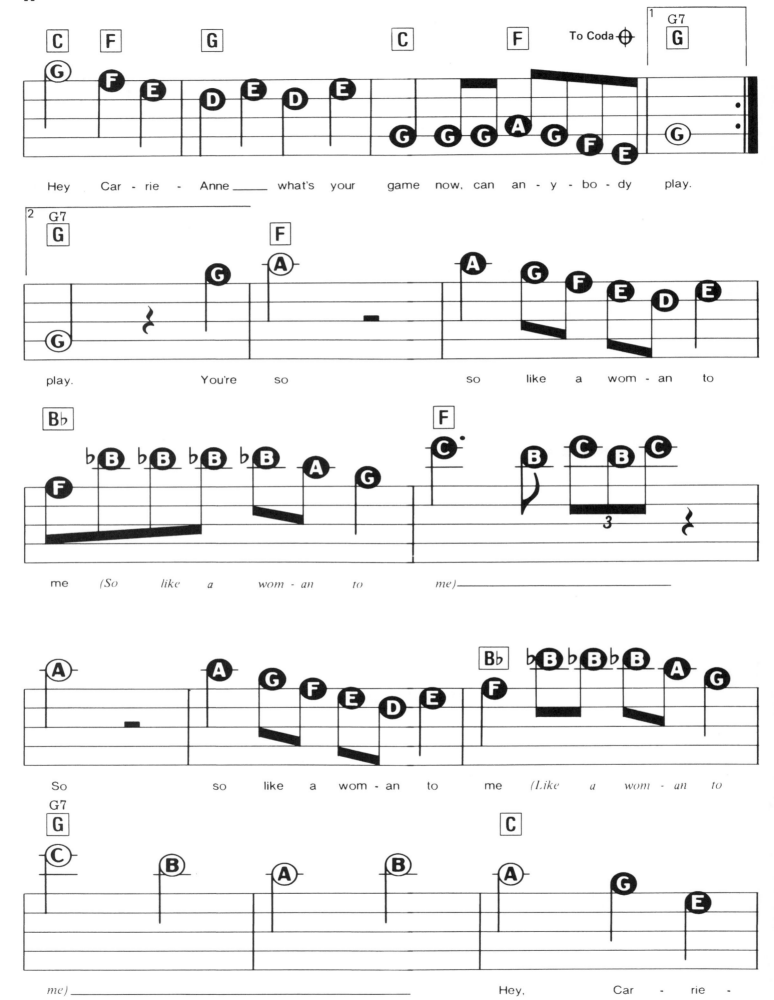

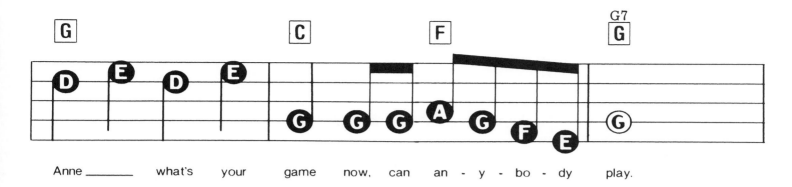

Anne _____ what's your game now, can an - y - bo - dy play.

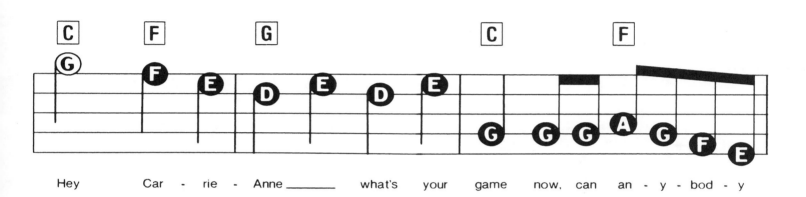

Hey Car - rie - Anne _____ what's your game now, can an - y - bod - y

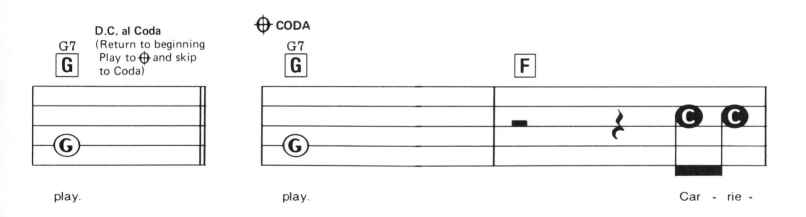

play. play. Car - rie -

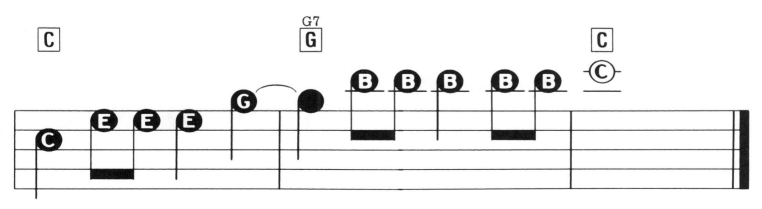

Anne Car - rie - Anne _____ Car - rie - Anne Car - rie - Anne.

Cat's in the Cradle

Registration 2
Rhythm: Rock

Words and Music by Harry Chapin
and Sandy Chapin

My child ar - rived just the oth - er day. He
son turned ten just the oth - er day. He said,
came from col - lege just the oth - er day. So

came to the world in the u - su - al way, but there were
"Thanks for the ball, Dad. Come on, let's play. Can you
much like a man I just had to say, "Son, I'm

planes to catch and bills to pay.
teach me to throw?" I said, "Not to - day, I got a
proud of you, can you sit for a - while?"

He learned to walk while I was a - way. And he was
lot to do." He said, "That's o - kay." And he,
He shook his head and he said with a smile, "What I'd

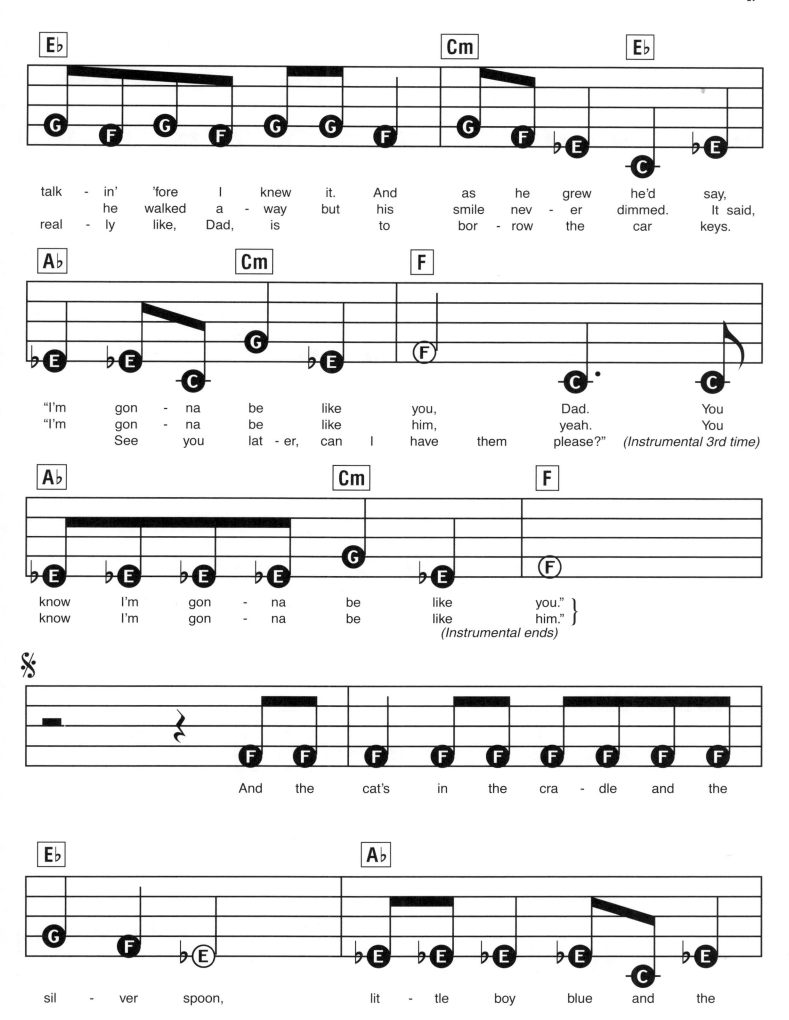

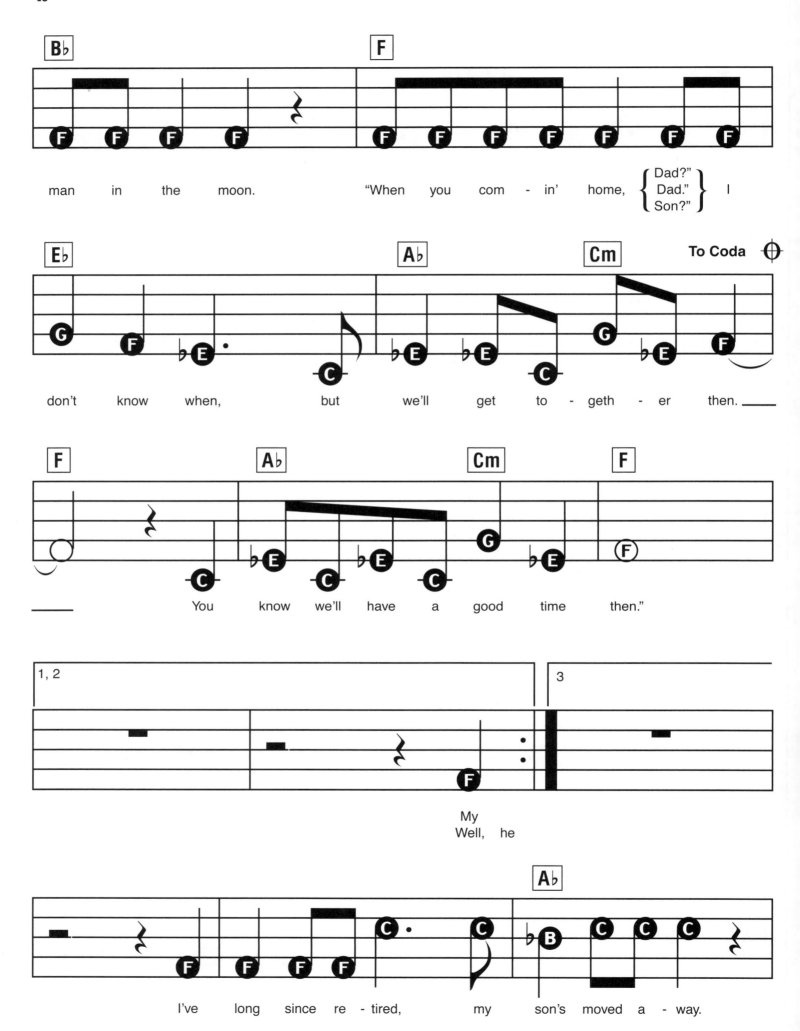

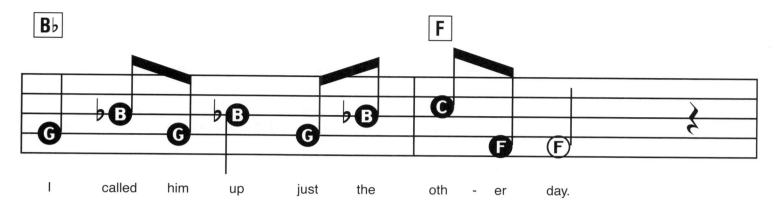

I called him up just the oth - er day.

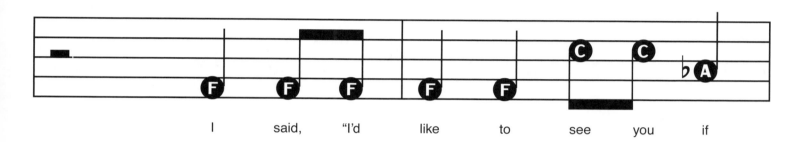

I said, "I'd like to see you if

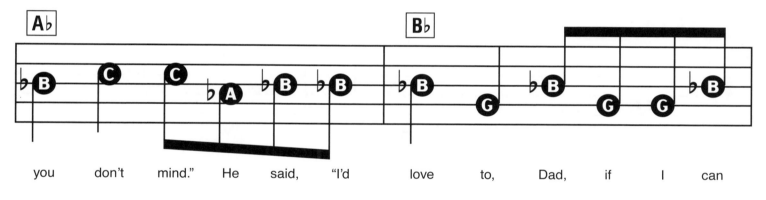

you don't mind." He said, "I'd love to, Dad, if I can

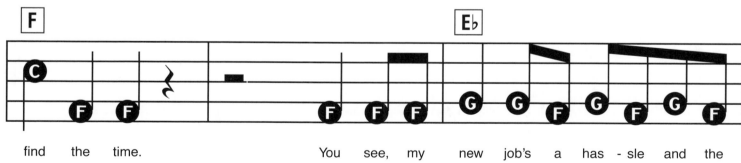

find the time. You see, my new job's a has - sle and the

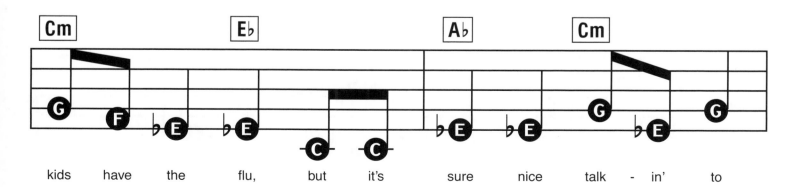

kids have the flu, but it's sure nice talk - in' to

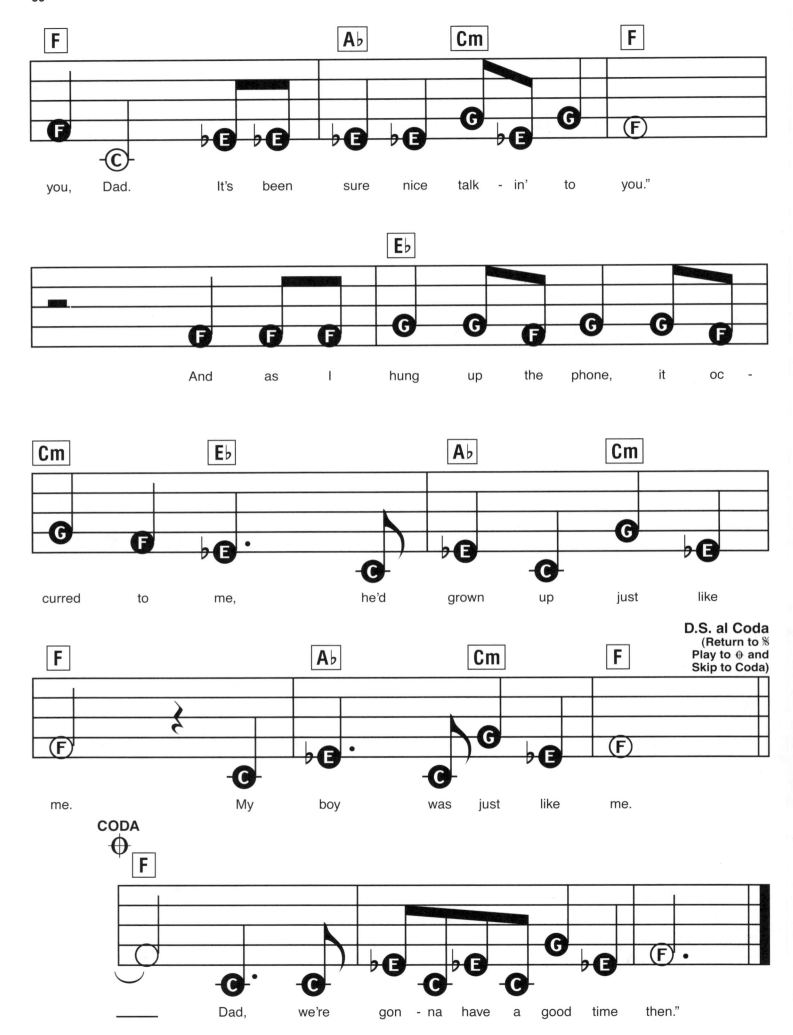

Daydream

Registration 5
Rhythm: Swing

Words and Music by
John Sebastian

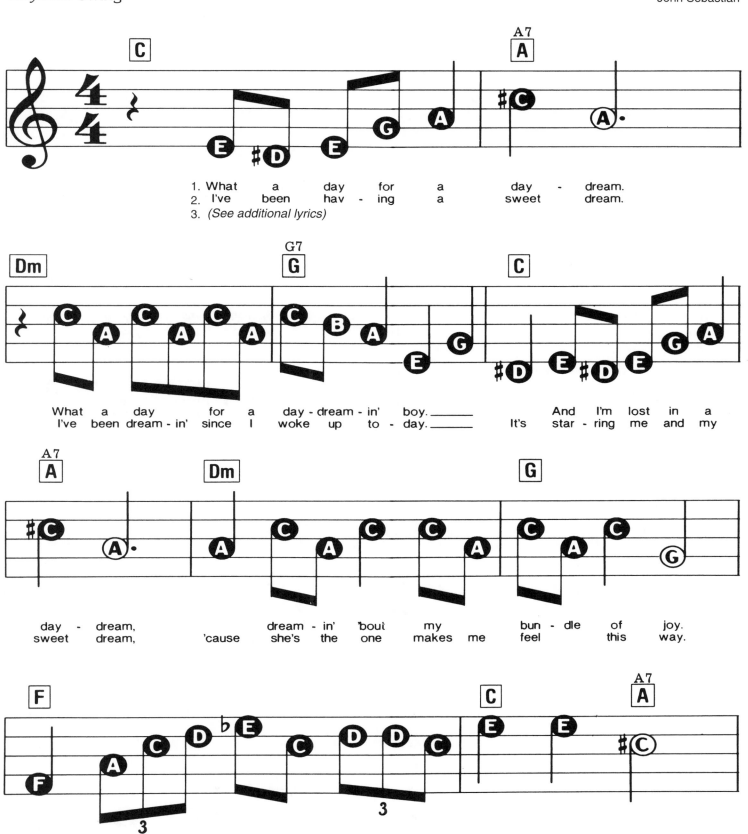

1. What a day for a day - dream.
2. I've been hav - ing a sweet dream.
3. *(See additional lyrics)*

What a day for a day - dream - in' boy. _____ And I'm lost in a
I've been dream - in' since I woke up to - day. _____ It's star - ring me and my

day - dream, dream - in' 'bout my bun - dle of joy.
sweet dream, 'cause she's the one makes me feel this way.

And ev - en if time ain't real - ly on my side,
And ev - en if time is pass - ing by a lot,

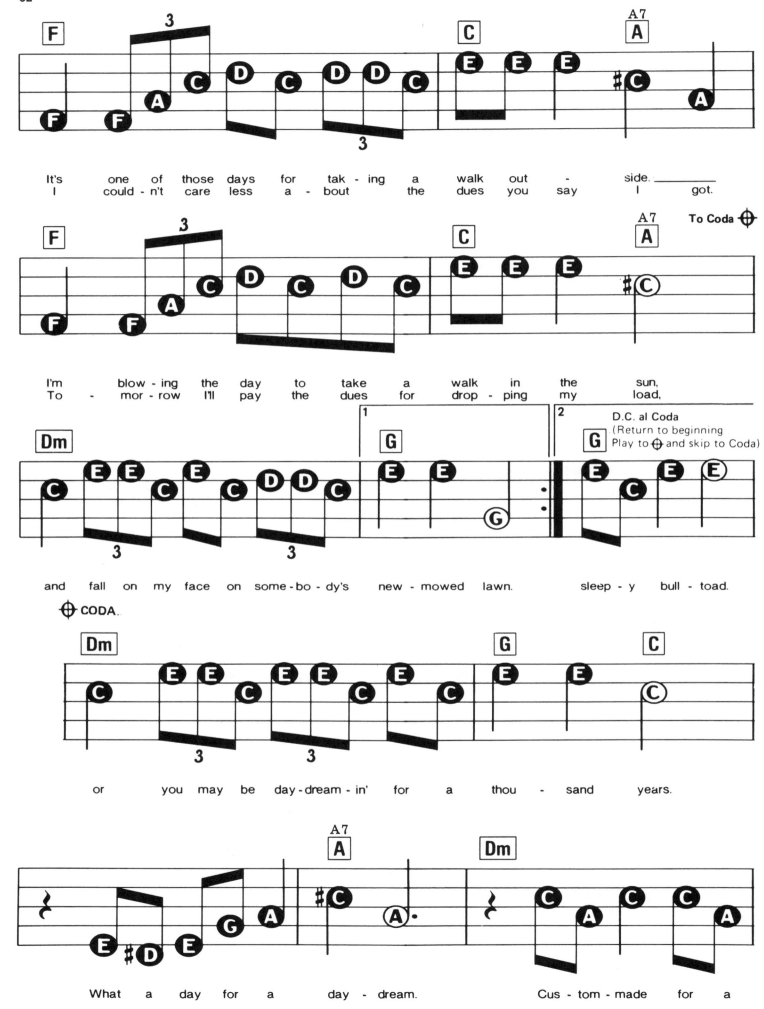

It's   one   of   those days for   tak - ing   a   walk   out -   side. _____
I   could - n't care less   a - bout   the   dues you   say   I   got.

I'm   blow - ing the   day   to   take   a   walk   in   the   sun,
To - mor - row I'll   pay   the dues   for drop - ping   my   load,

and   fall on   my   face on some - bo - dy's new - mowed lawn.   sleep - y   bull - toad.

CODA.

or   you   may be day - dream - in' for   a   thou - sand   years.

What   a   day   for   a   day - dream.   Cus - tom - made   for   a

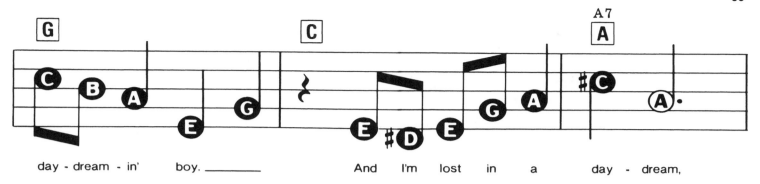

day - dream - in' boy. _____ And I'm lost in a day - dream,

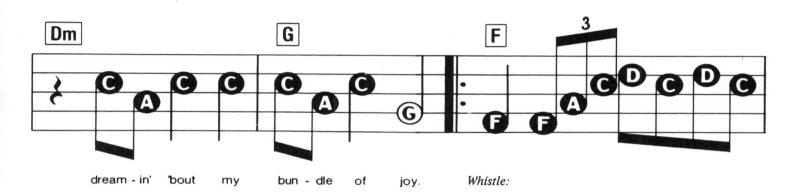

dream - in' 'bout my bun - dle of joy. *Whistle:*

Repeat and Fade

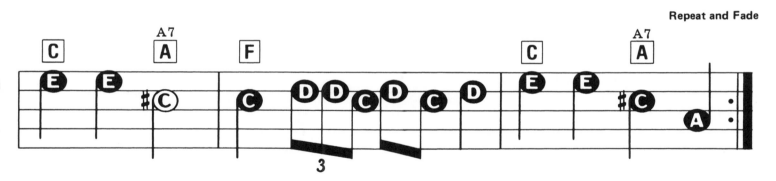

Additional Lyrics

Verse 3. (Whistle)
(Whistle)
(Whistle)
(Whistle)

And you can be sure that if you're feelin' right,
A Daydream will last till long into the night.
Tomorrow at breakfast you may pick up your ears,
Or you may be daydreamin' for a thousand years.

Daydream Believer

54

Registration 1
Rhythm: Fox Trot or Swing

Words and Music by
John Stewart

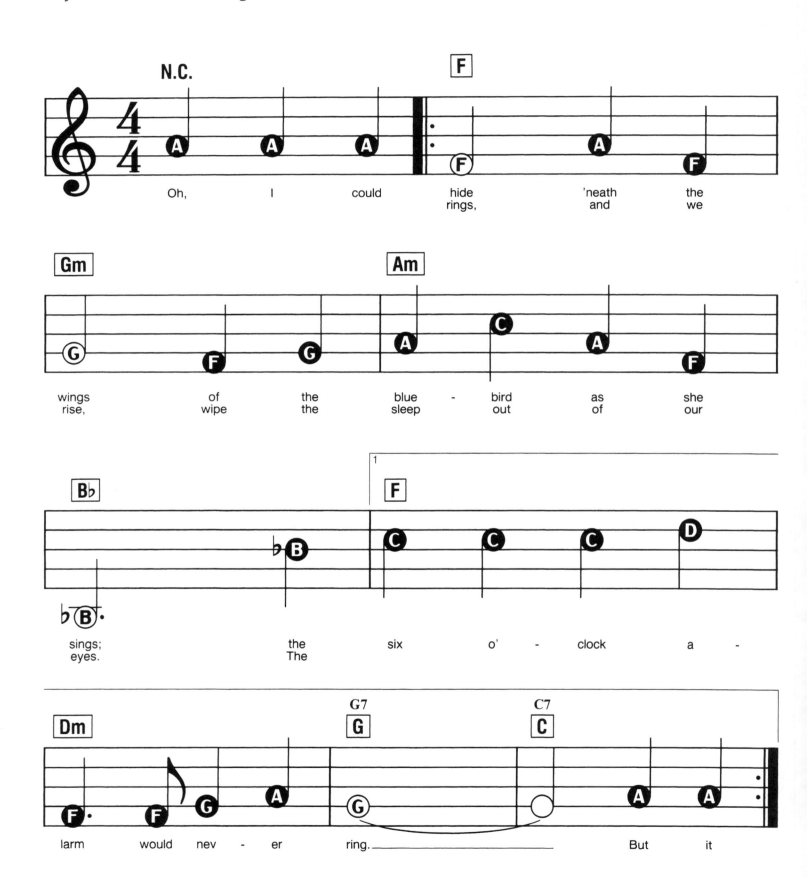

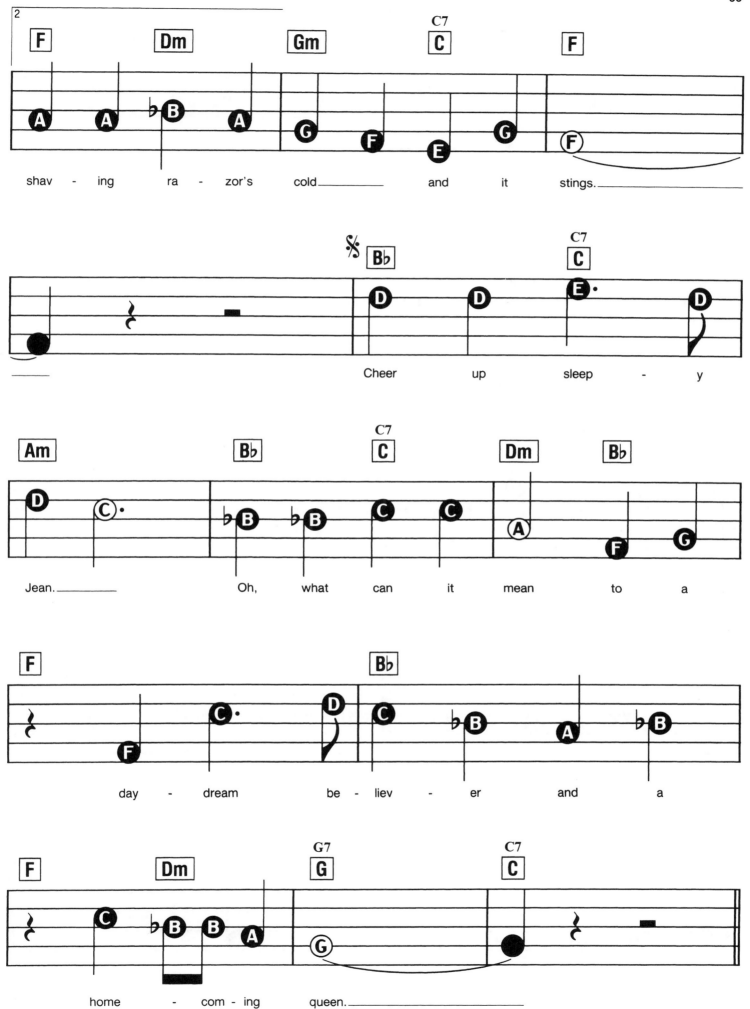

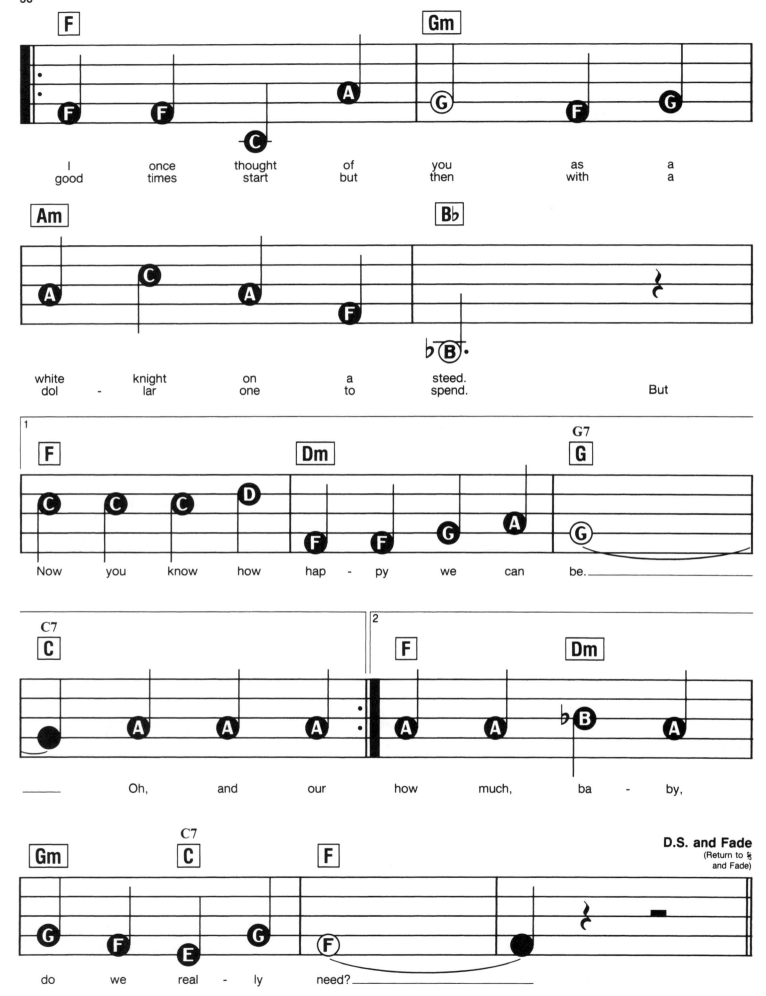

Everyday People

Registration 4
Rhythm: Rock or 8-Beat

Words and Music by
Sylvester Stewart

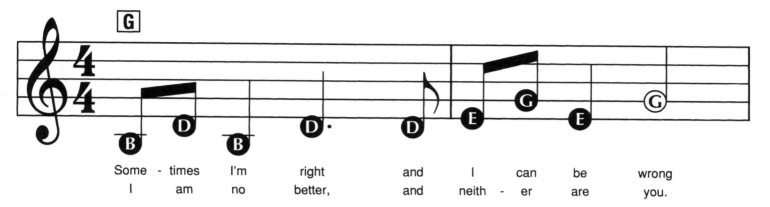

Some - times I'm right and I can be wrong
I am no better, and neith - er are you.

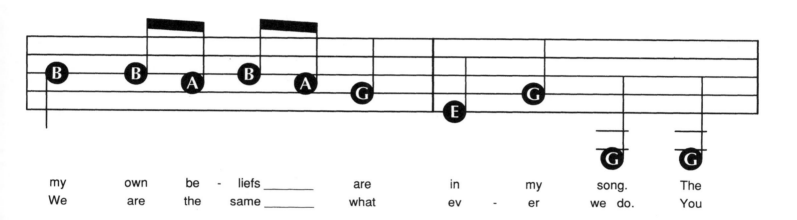

my own be - liefs _____ are in my song. The
We are the same _____ what ev - er we do. The You

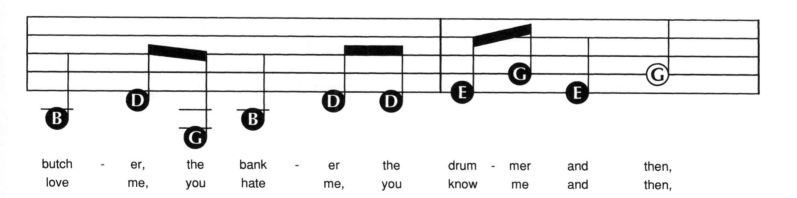

butch - er, the bank - er the drum - mer and then,
love me, you hate me, you know me and then,

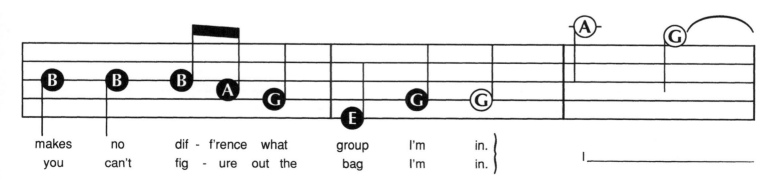

makes no dif - f'rence what group I'm in.
you can't fig - ure out the bag I'm in.

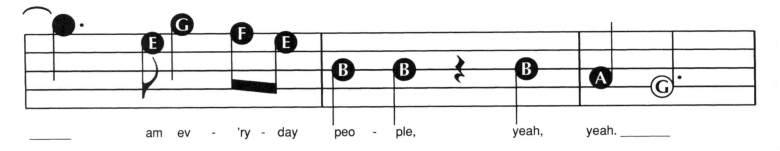

_____ am ev - 'ry - day peo - ple, yeah, yeah. _____

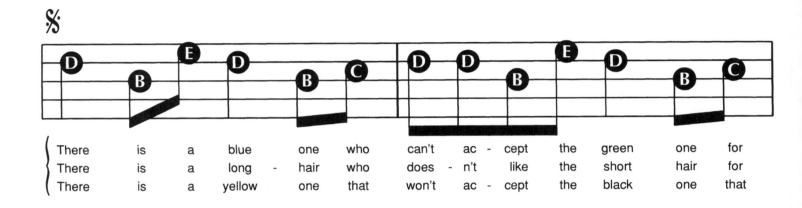

There	is	a	blue	one	who	can't	ac	-	cept	the	green	one	for
There	is	a	long	-	hair	who	does	-	n't	like	the	short	hair	for
There	is	a	yellow	one	that	won't	ac	-	cept	the	black	one	that

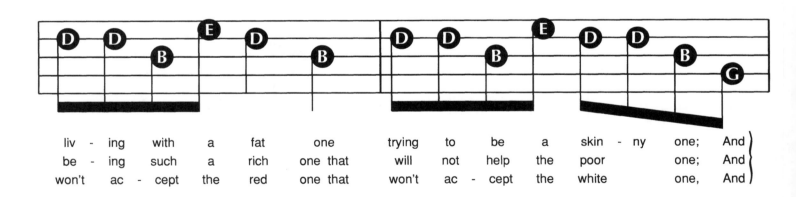

liv	-	ing	with	a	fat	one	trying	to	be	a	skin	-	ny	one;	And
be	-	ing	such	a	rich	one	that	will	not	help	the	poor	one;	And
won't	ac	-	cept	the	red	one	that	won't	ac	-	cept	the	white	one,	And

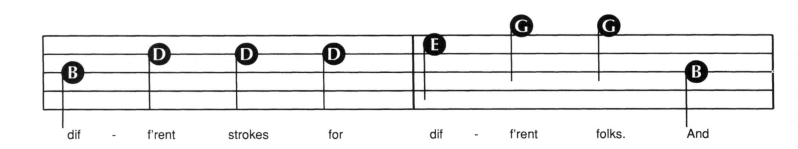

dif - f'rent strokes for dif - f'rent folks. And

59

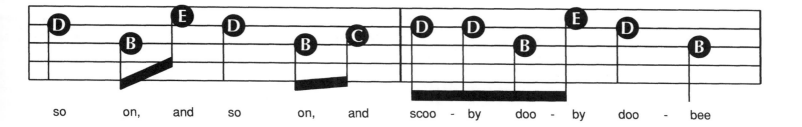

so on, and so on, and scoo - by doo - by doo - bee

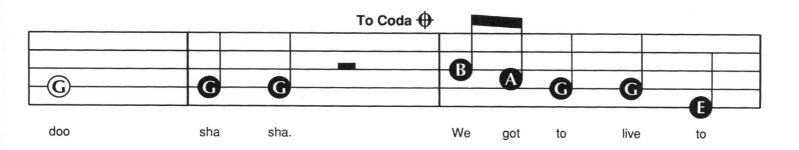

To Coda ⊕

doo   sha   sha.   We got to live to

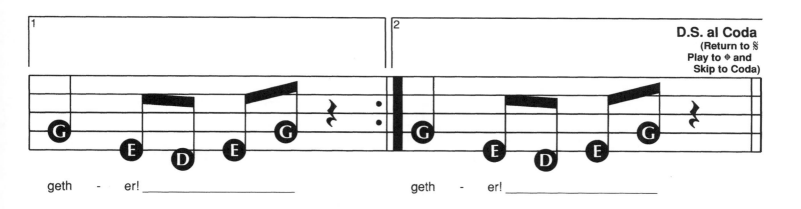

1   2   **D.S. al Coda**
(Return to 𝄋
Play to ⊕ and
Skip to Coda)

geth - er! _____   geth - er! _____

CODA
⊕

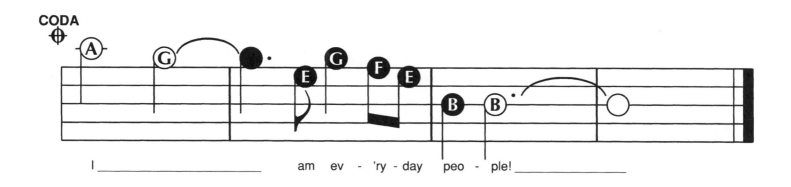

I _____   am ev - 'ry - day peo - ple! _____

The 59th Street Bridge Song
(Feelin' Groovy)

Registration 8
Rhythm: Rock

Words and Music by
Paul Simon

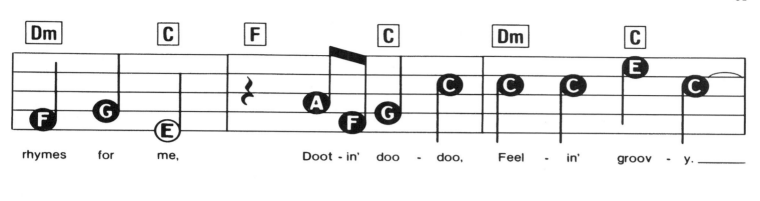

rhymes   for   me,   Doot-in' doo-doo, Feel-in' groov-y. _____

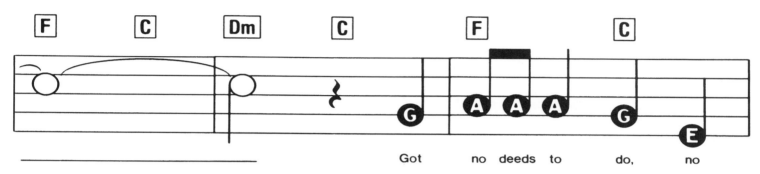

_____ Got   no deeds to   do,   no

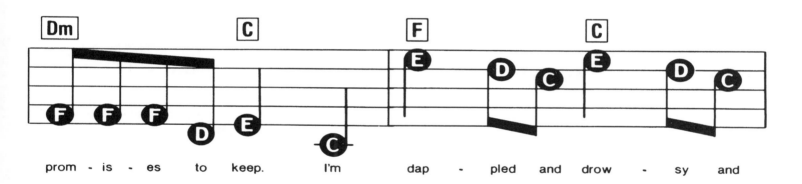

prom-is-es   to   keep.   I'm   dap-pled and drow-sy and

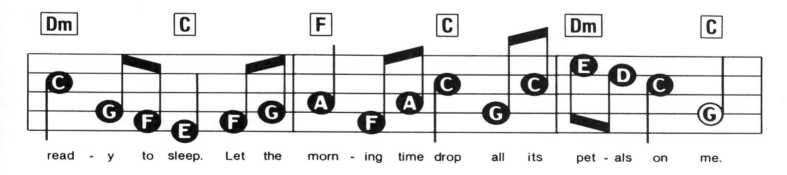

read-y   to sleep. Let the morn-ing time drop   all   its   pet-als on   me.

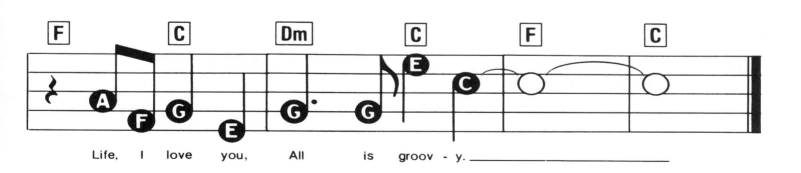

Life,   I   love   you,   All   is   groov-y. _____

Gimme Some Lovin'

Registration 2
Rhythm: Rock

Words and Music by Steve Winwood,
Muff Winwood and Spencer Davis

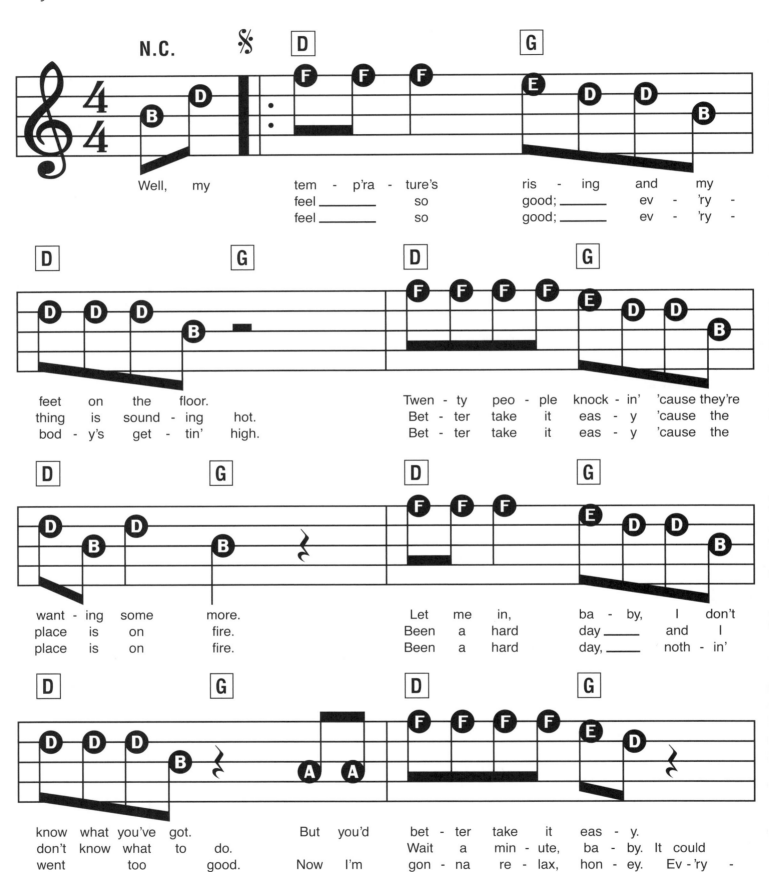

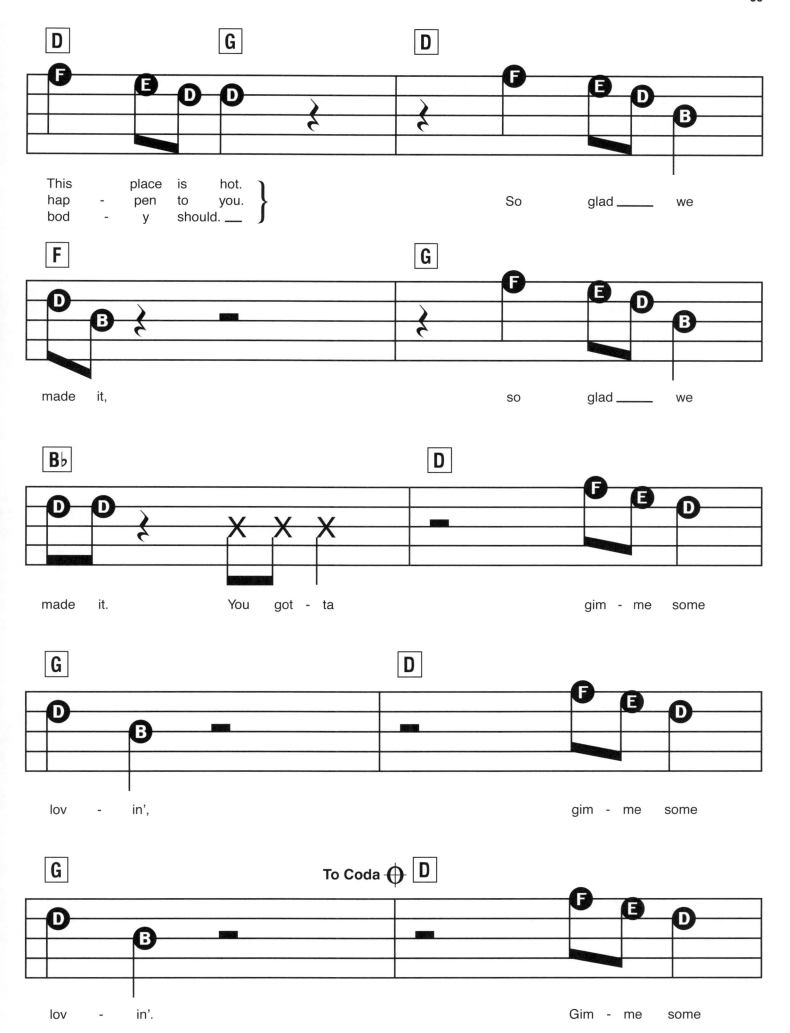

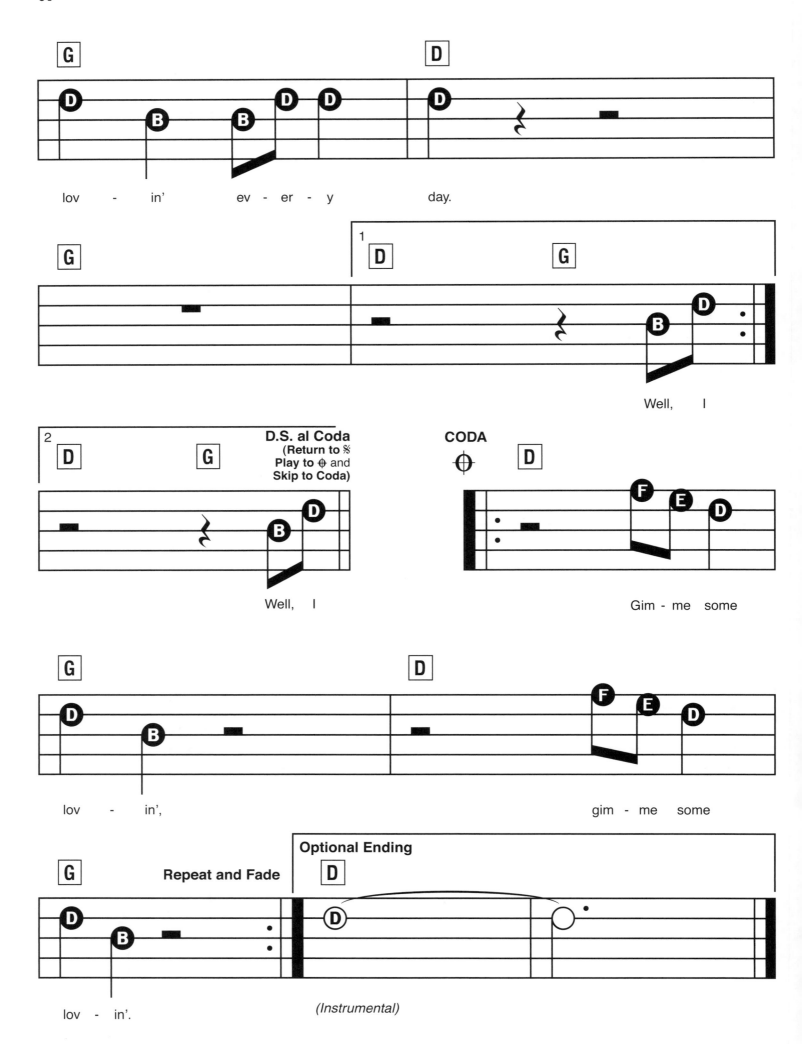

Good Morning Starshine
from the Broadway Musical Production HAIR

Registration 4
Rhythm: Rock

Words by James Rado
and Gerome Ragni
Music by Galt MacDermot

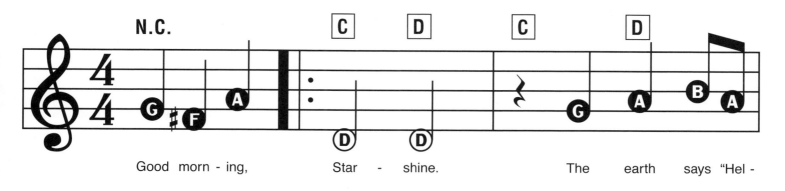

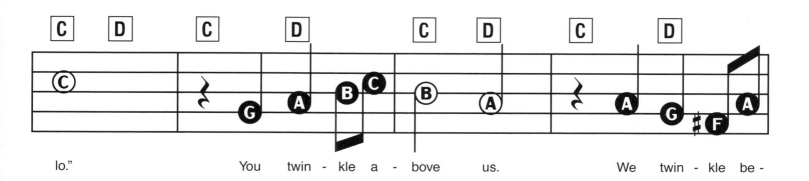

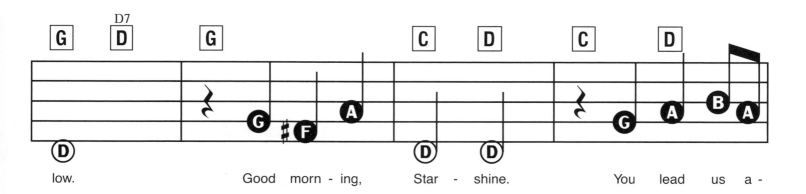

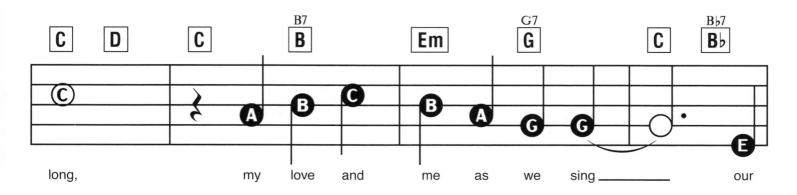

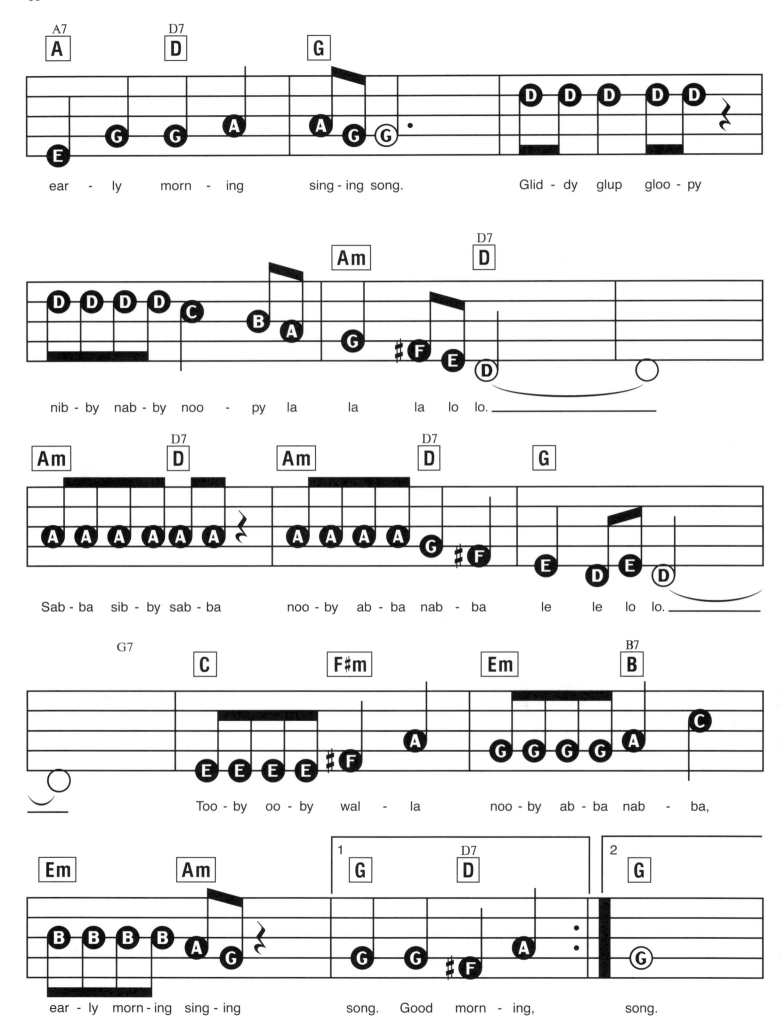

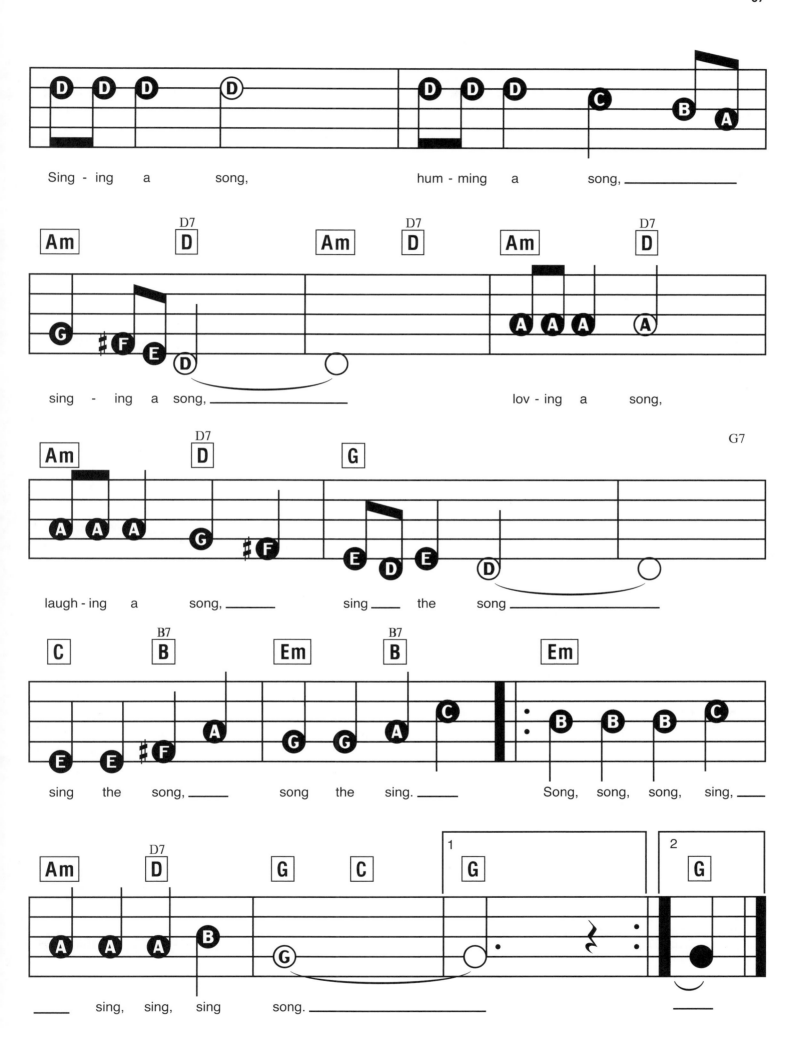

Good Vibrations

Registration 7
Rhythm: Rock

Words and Music by Brian Wilson
and Mike Love

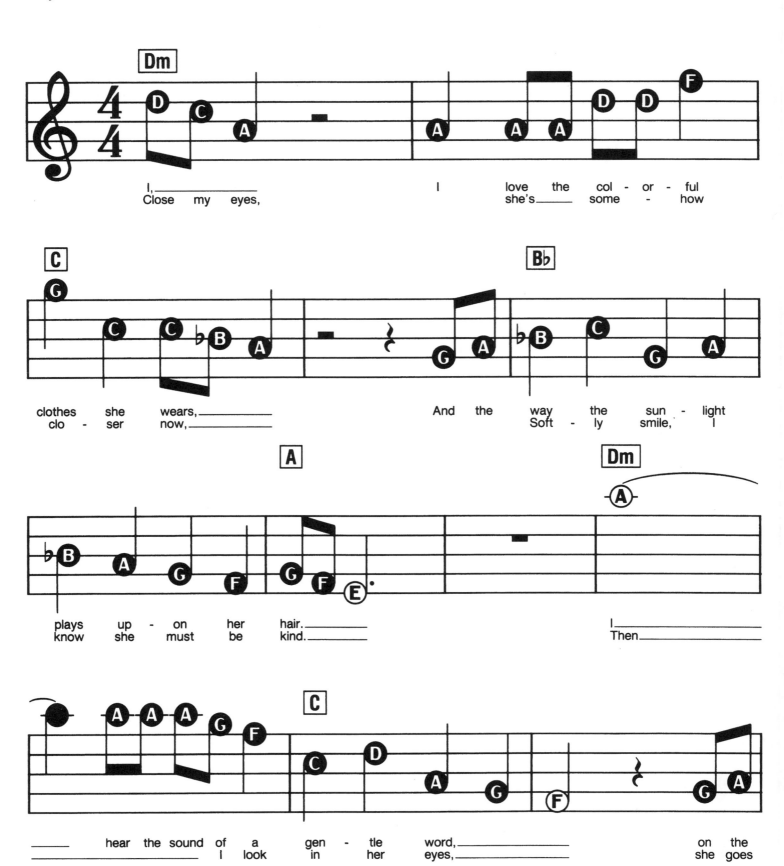

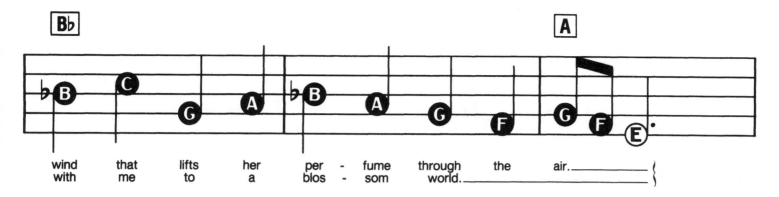

wind that lifts her per - fume through the air.
with me to a blos - som world.

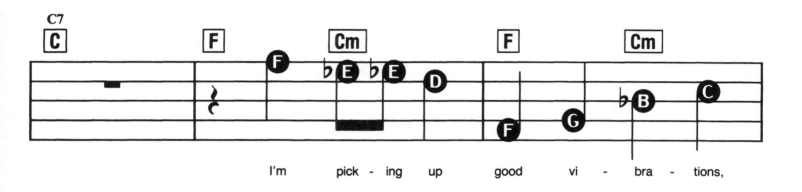

I'm pick - ing up good vi - bra - tions,

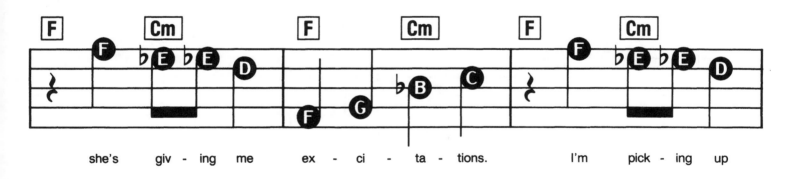

she's giv - ing me ex - ci - ta - tions. I'm pick - ing up

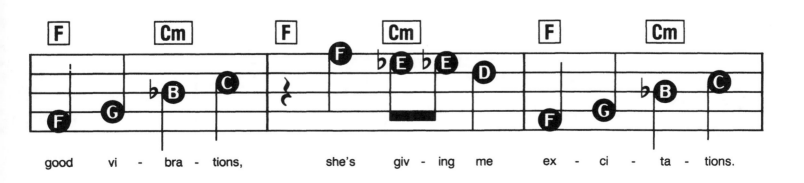

good vi - bra - tions, she's giv - ing me ex - ci - ta - tions.

70

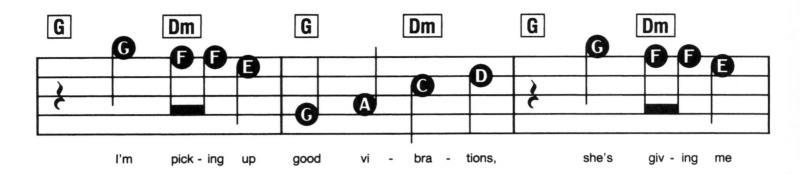

I'm pick - ing up good vi - bra - tions, she's giv - ing me

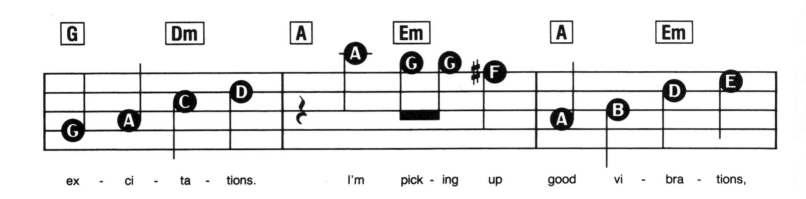

ex - ci - ta - tions. I'm pick - ing up good vi - bra - tions,

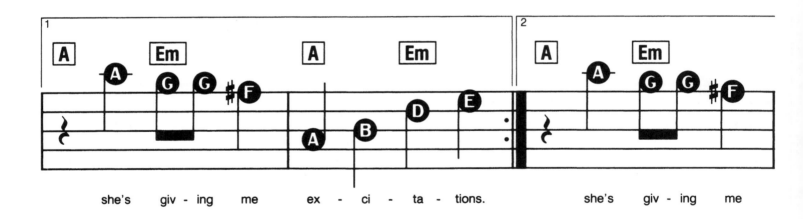

she's giv - ing me ex - ci - ta - tions. she's giv - ing me

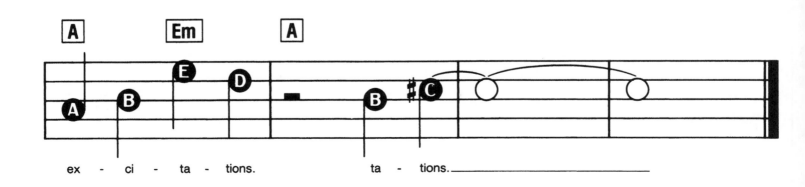

ex - ci - ta - tions. ta - tions._____

Groovin'

Registration 2
Rhythm: Slow Rock or Ballad

Words and Music by Felix Cavaliere
and Edward Brigati, Jr.

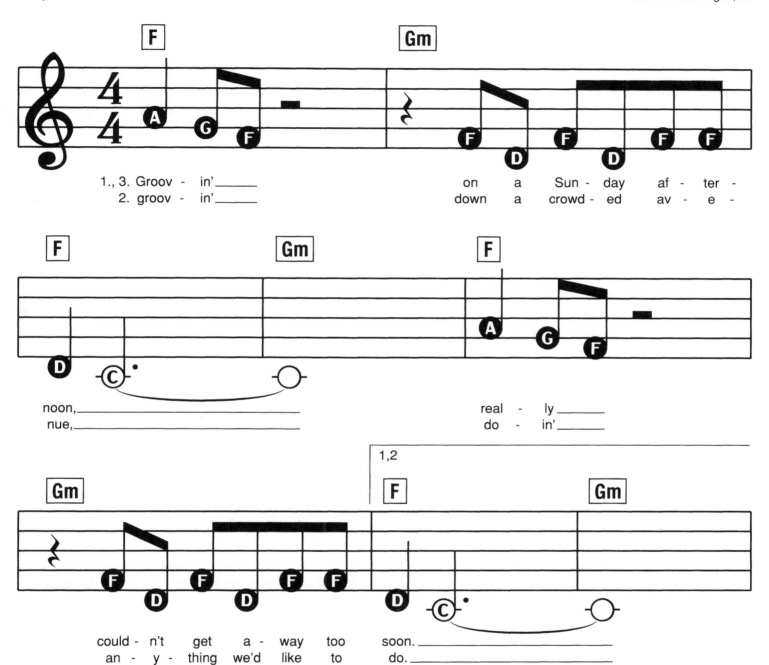

1., 3. Groov - in'_____   on a Sun - day af - ter -
2. groov - in'_____   down a crowd - ed av - e -

noon,_____   real - ly_____
nue,_____   do - in'_____

could - n't get a - way too soon._____
an - y - thing we'd like to do._____

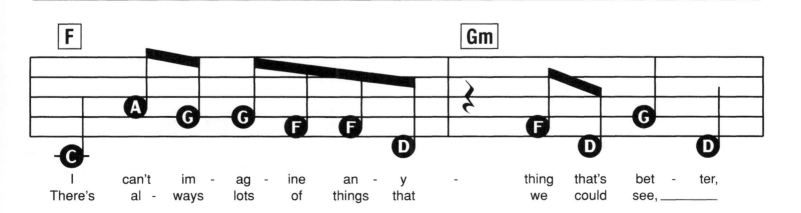

I can't im - ag - ine an - y - thing that's bet - ter,
There's al - ways lots of things that we could see,_____

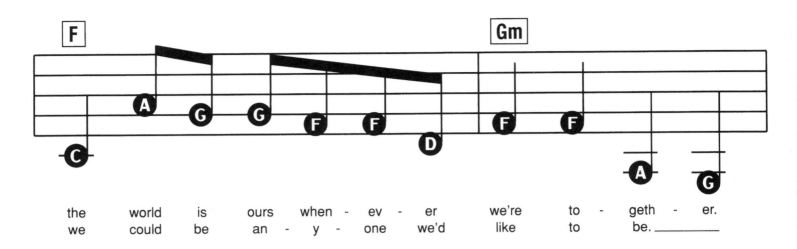

the world is ours when - ev - er we're to - geth - er.
we could be an - y - one we'd like to be. _____

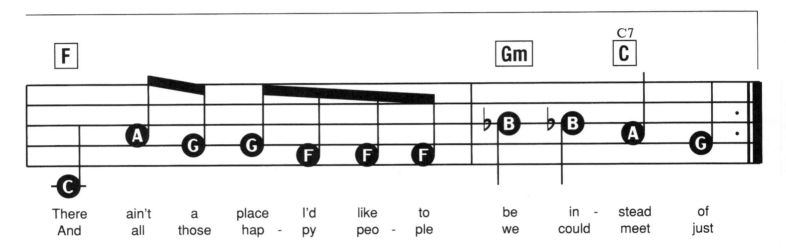

There ain't a place I'd like to be in - stead of
And all those hap - py peo - ple we could meet just

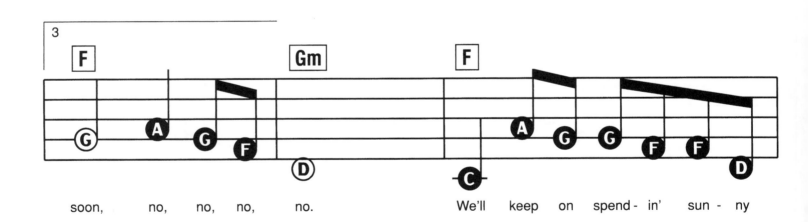

soon, no, no, no, no. We'll keep on spend - in' sun - ny

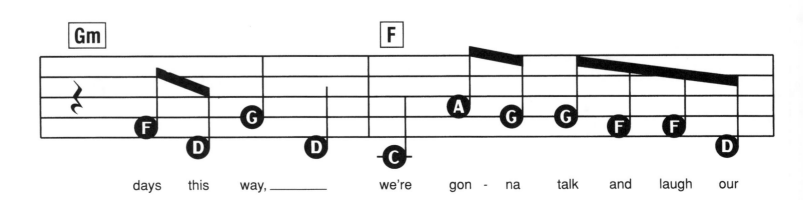

days this way, _____ we're gon - na talk and laugh our

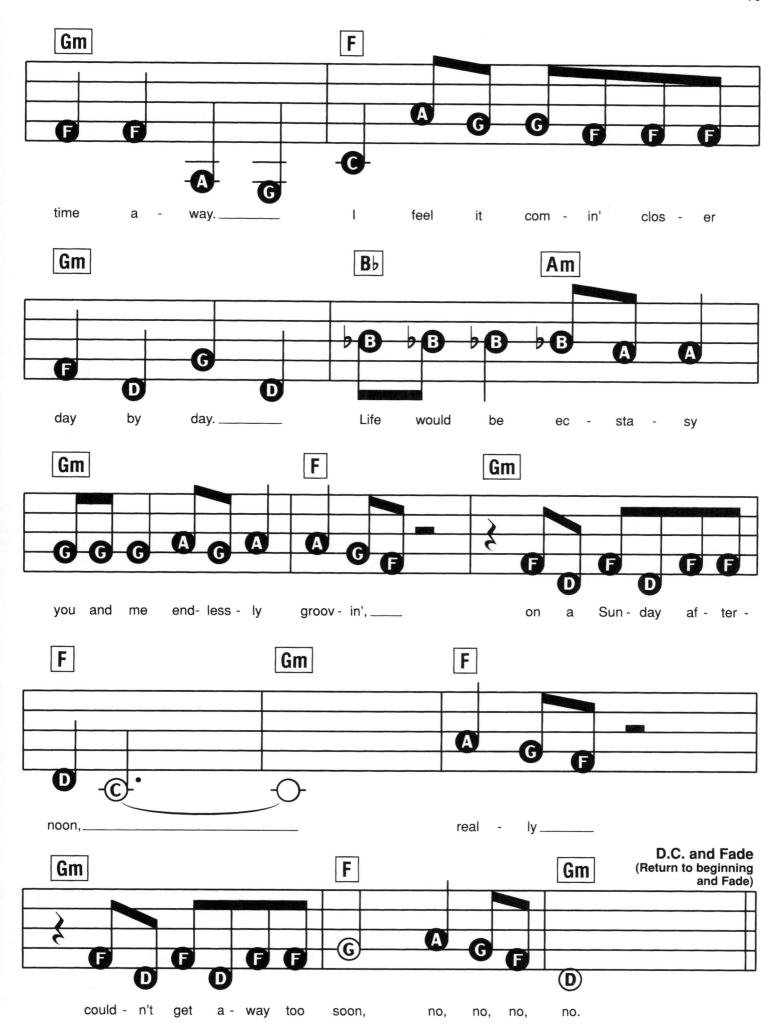

Hang On Sloopy

Registration 2
Rhythm: Rock

Words and Music by Wes Farrell
and Bert Russell

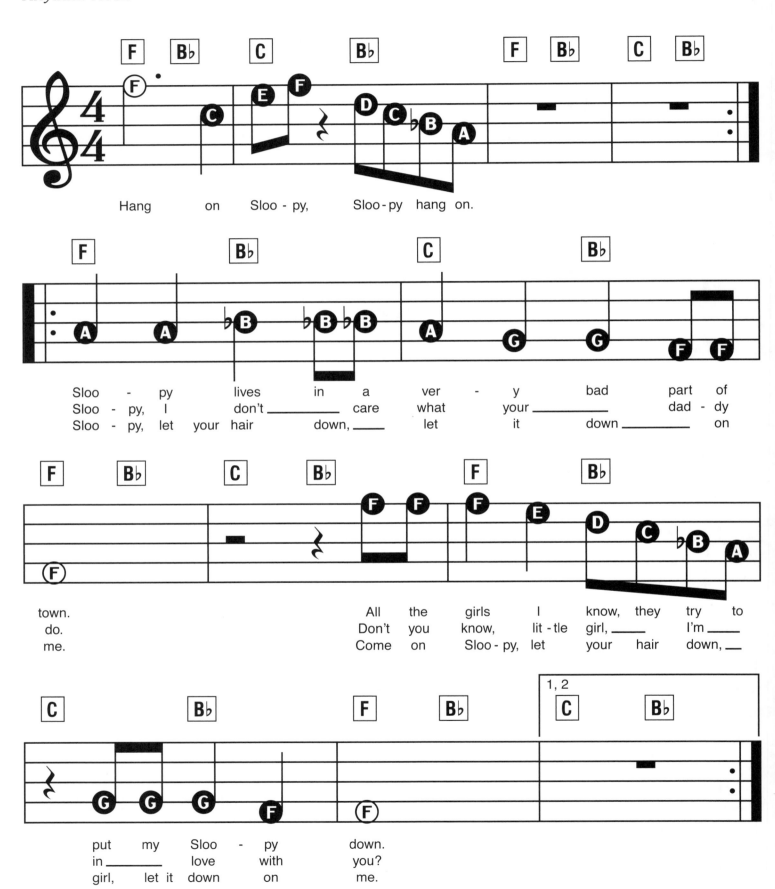

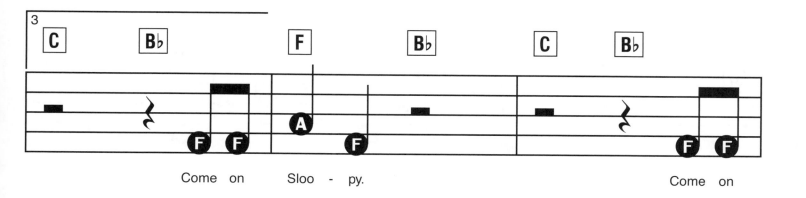

Come on Sloo - py.   Come on

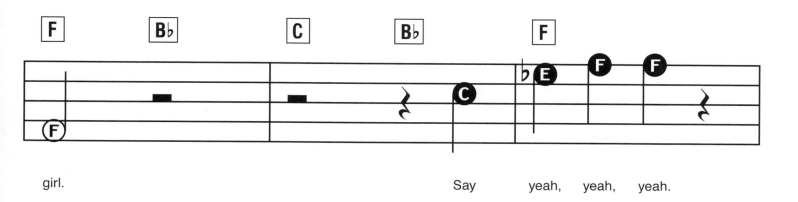

girl.   Say   yeah,   yeah,   yeah.

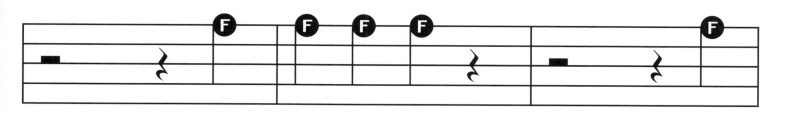

Good,   good,   good,   good.   Good,

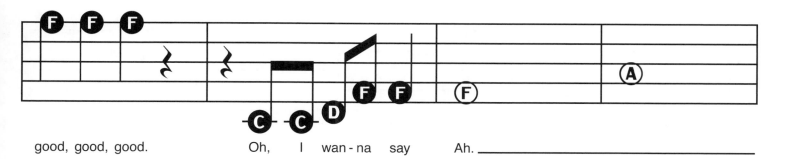

good, good, good.   Oh,   I wan-na say   Ah. _____

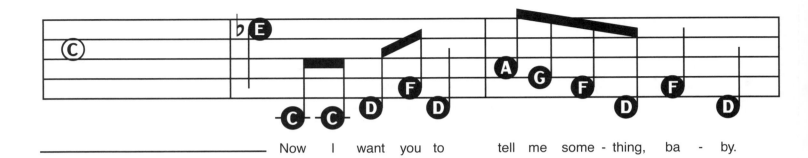

Now I want you to tell me some - thing, ba - by.

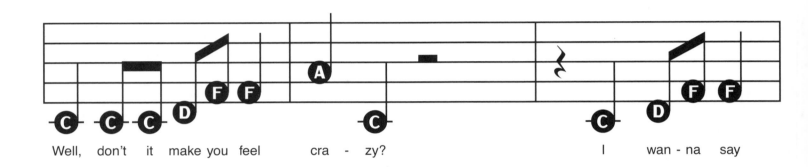

Well, don't it make you feel cra - zy? I wan - na say

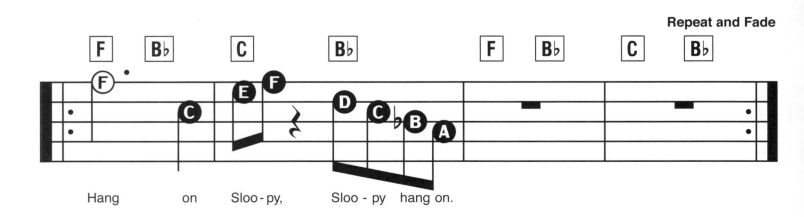

Ah.

Repeat and Fade

Hang on Sloo - py, Sloo - py hang on.

He Ain't Heavy, He's My Brother

Registration 4
Rhythm: Pops or 8-Beat

Words and Music by Bob Russell
and Bobby Scott

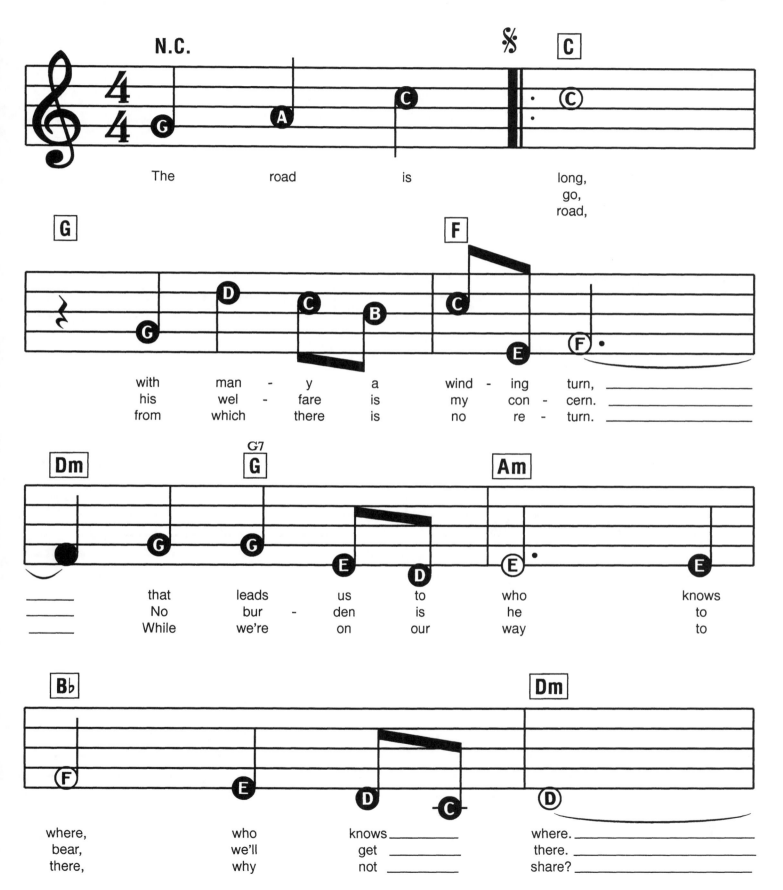

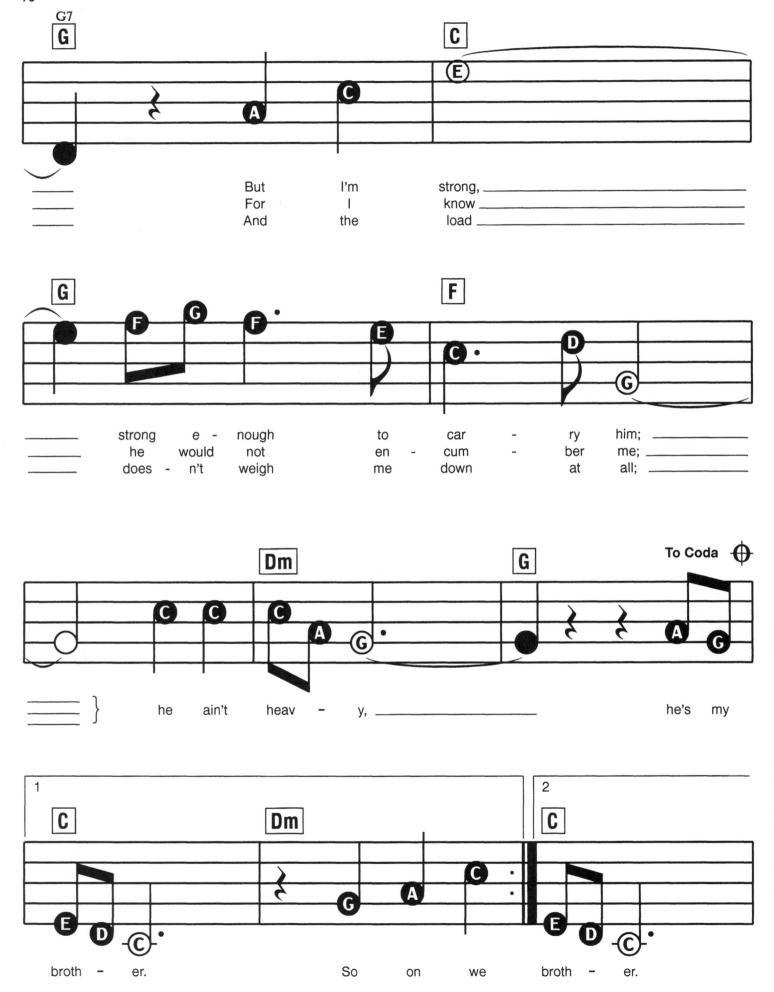

But   I'm   strong, _____
For   I   know _____
And   the   load _____

strong e - nough   to   car   -   ry   him; _____
he   would   not   en - cum   -   ber   me; _____
does - n't   weigh   me   down   at   all; _____

he   ain't   heav - y, _____   he's   my

To Coda ⊕

1

broth – er.   So   on   we

2

broth – er.

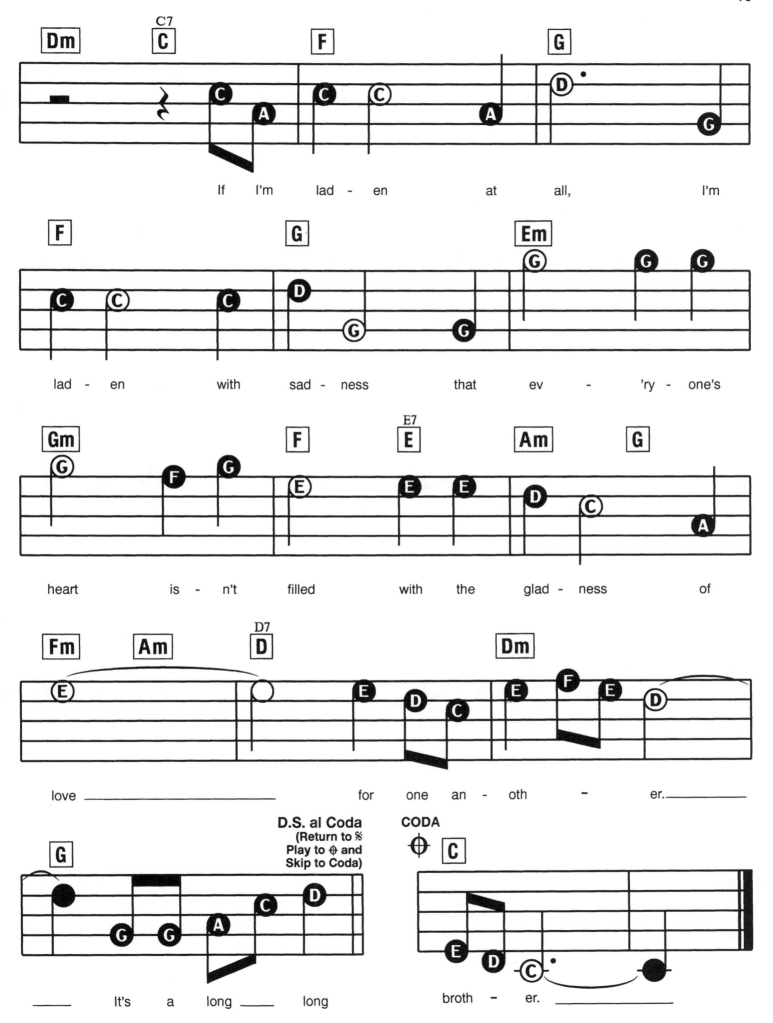

Happy Together

Registration 4
Rhythm: Rock

Words and Music by Garry Bonner
and Alan Gordon

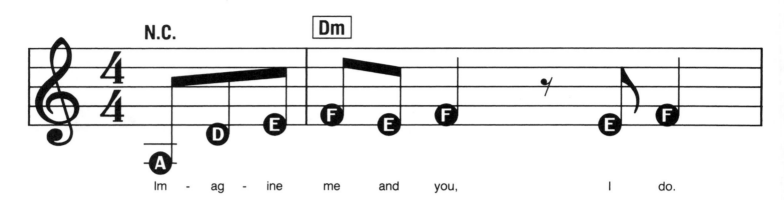

Im - ag - ine me and you, I do.

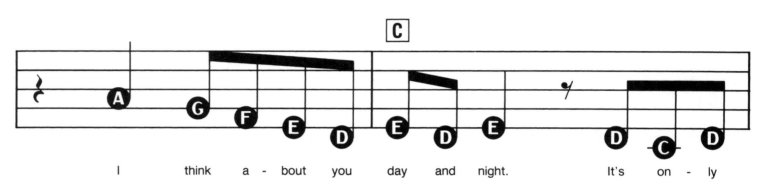

I think a - bout you day and night. It's on - ly

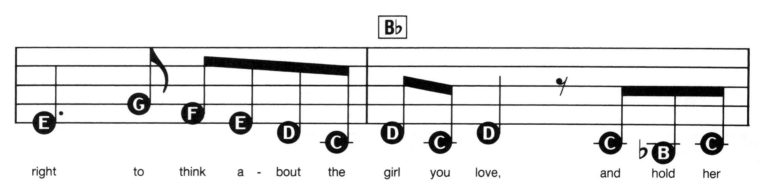

right to think a - bout the girl you love, and hold her

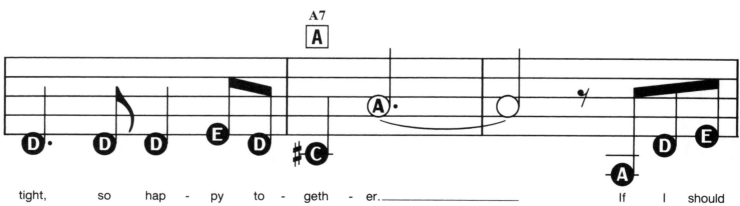

tight, so hap - py to - geth - er. If I should

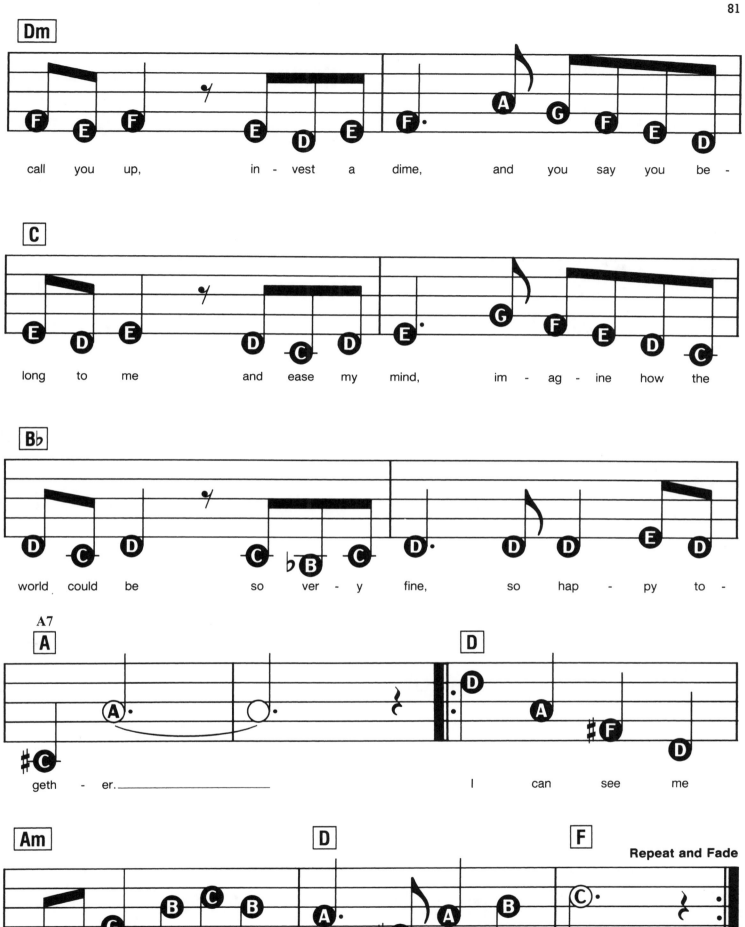

How Can I Be Sure

Registration 2
Rhythm: Waltz

Words and Music by Felix Cavaliere
and Edward Brigati, Jr.

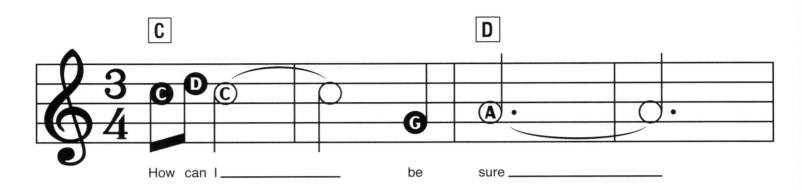

How can I _____ be sure _____

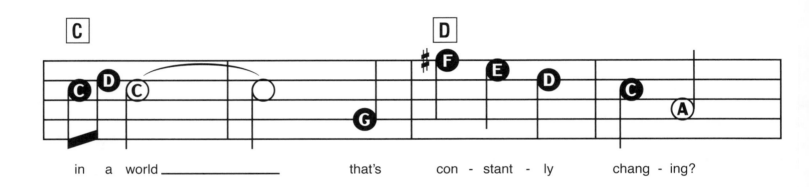

in a world _____ that's con - stant - ly chang - ing?

To Coda ⊕

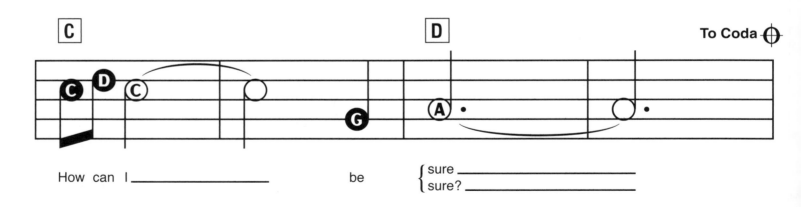

How can I _____ be ⎰ sure _____
⎱ sure? _____

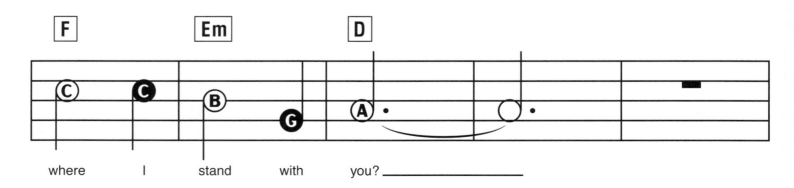

where I stand with you? _____

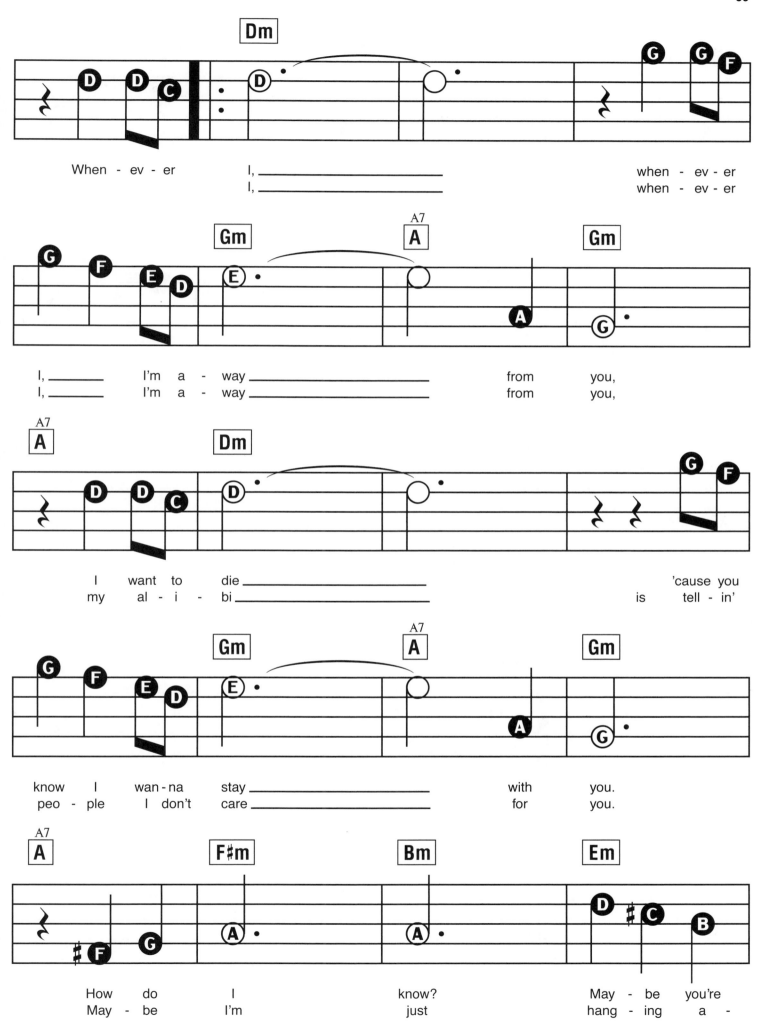

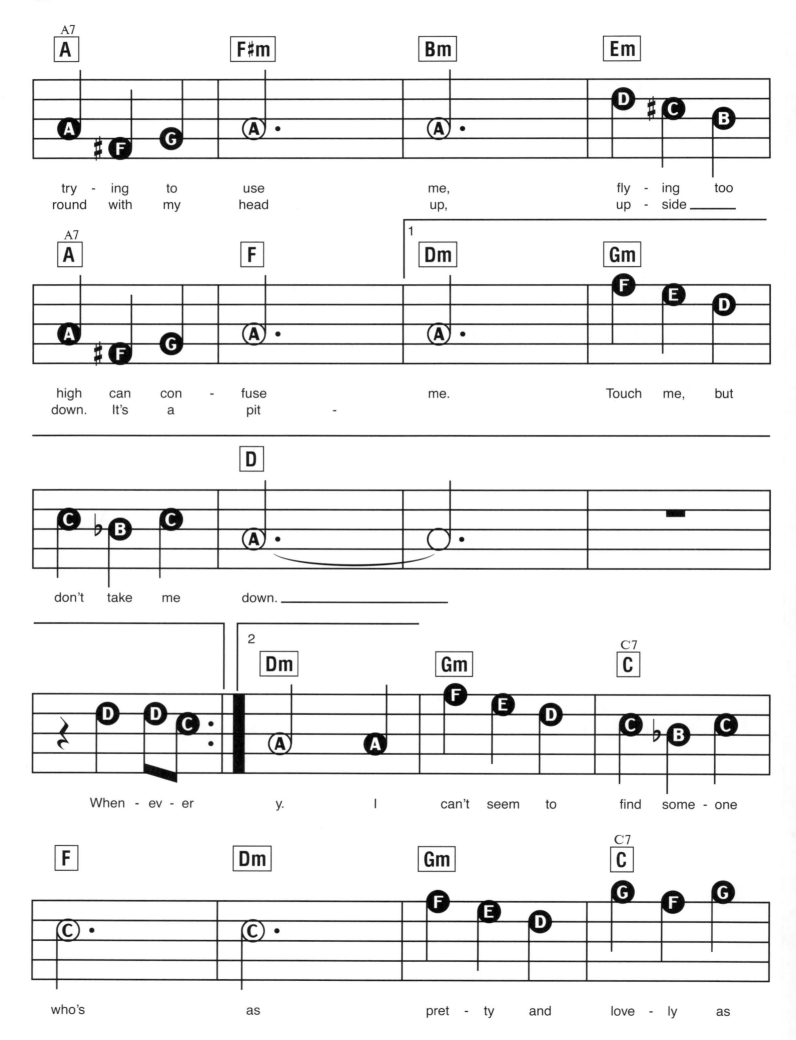

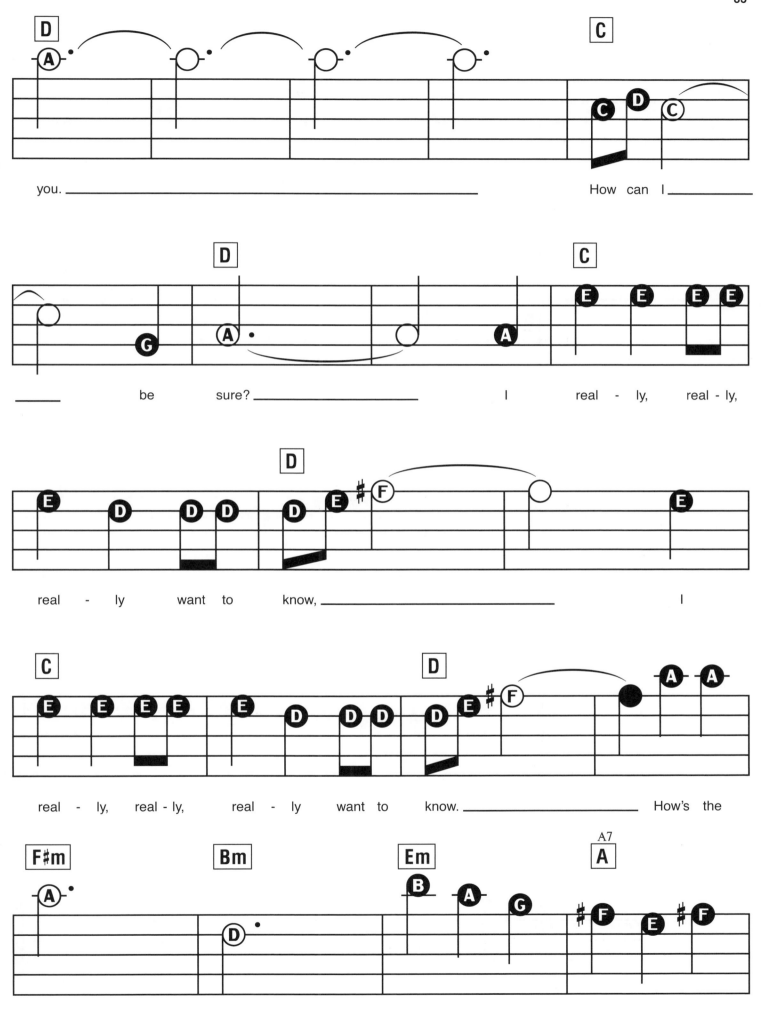

you. _____ How can I _____

_____ be sure? _____ I real - ly, real - ly,

real - ly want to know, _____ I

real - ly, real - ly, real - ly want to know. _____ How's the

weath - er? Wheth - er or not we're to -

86

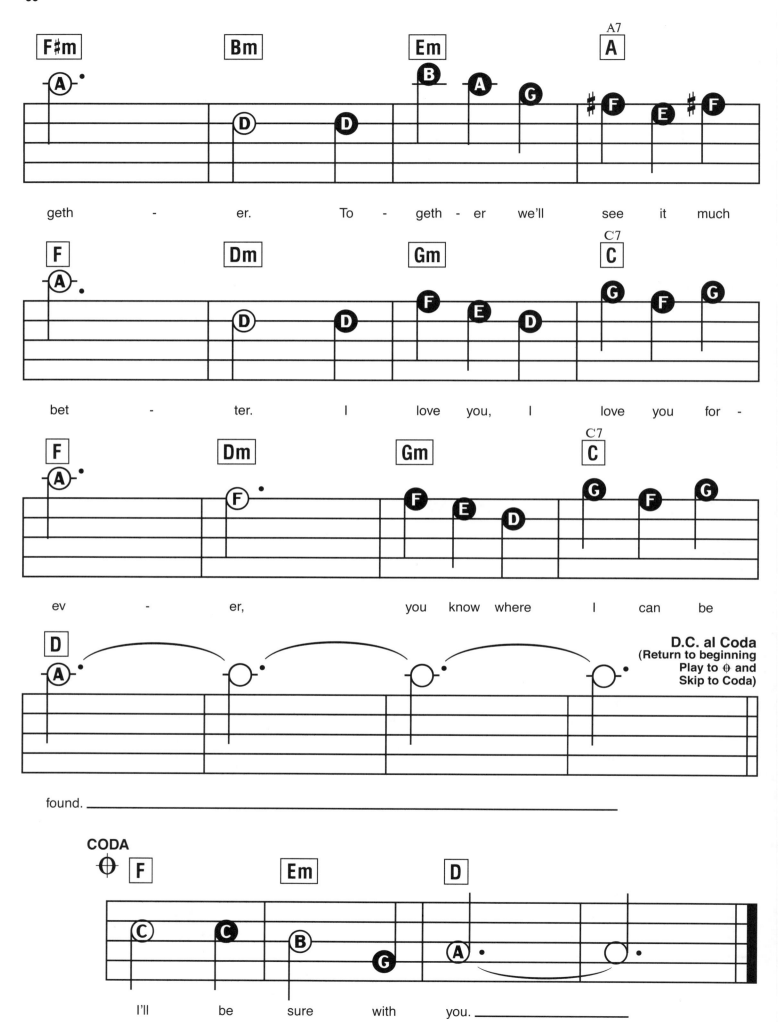

Imagine

Registration 8
Rhythm: 8-Beat or Rock

Words and Music by
John Lennon

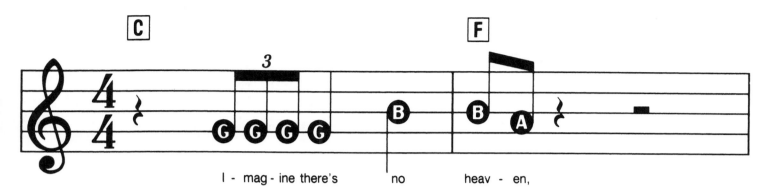

I - mag - ine there's no heav - en,

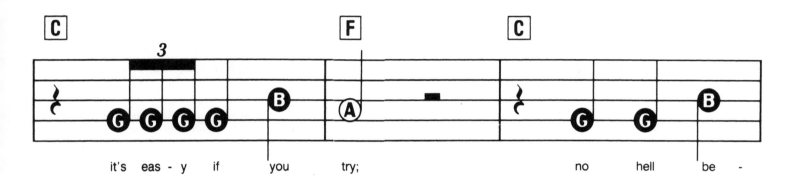

it's eas - y if you try; no hell be -

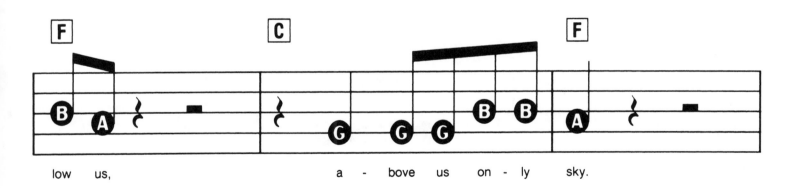

low us, a - bove us on - ly sky.

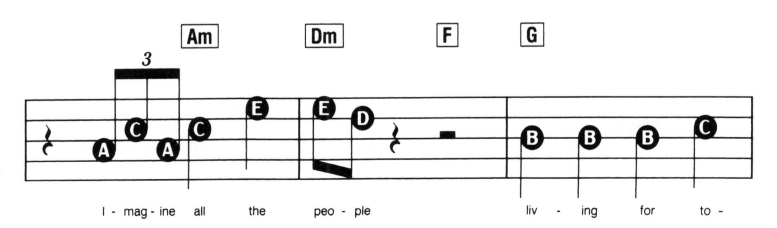

I - mag - ine all the peo - ple liv - ing for to -

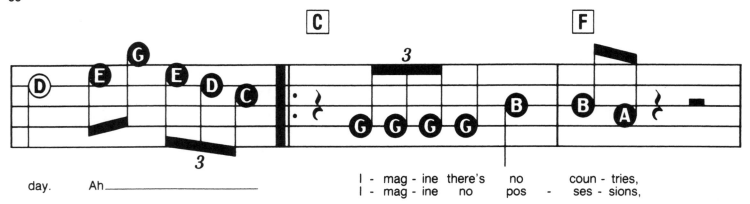

day.　　Ah

I - mag - ine there's　no　　coun - tries,
I - mag - ine　no　pos - ses - sions,

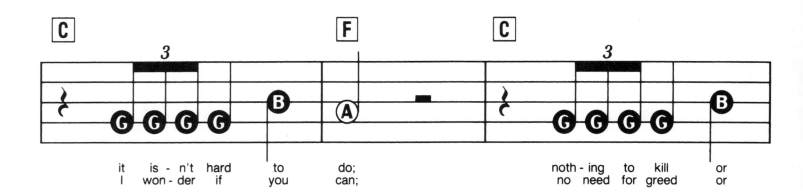

it　is - n't hard　to　do;
I　won - der　if　you　can;

noth - ing　to　kill　or
no need for greed　or

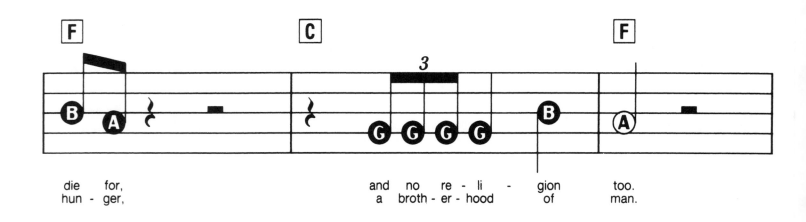

die　for,
hun - ger,

and　no　re - li - gion　too.
a　broth - er - hood　of　man.

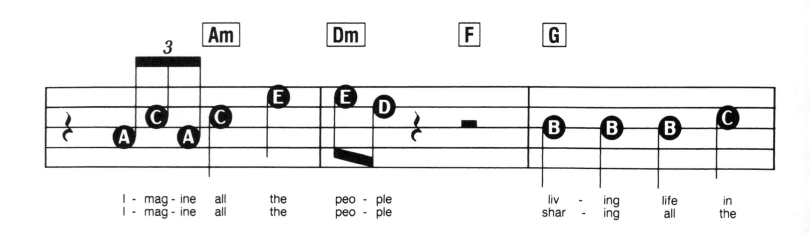

I - mag - ine　all　the　peo - ple
I - mag - ine　all　the　peo - ple

liv - ing　life　in
shar - ing　all　in the

89

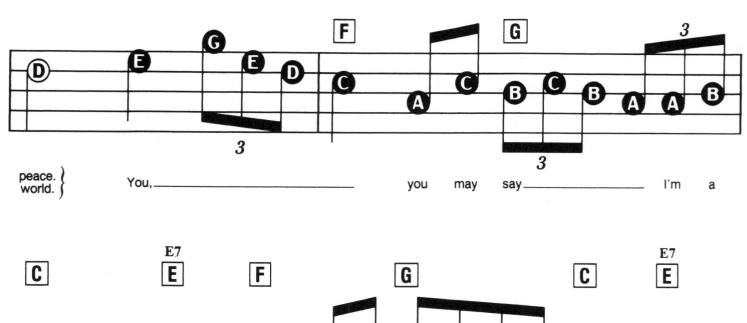

peace. } You,_____ you may say_____ I'm a
world. }

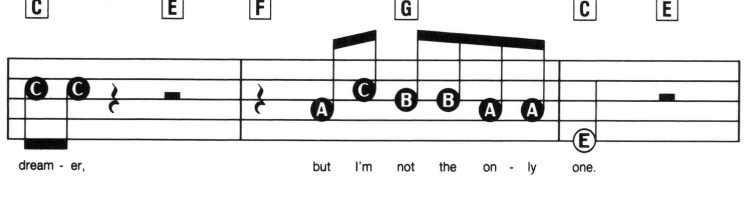

dream - er, but I'm not the on - ly one.

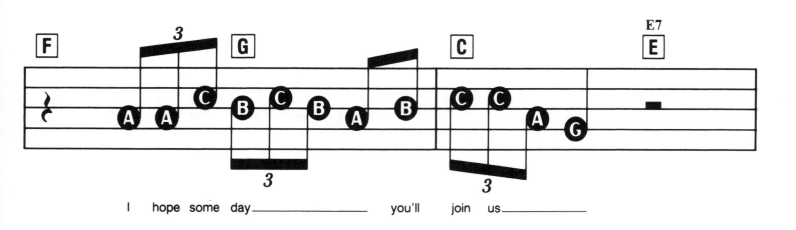

I hope some day_____ you'll join us_____

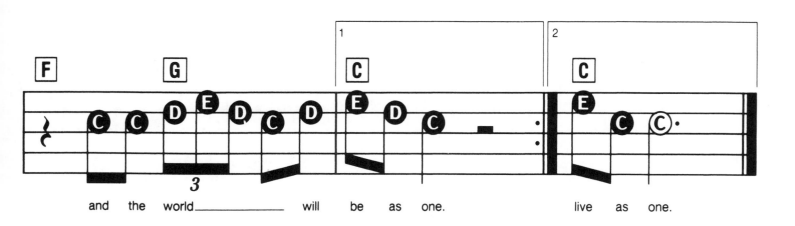

and the world_____ will be as one. live as one.

I'd Like to Teach the World to Sing

Registration 4
Rhythm: Rock

Words and Music by Bill Backer,
Roquel Davis, Roger Cook
and Roger Greenaway

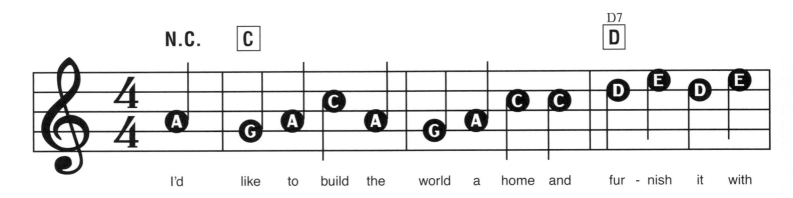

I'd like to build the world a home and fur - nish it with

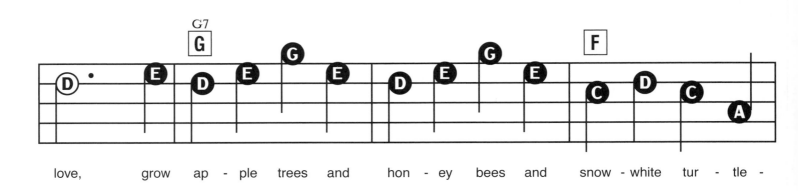

love, grow ap - ple trees and hon - ey bees and snow - white tur - tle -

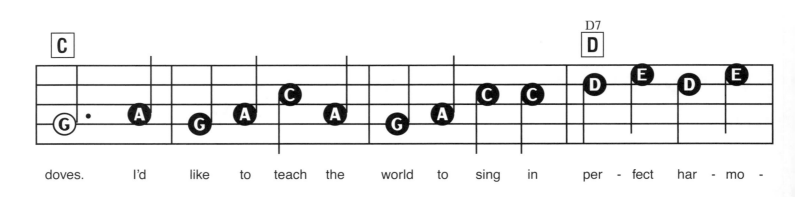

doves. I'd like to teach the world to sing in per - fect har - mo -

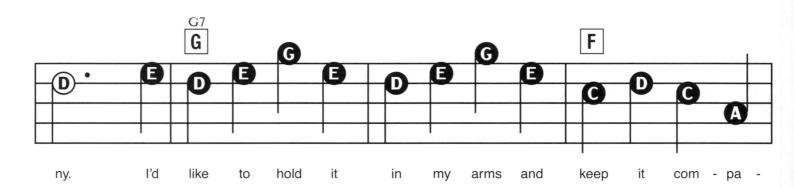

ny. I'd like to hold it in my arms and keep it com - pa -

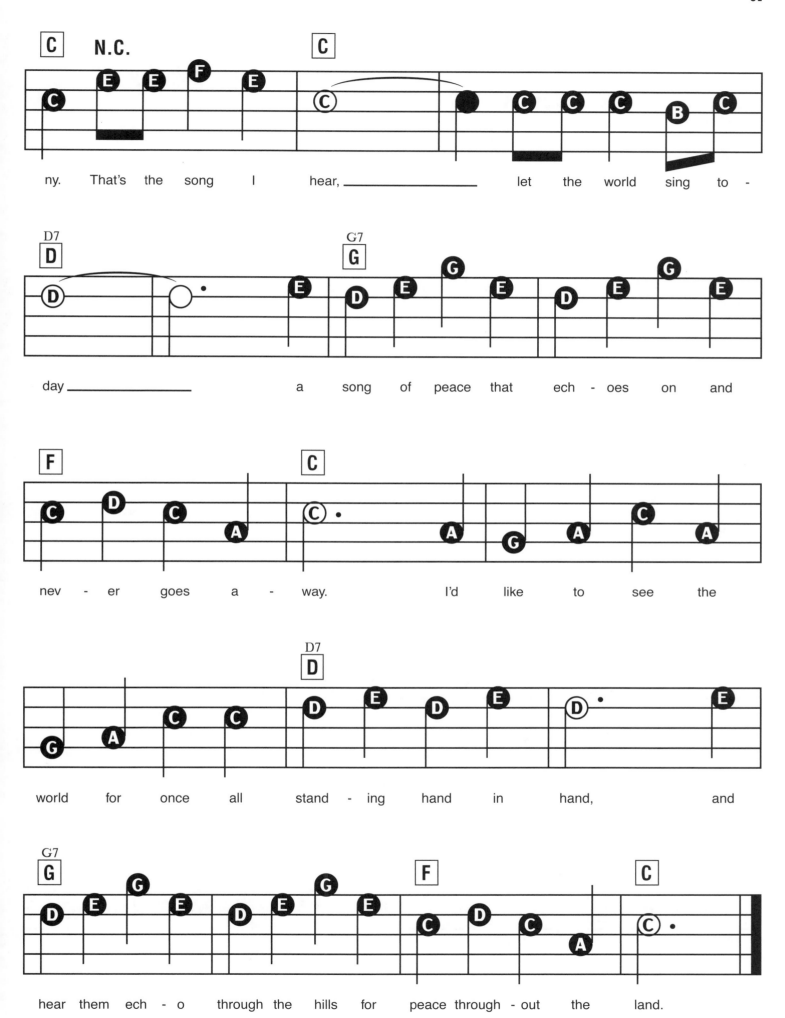

Incense and Peppermints

Registration 1
Rhythm: Rock

Words and Music by John Carter
and Tim Gilbert

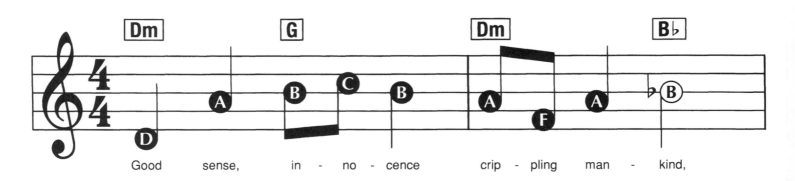

Good sense, in - no - cence crip - pling man - kind,

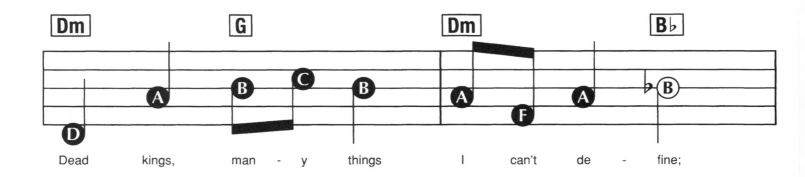

Dead kings, man - y things I can't de - fine;

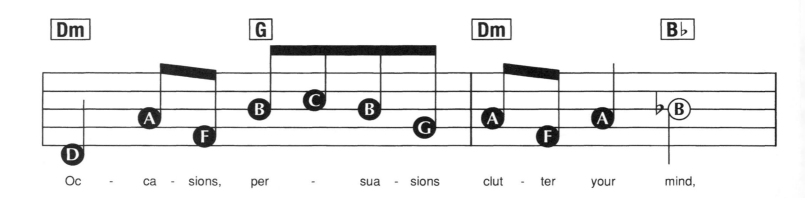

Oc - ca - sions, per - sua - sions clut - ter your mind,

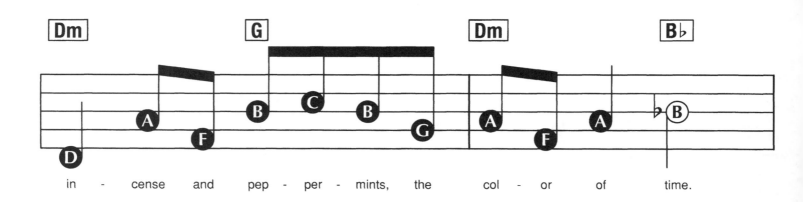

in - cense and pep - per - mints, the col - or of time.

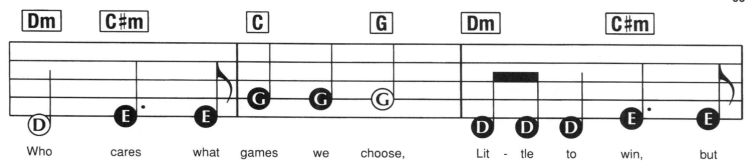

Who cares what games we choose, Lit - tle to win, but

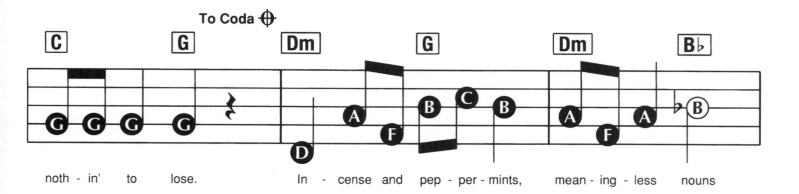

noth - in' to lose. In - cense and pep - per - mints, mean - ing - less nouns

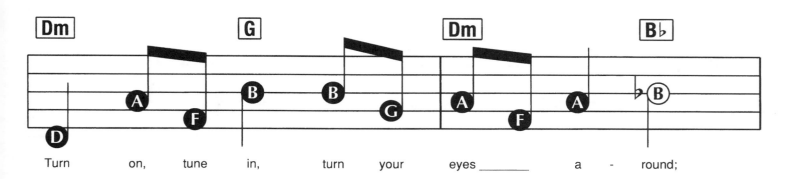

Turn on, tune in, turn your eyes_____ a - round;

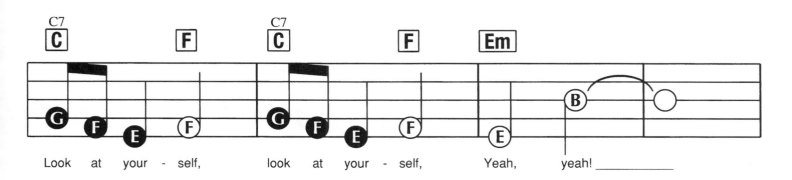

Look at your - self, look at your - self, Yeah, yeah!_____

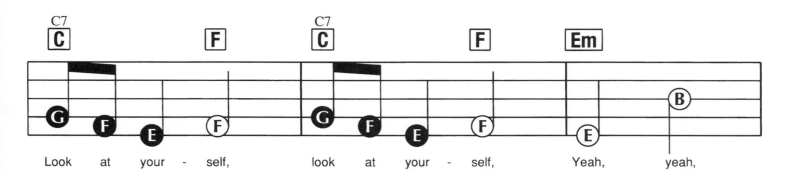

Look at your - self, look at your - self, Yeah, yeah,

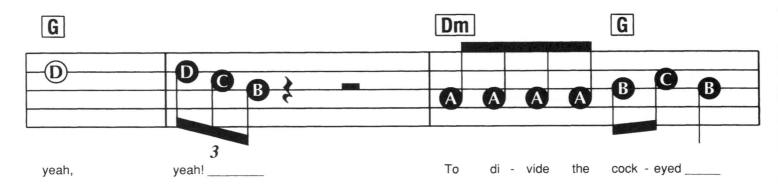

yeah, yeah! _____ To di - vide the cock - eyed ____

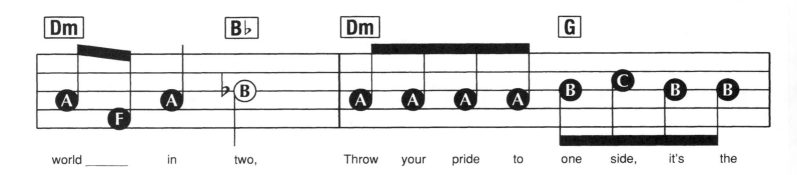

world ____ in two, Throw your pride to one side, it's the

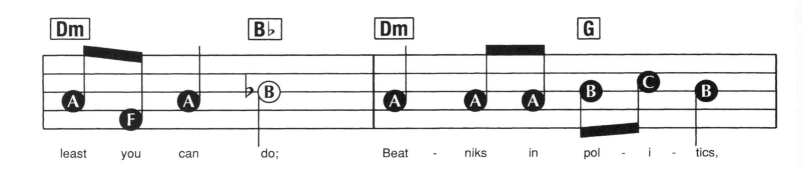

least you can do; Beat - niks in pol - i - tics,

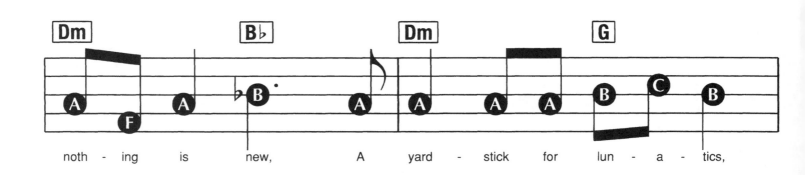

noth - ing is new, A yard - stick for lun - a - tics,

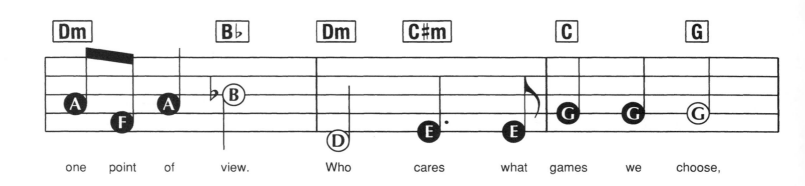

one point of view. Who cares what games we choose,

D.C. al Coda
(Return to beginning
Play to ✛ and
Skip to Coda)

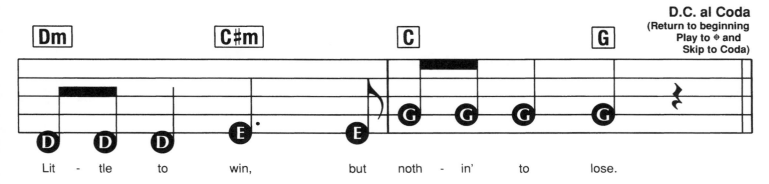

Lit - tle to win, but noth - in' to lose.

CODA ✛

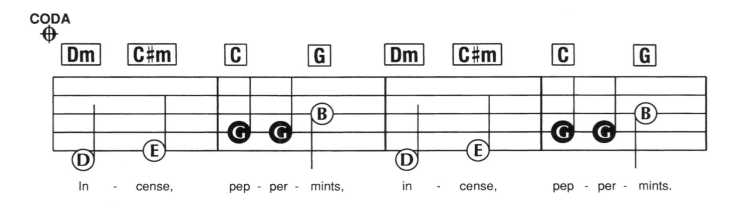

In - cense, pep - per - mints, in - cense, pep - per - mints.

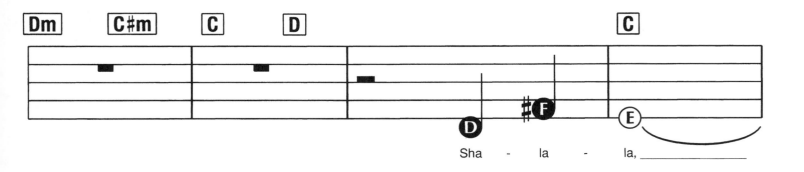

Sha - la - la, _____

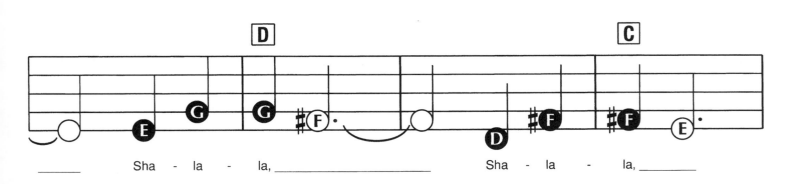

_____ Sha - la - la, _____ Sha - la - la, _____

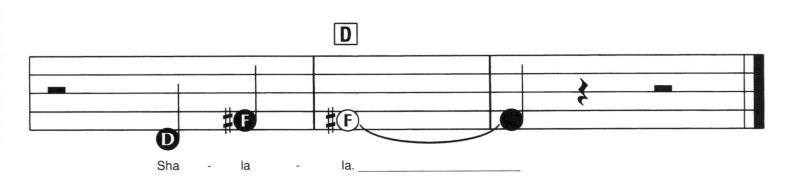

Sha - la - la. _____

It Never Rains in Southern California

Registration 8
Rhythm: Rock

Words and Music by Albert Hammond
and Michael Hazlewood

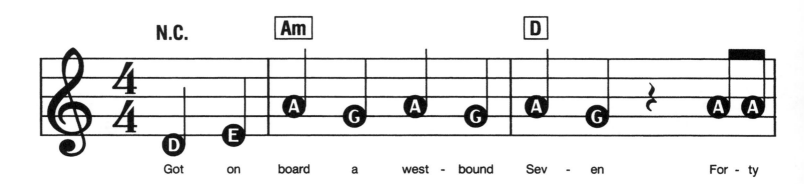

Got on board a west-bound Sev-en For-ty

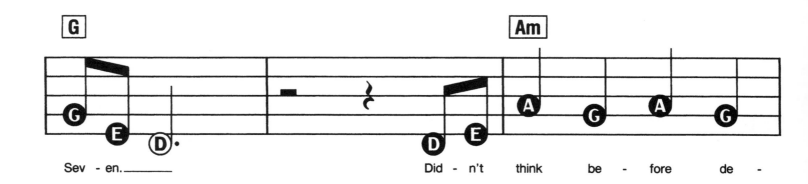

Sev-en. Did-n't think be-fore de-

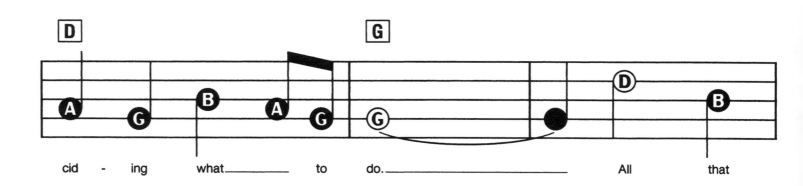

cid-ing what to do. All that

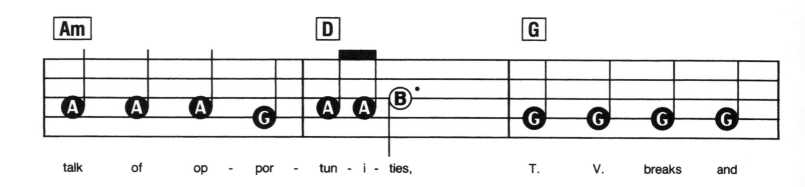

talk of op-por-tun-i-ties, T. V. breaks and

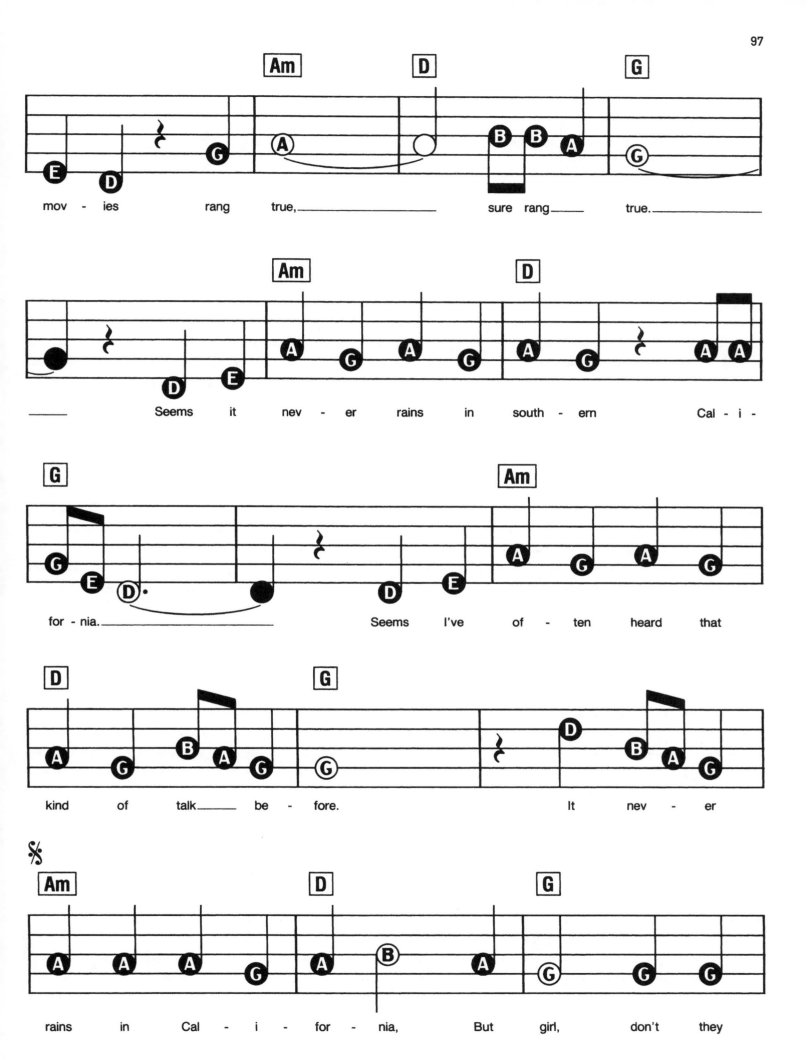

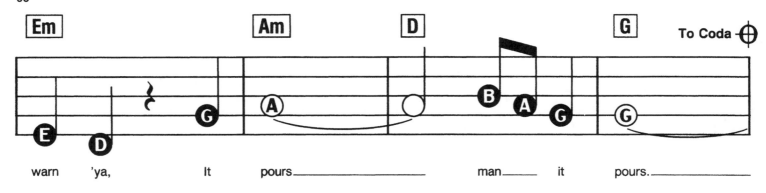

warn 'ya,   It   pours_____   man____ it   pours._____

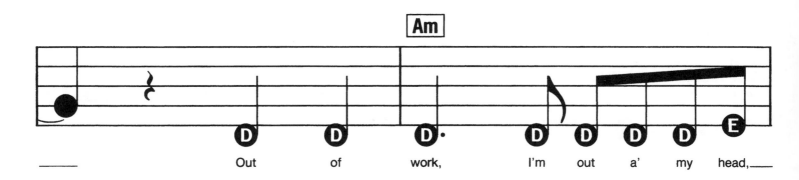

_____   Out   of   work,   I'm   out   a'   my   head,____

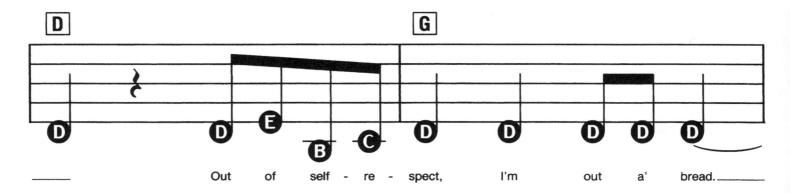

_____   Out   of   self - re - spect,   I'm   out   a'   bread._____

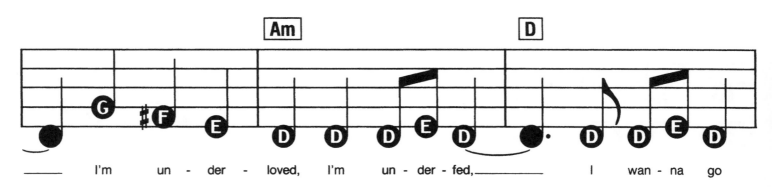

_____   I'm   un - der - loved,   I'm   un - der - fed,_____   I   wan - na   go

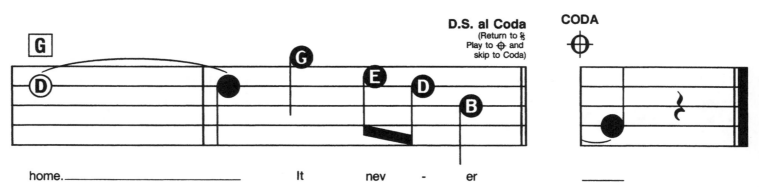

home._____   It   nev - er   _____

Joy to the World

Registration 2
Rhythm: Rock

Words and Music by
Hoyt Axton

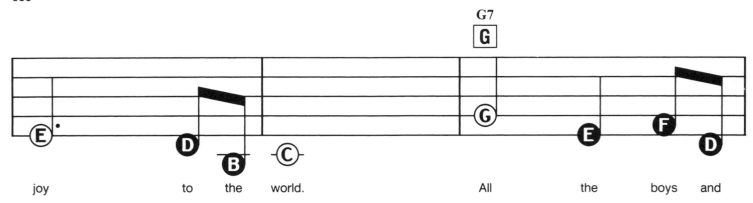

joy to the world. All the boys and

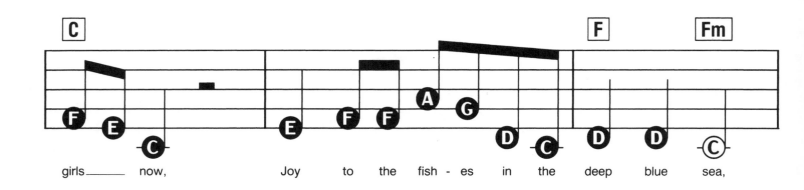

girls___ now, Joy to the fish - es in the deep blue sea,

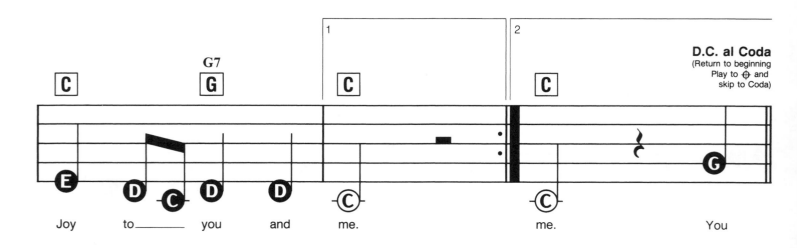

Joy to___ you and me. me. You

CODA

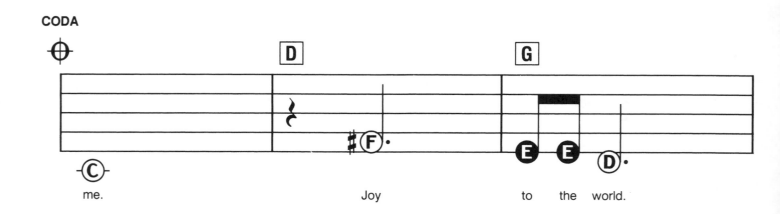

me. Joy to the world.

101

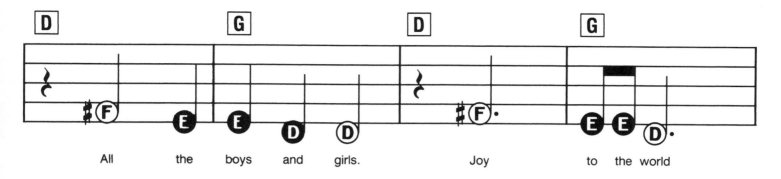

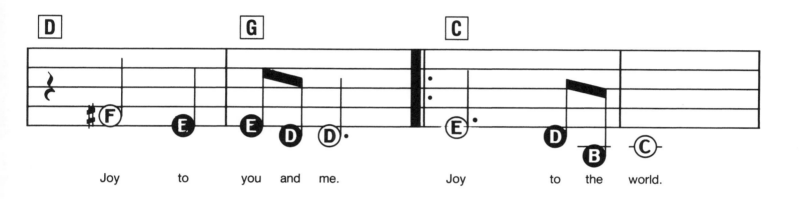

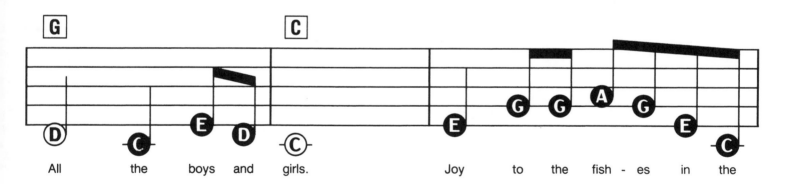

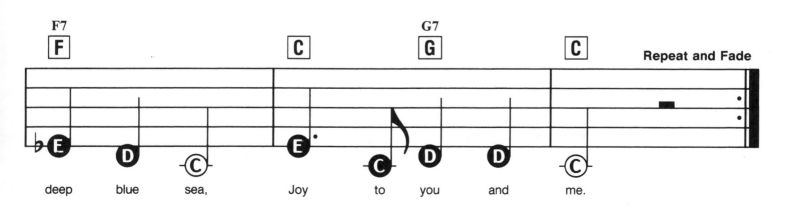

Leaving on a Jet Plane

Registration 1
Rhythm: Rock or Slow Rock

Words and Music by
John Denver

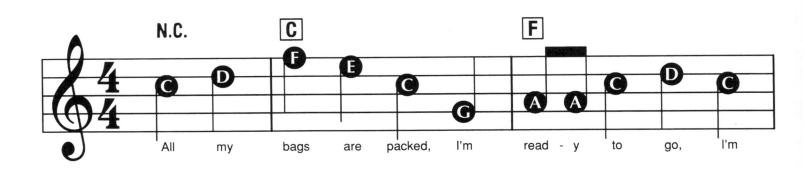

All my bags are packed, I'm read - y to go, I'm

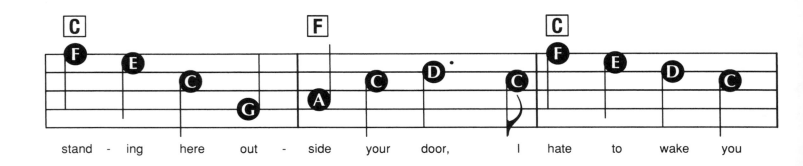

stand - ing here out - side your door, I hate to wake you

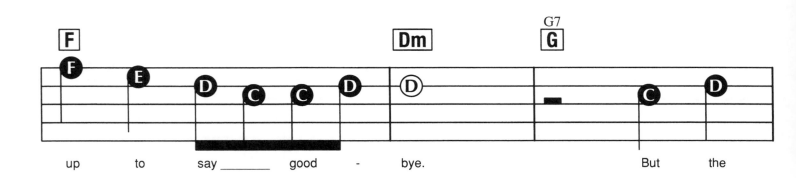

up to say _____ good - bye. But the

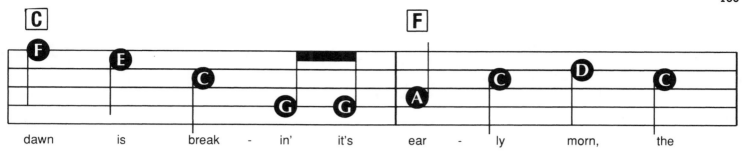

dawn is break - in' it's ear - ly morn, the

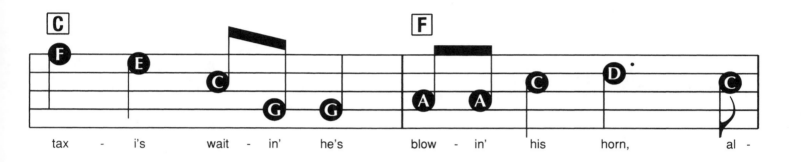

tax - i's wait - in' he's blow - in' his horn, al -

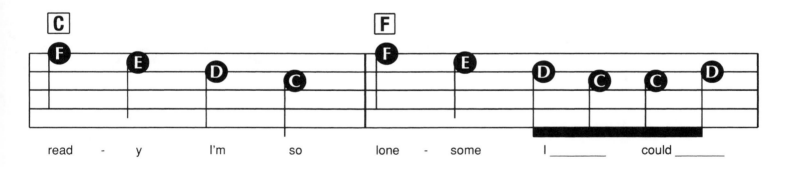

read - y I'm so lone - some I _____ could _____

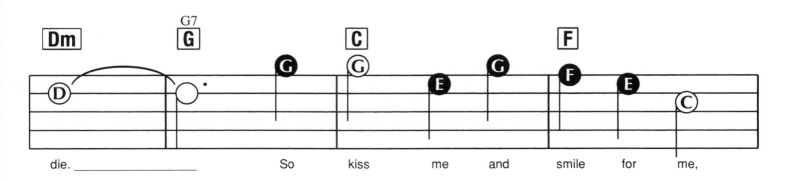

die. _____ So kiss me and smile for me,

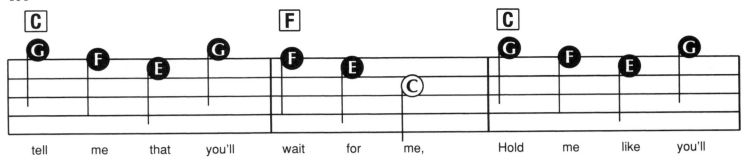

tell me that you'll wait for me, Hold me like you'll

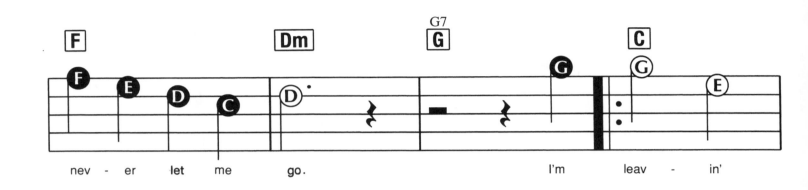

nev - er let me go. I'm leav - in'

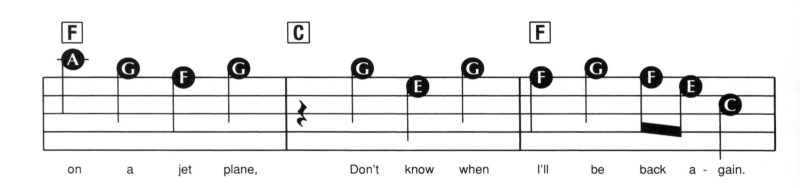

on a jet plane, Don't know when I'll be back a - gain.

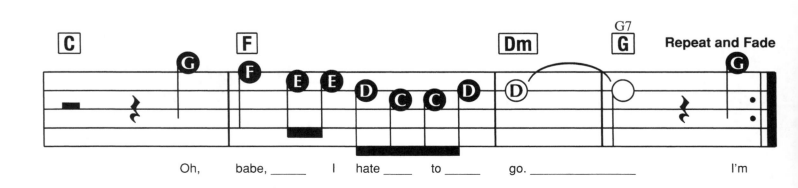

Oh, babe, _____ I hate _____ to _____ go. _____ I'm

Magic Carpet Ride

Registration 5
Rhythm: Rock or Hark Rock

Words and Music by John Kay
and Rushton Moreve

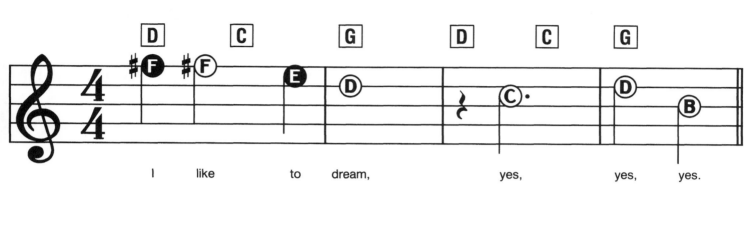

I like to dream, yes, yes, yes.

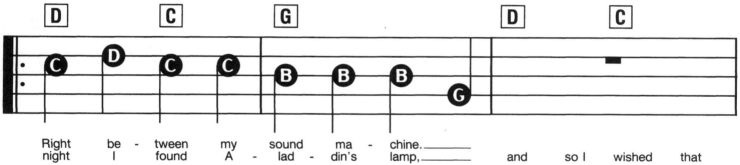

Right be - tween my sound ma - chine._____
night I found A - lad - din's lamp,_____ and so I wished that

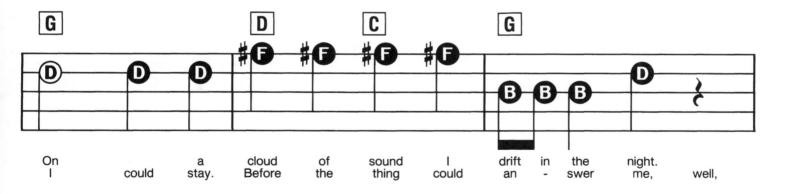

On a cloud of sound I drift in the night.
I could stay. Before the thing I could an - swer me, well,

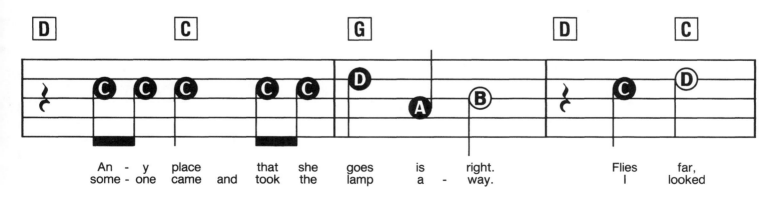

An - y place that she goes is right. Flies far,
some - one came and took the lamp a - way. I looked

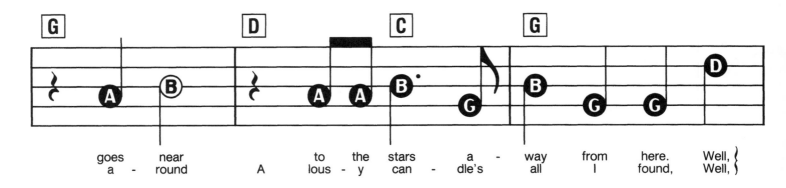

goes   near   to the stars   a - way from here.   Well,
a - round   A   lous - y can - dle's   all   I   found,   Well,

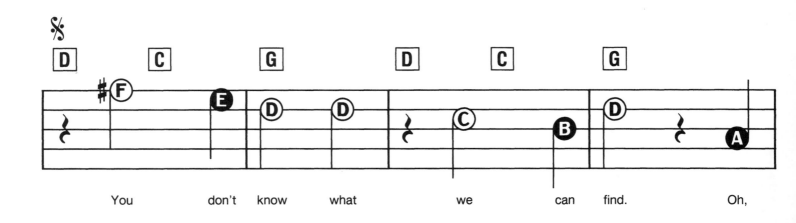

You   don't know   what   we   can   find.   Oh,

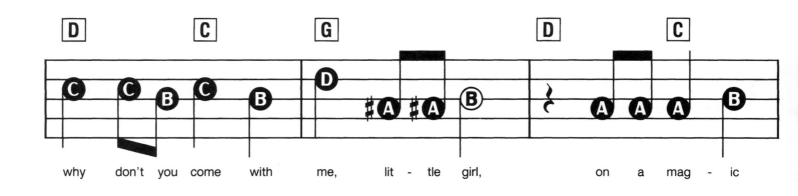

why   don't you come   with   me,   lit - tle girl,   on   a   mag - ic

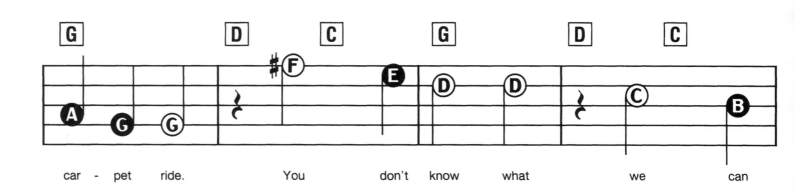

car - pet ride.   You   don't   know   what   we   can

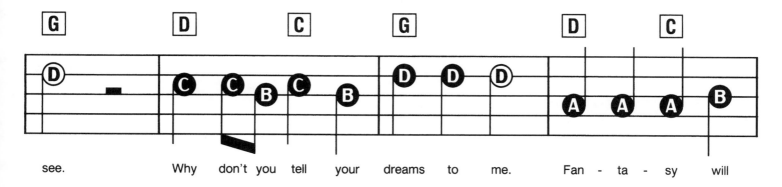

see.   Why   don't you   tell   your   dreams   to   me.   Fan - ta - sy   will

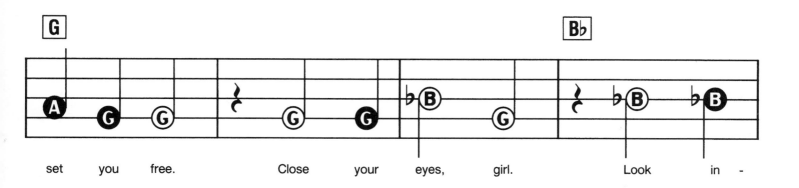

set   you   free.   Close   your   eyes,   girl.   Look   in -

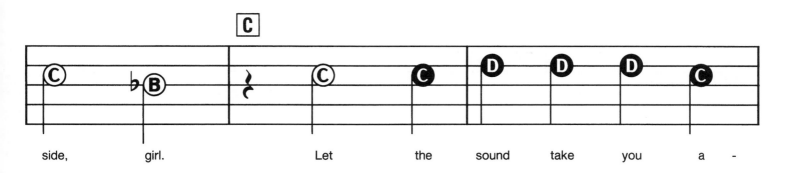

side,   girl.   Let   the   sound   take   you   a -

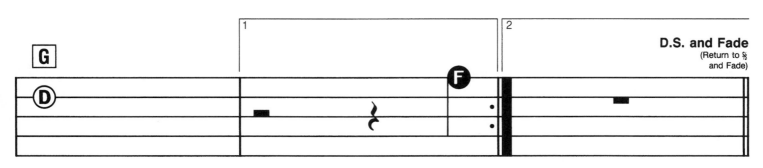

D.S. and Fade
(Return to 𝄋 and Fade)

way.   Last

Lucy in the Sky with Diamonds

Registration 8
Rhythm: Waltz

Words and Music by John Lennon
and Paul McCartney

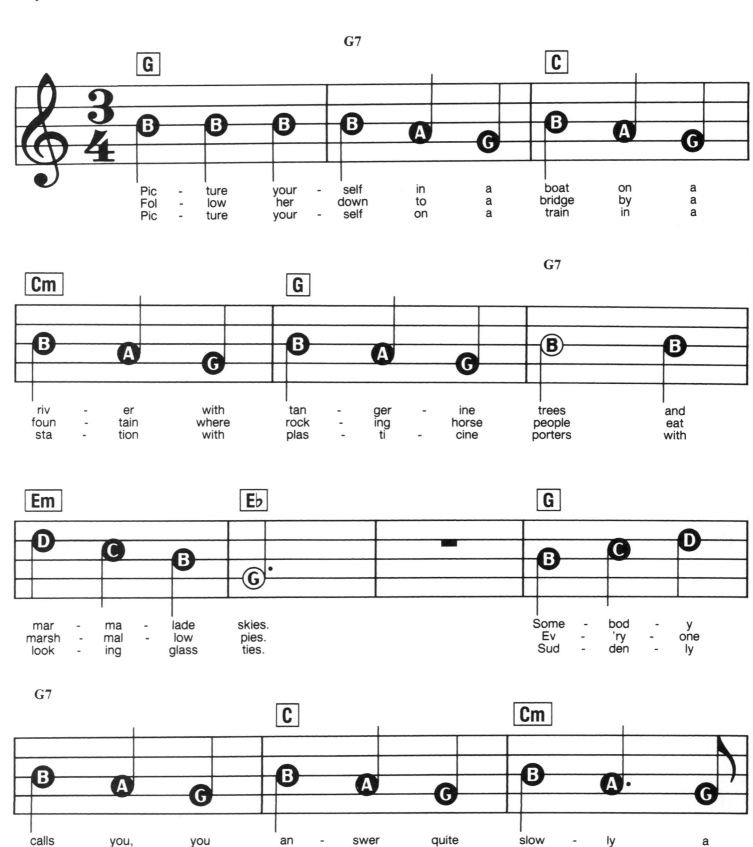

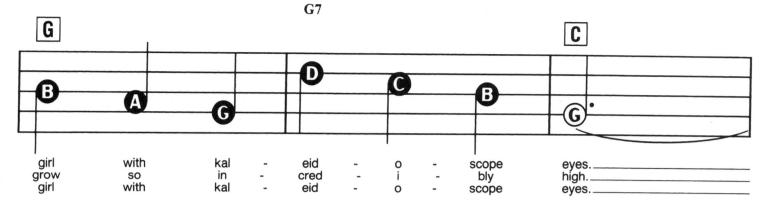

girl   with   kal - eid - o - scope   eyes.
grow   so   in - cred - i - bly   high.
girl   with   kal - eid - o - scope   eyes.

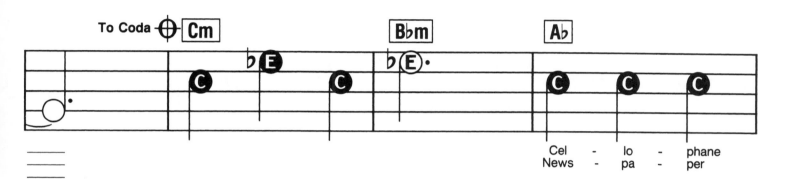

Cel - lo - phane
News - pa - per

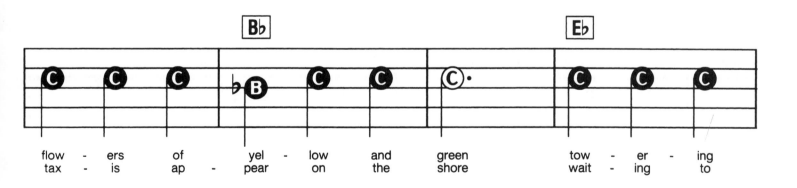

flow - ers   of   ap - yel - low   and   the   green   tow - er - ing
tax - is   ap - pear   on   the   shore   wait - ing - to

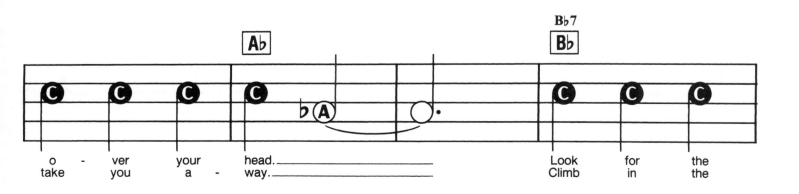

o - ver   your   head.   Look   for   the
take you   a - way.   Climb in   the

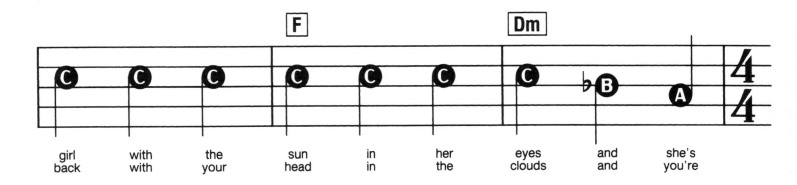

girl with the sun in her eyes and she's
back with your head in the clouds and you're

Rhythm: Rock

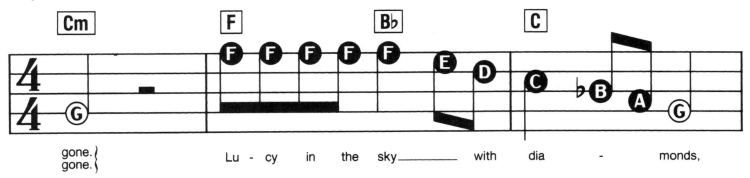

gone.
gone. } Lu - cy in the sky_____ with dia - monds,

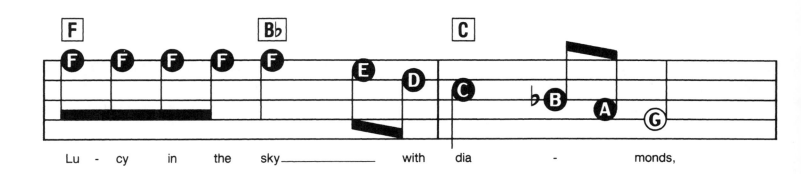

Lu - cy in the sky_____ with dia - monds,

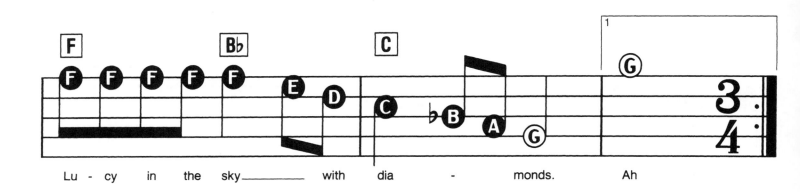

Lu - cy in the sky_____ with dia - monds. Ah

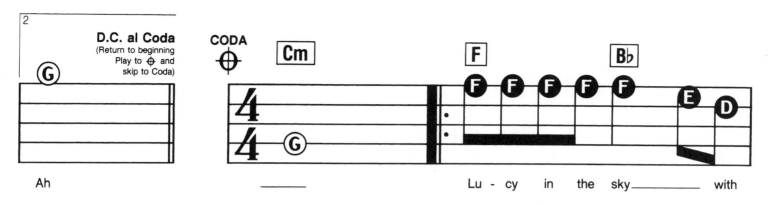

Ah ____ Lu - cy in the sky ____ with

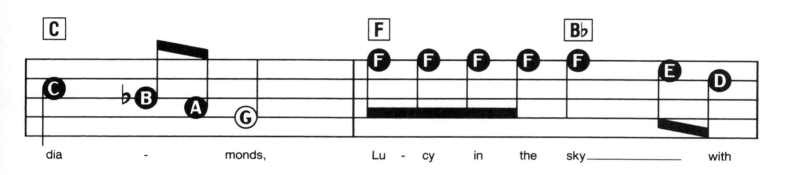

dia - monds, Lu - cy in the sky ____ with

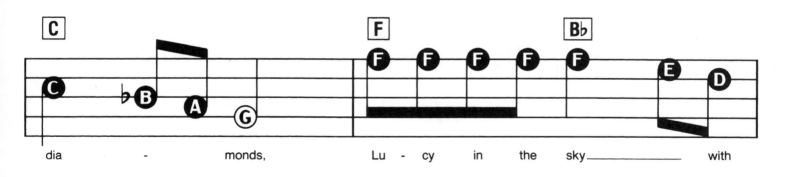

dia - monds, Lu - cy in the sky ____ with

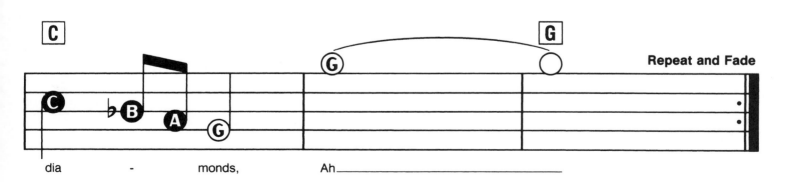

dia - monds, Ah ____

Me and You and a Dog Named Boo

Registration 1
Rhythm: Rock, March or Polka

Words and Music by
Lobo

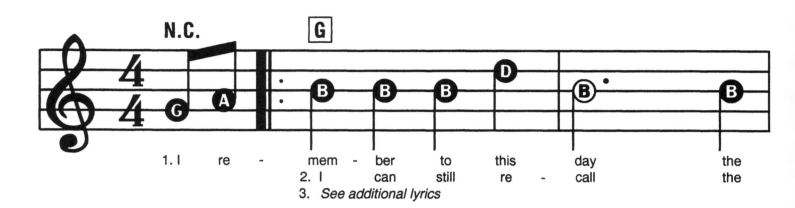

1. I re - mem - ber to this day the
2. I can still re - call the
3. *See additional lyrics*

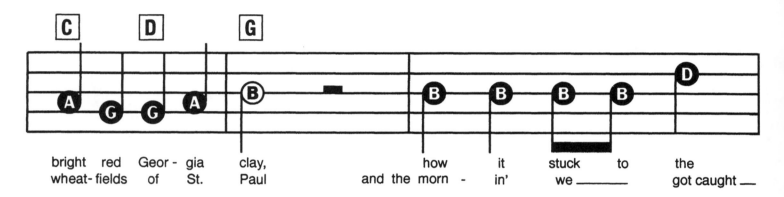

bright red Geor - gia clay, how it stuck to the
wheat- fields of St. Paul and the morn - in' we _____ got caught _____

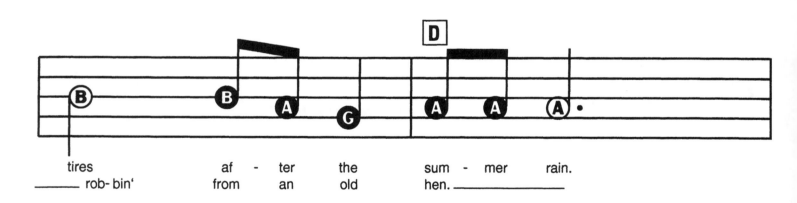

tires af - ter the sum - mer rain.
_____ rob- bin' from an old hen. _____

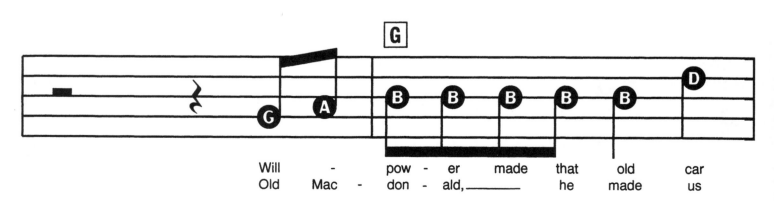

Will - pow - er made that old car
Old Mac - don - ald, _____ he made us

113

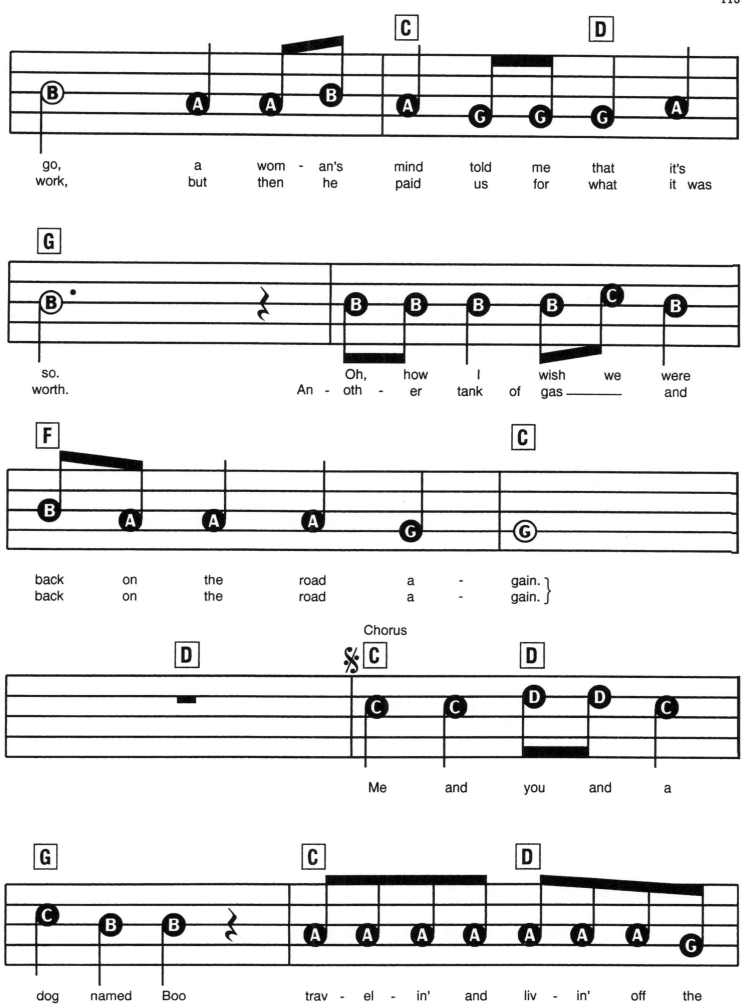

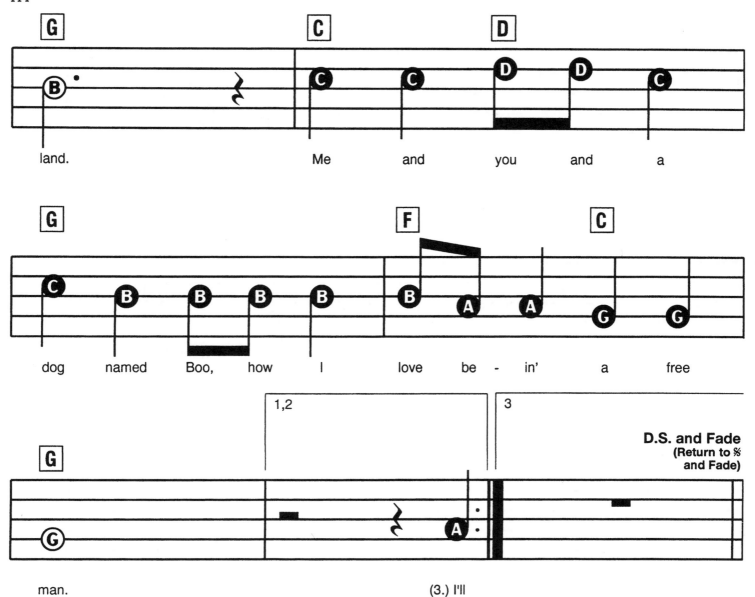

D.S. and Fade
(Return to % and Fade)

land.   Me   and   you   and   a

dog   named   Boo,   how   I   love   be - in'   a   free

man.   (3.) I'll

Additional Lyrics

3. I'll never forget that day,
   We motored stately into L.A.
   The lights of the city put setttlin' down in my brain.
   Though it's only been a month or so,
   That old car's buggin' us to go.
   You gotta get away and get back on the road again.
   To Chorus:

New World Coming

Registration 4
Rhythm: Pops or 8-Beat

Words and Music by Barry Mann
and Cynthia Weil

There's a new world com - ing and it's

just a - round the bend. There's a new world

com - ing, this one's com - ing to an end. There's a

new voice call - ing, you can hear it if you

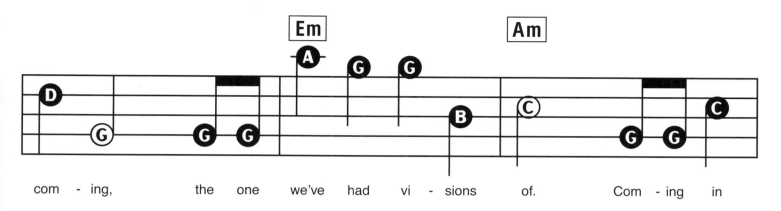

com - ing, the one we've had vi - sions of. Com - ing in

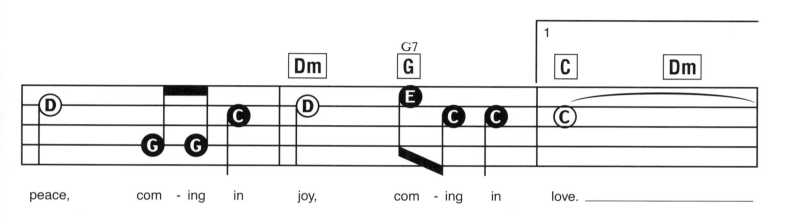

peace, com - ing in joy, com - ing in love. _____

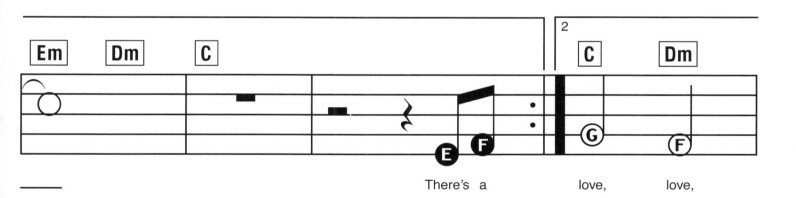

_____ There's a love, love,

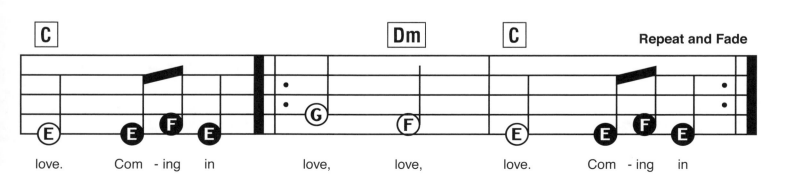

love. Com - ing in love, love, love. Com - ing in

Mellow Yellow

Registration 1
Rhythm: 8-Beat or Rock

Words and Music by
Donovan Leitch

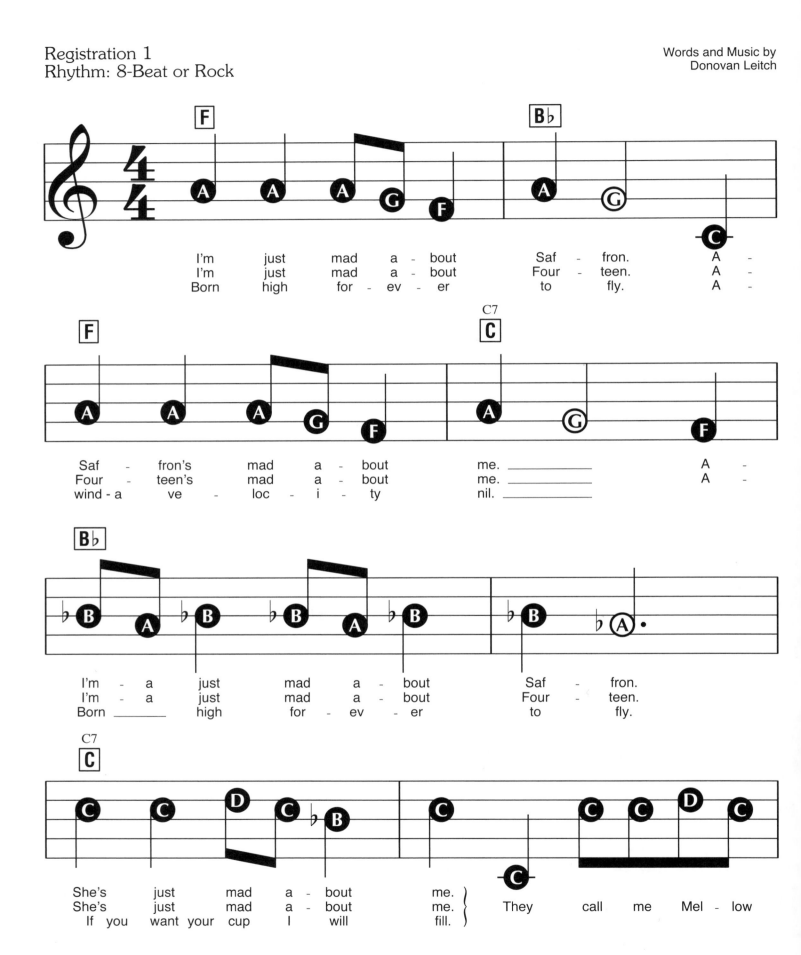

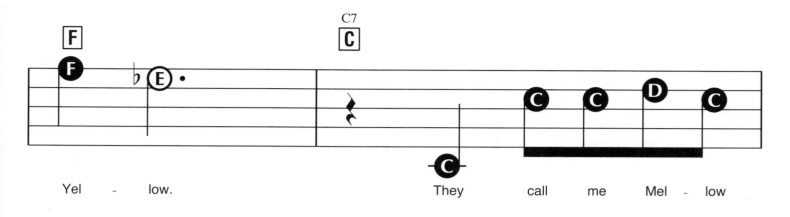

Yel - low. They call me Mel - low

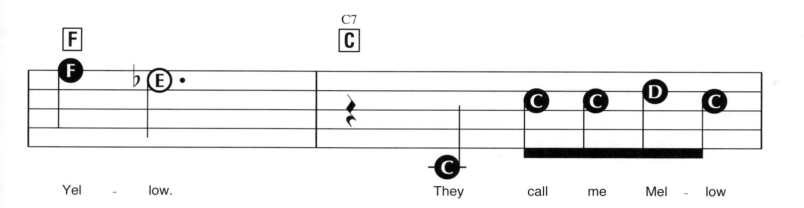

Yel - low. They call me Mel - low

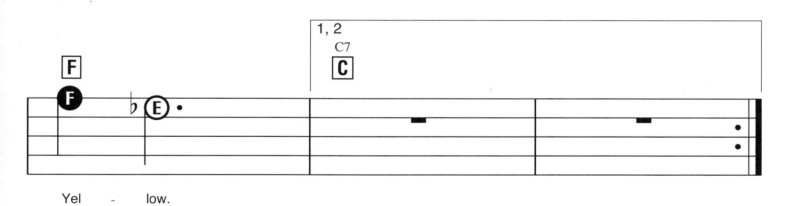

Yel - low.

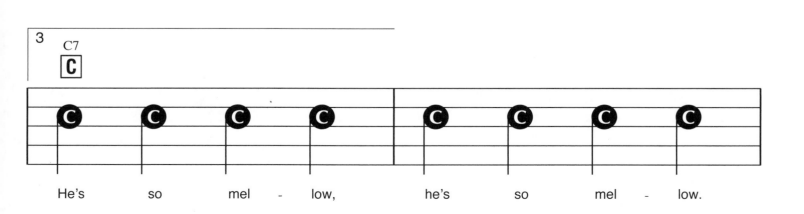

He's   so   mel - low,   he's   so   mel - low.

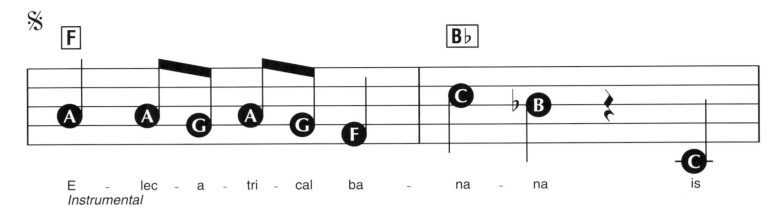

E - lec - a - tri - cal ba - na - na is
Instrumental

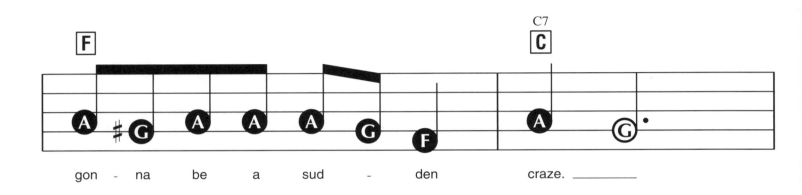

gon - na be a sud - den craze. _____

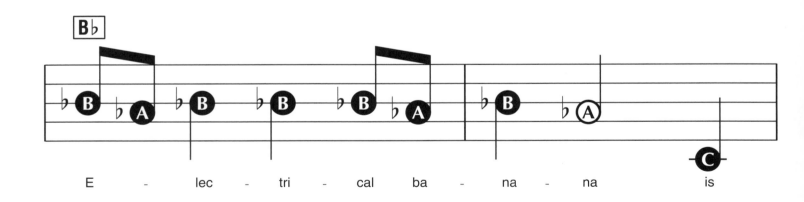

E - lec - tri - cal ba - na - na is

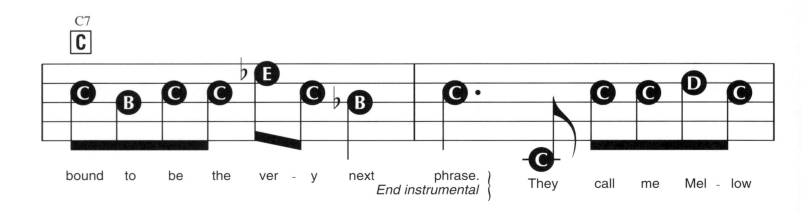

bound to be the ver - y next phrase. }
End instrumental { They call me Mel - low

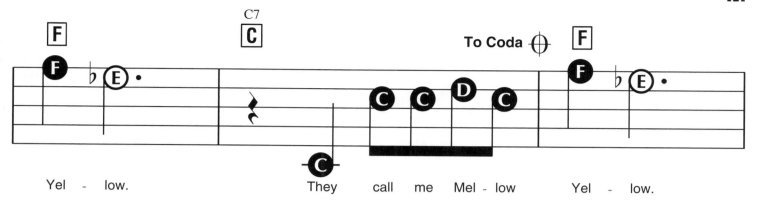

Yel - low.   They call me Mel - low   Yel - low.

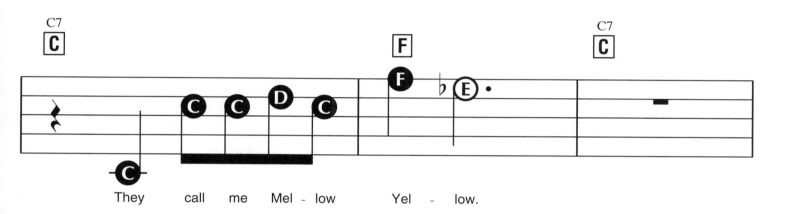

They call me Mel - low   Yel - low.

D.S. al Coda
(Return to 𝄋
Play to ⨁ and
Skip to Coda)

CODA

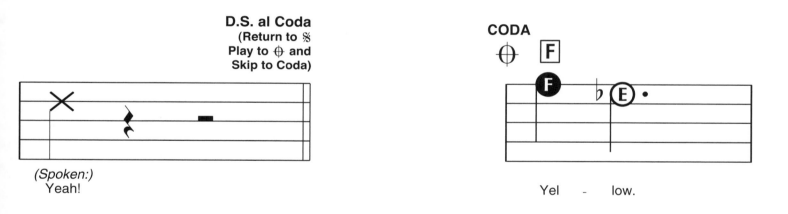

(Spoken:)
Yeah!

Yel - low.

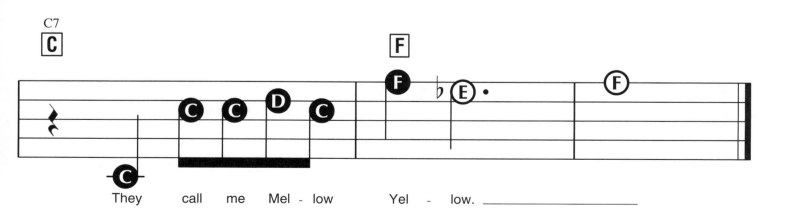

They call me Mel - low   Yel - low. _____

Mr. Tambourine Man

Registration 8
Rhythm: Rock

Words and Music by
Bob Dylan

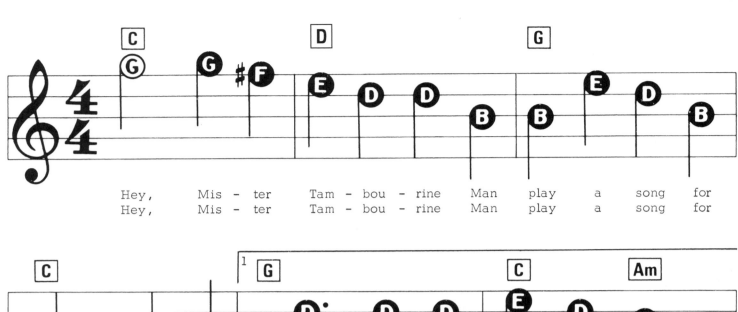

Hey,   Mis - ter   Tam - bou - rine   Man   play   a   song   for
Hey,   Mis - ter   Tam - bou - rine   Man   play   a   song   for

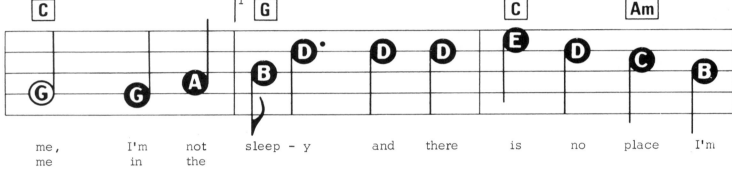

me,   I'm   not   sleep - y   and   there   is   no   place   I'm
me   in   not   the

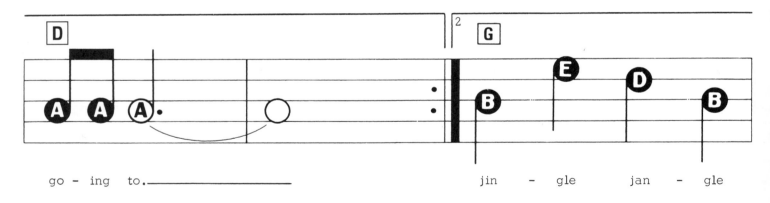

go - ing   to._____   jin - gle   jan - gle

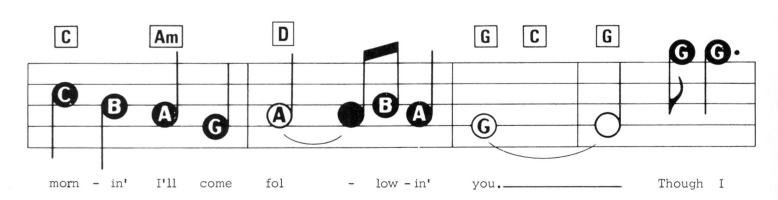

morn - in'   I'll   come   fol - low - in'   you._____   Though   I

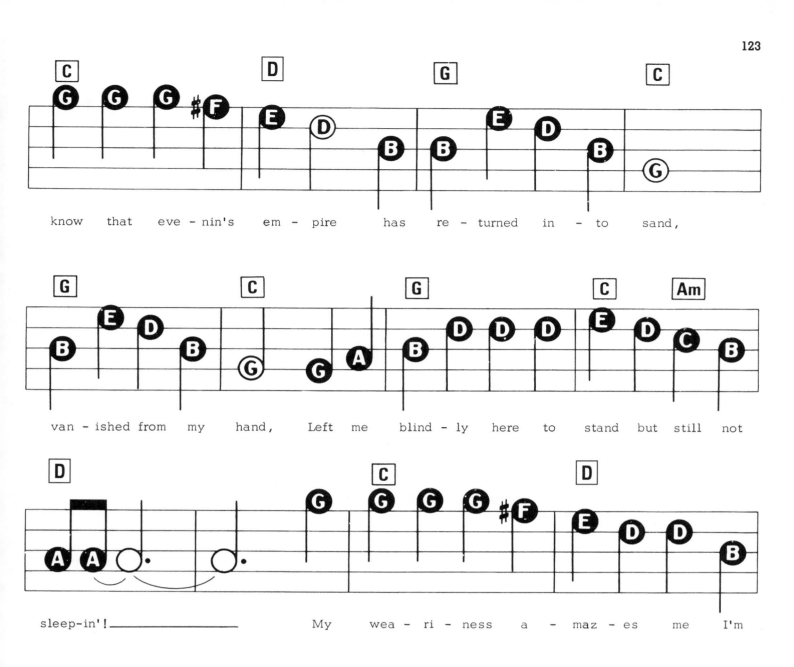

know that eve - nin's em - pire has re - turned in - to sand,

van - ished from my hand, Left me blind - ly here to stand but still not

sleep-in'!_____ My wea - ri - ness a - maz - es me I'm

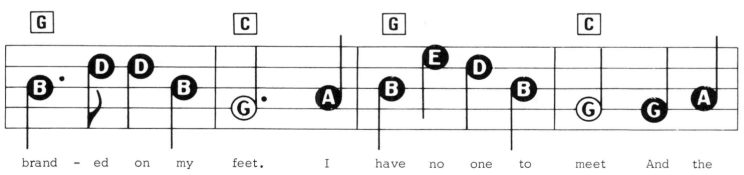

brand - ed on my feet. I have no one to meet And the

D.C. and Fade
(Return to beginning
and Fade)

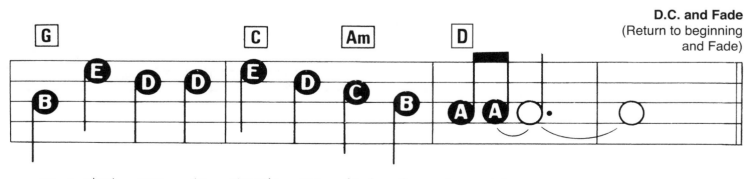

an - cient emp - ty street's too dead for dream-in'._____

Monday, Monday

Registration 4
Rhythm: Rock

Words and Music by
John Phillips

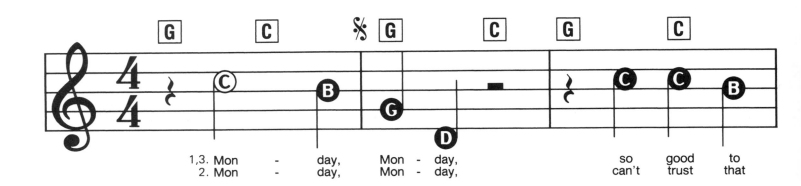

1,3. Mon - day, Mon - day,   so good to
2. Mon - day, Mon - day,   can't trust that

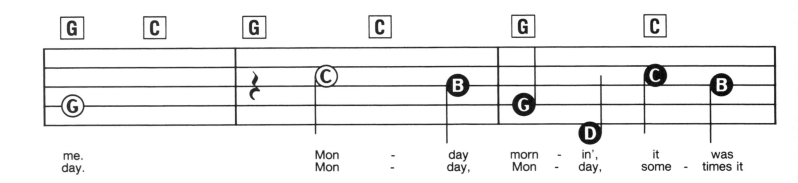

me.   Mon - day morn - in', it was
day.   Mon - day, Mon - day, some - times it

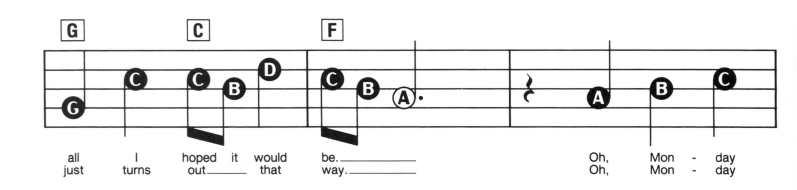

all I hoped it would be.   Oh, Mon - day
just turns out that way.   Oh, Mon - day

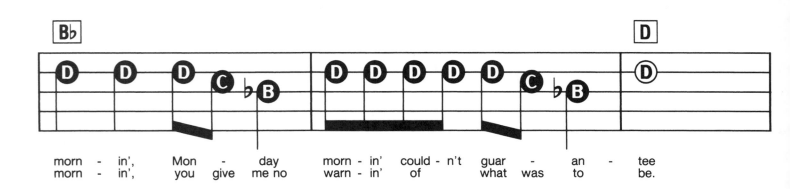

morn - in', Mon - day morn - in' could - n't guar - an - tee
morn - in', you give me no warn - in' of what was to be.

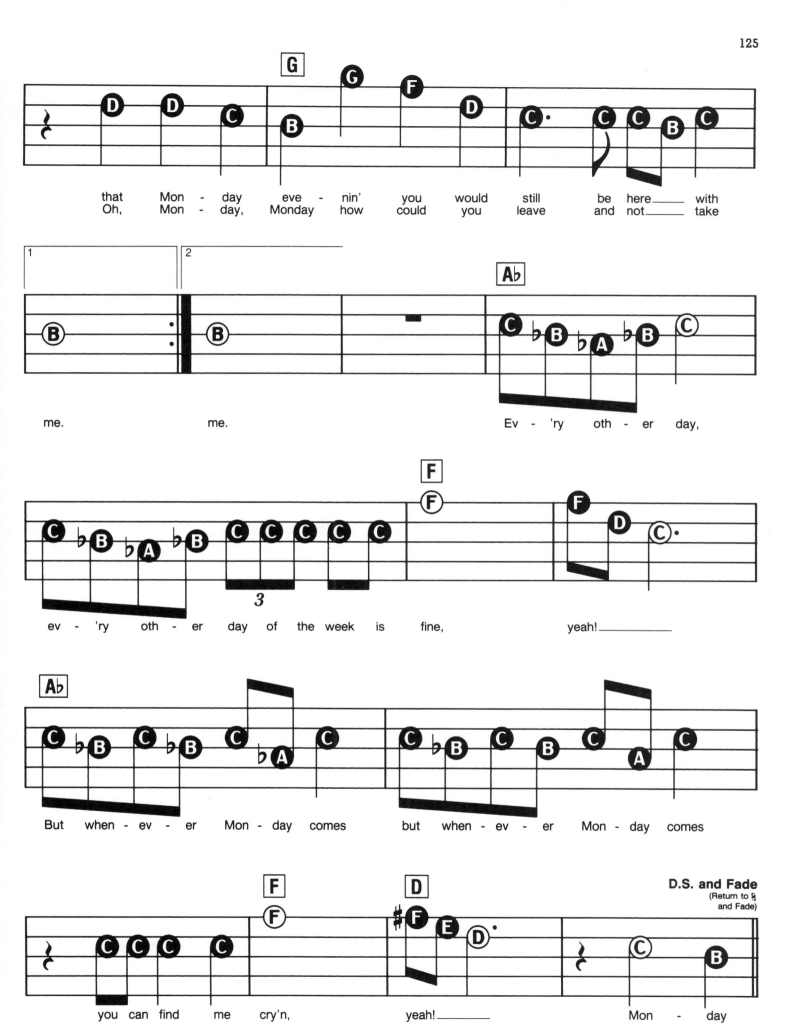

Morning Has Broken

Registration 10
Rhythm: Waltz

Words by Eleanor Farjeon
Music by Yusuf Islam

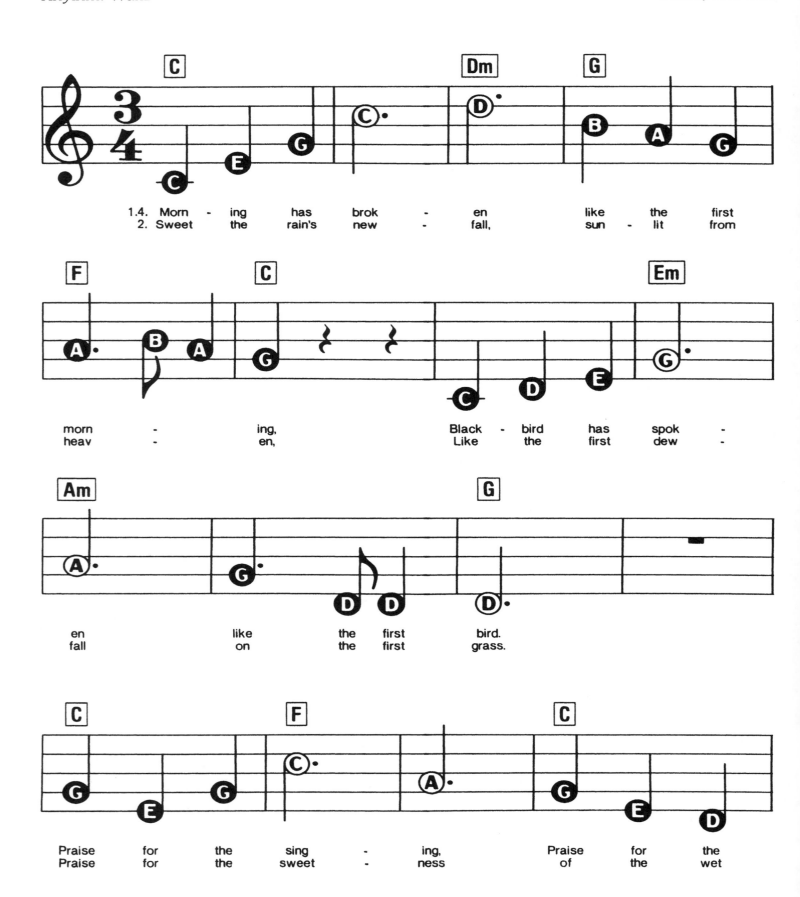

127

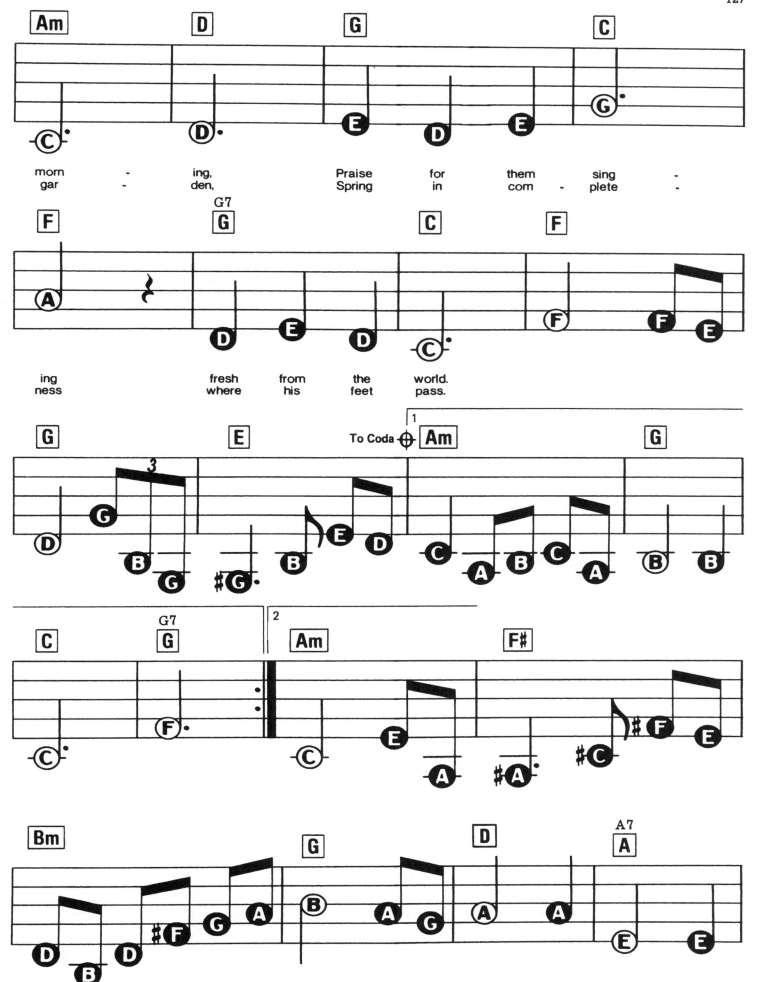

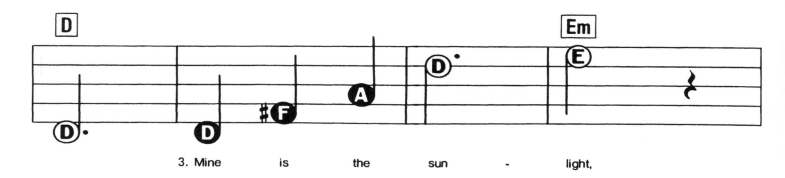

3. Mine   is   the   sun - light,

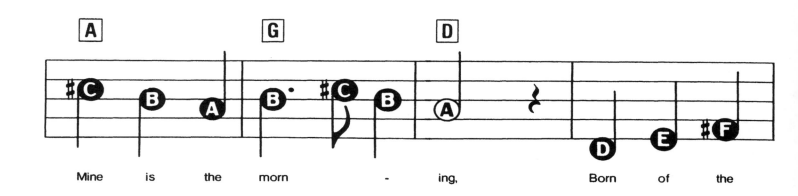

Mine   is   the   morn - ing,   Born   of   the

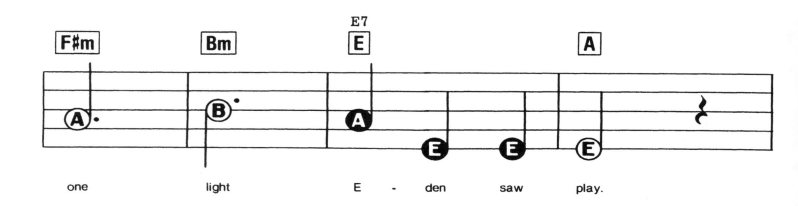

one   light   E - den   saw   play.

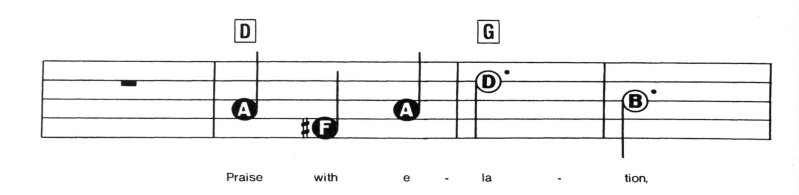

Praise   with   e - la - tion,

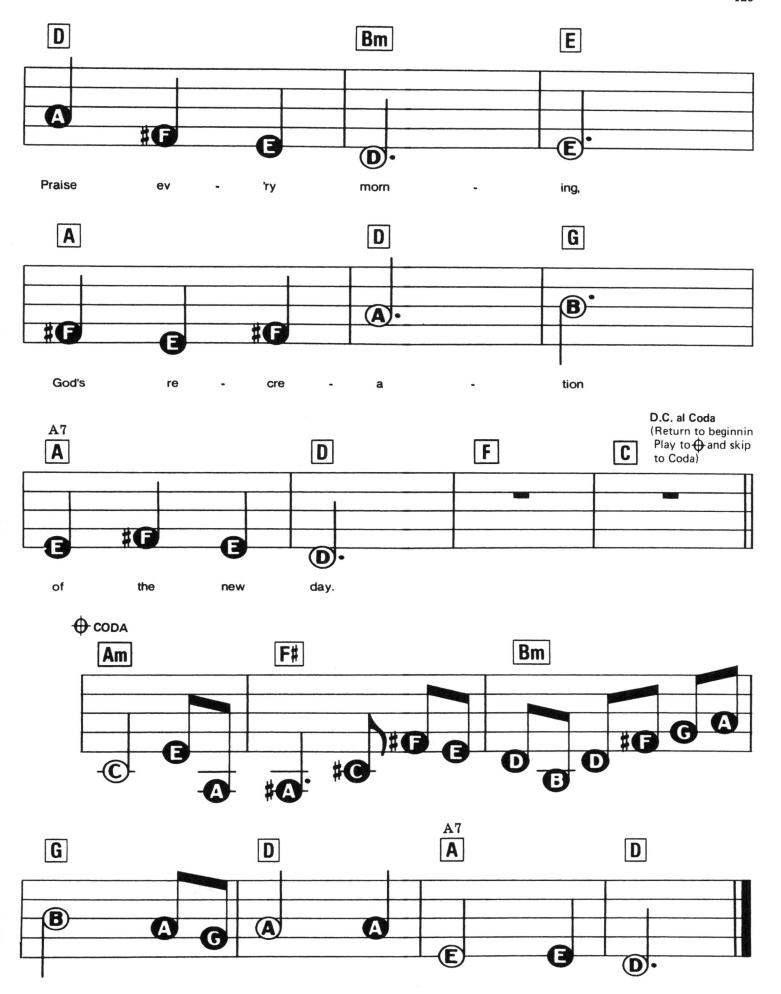

The Night They Drove Old Dixie Down

Registration 4
Rhythm: Country Rock or Rock

Words and Music by
Robbie Robertson

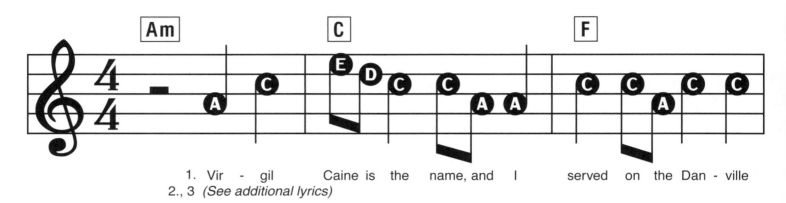

1. Vir - gil   Caine is the   name, and I   served on the Dan - ville
2., 3 *(See additional lyrics)*

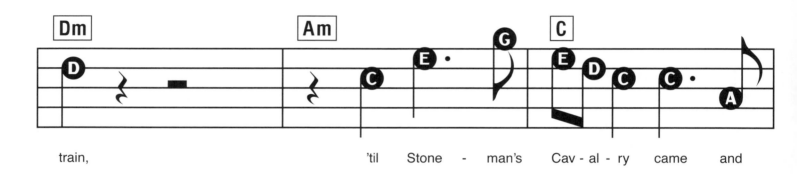

train,   'til Stone - man's   Cav - al - ry   came and

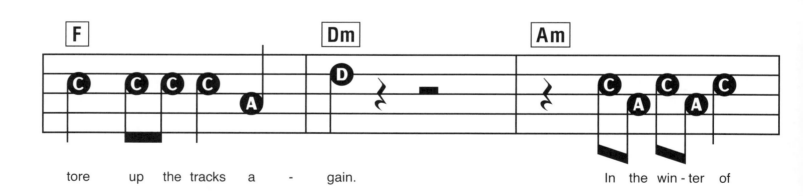

tore   up the   tracks a - gain.   In the win - ter of

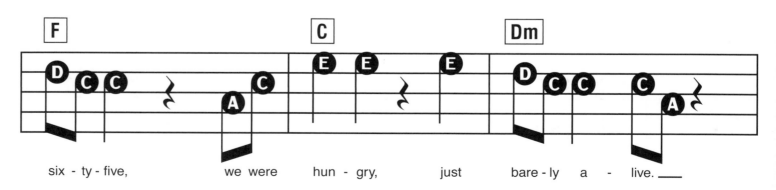

six - ty - five,   we were hun - gry,   just bare - ly a - live. ___

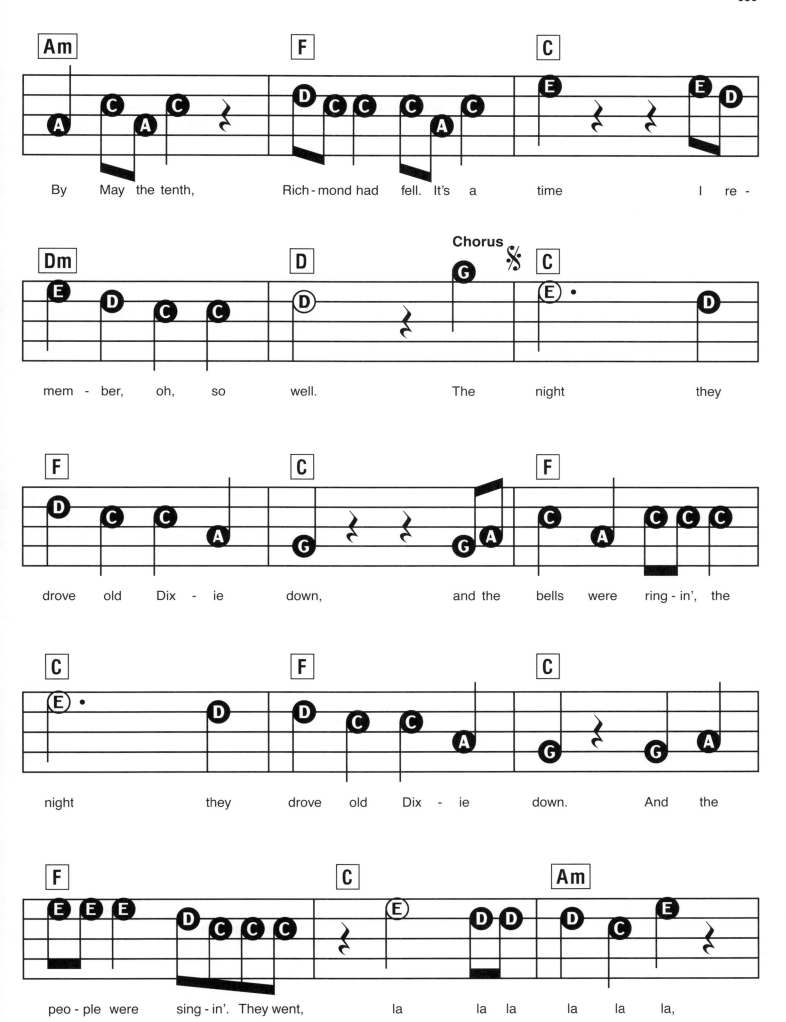

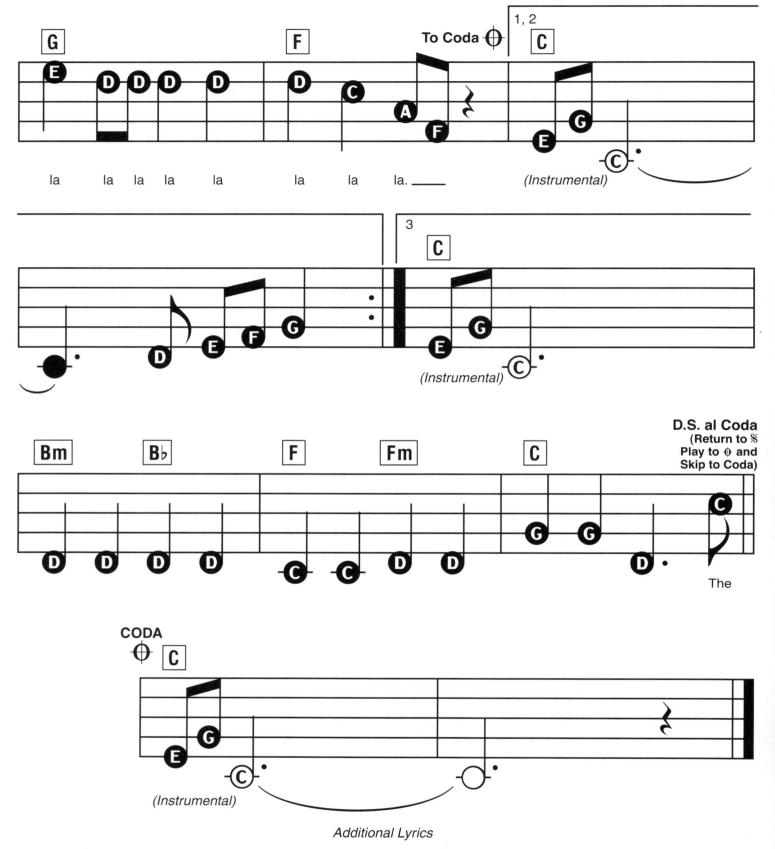

Additional Lyrics

2. Back with my wife in Tennessee
   When one day she called to me,
   "Virgil, quick, come see:
   There goes Robert E. Lee!"
   Now, I don't mind choppin' wood
   And I don't care if the money's no good.
   Ya take what ya need and ya leave the rest,
   But they should never have taken
   The very best.
   Chorus

3. Like my father before me,
   I will work the land.
   And like my brother above me,
   Who took a rebel stand.
   He was just eighteen, proud and brave,
   But a Yankee laid him in his grave.
   I swear by the mud below my feet,
   You can't raise a Caine back up
   When he's in defeat.
   Chorus

Oh Happy Day

Registration 8
Rhythm: Gospel or Rock

Words and Music by
Edwin R. Hawkins

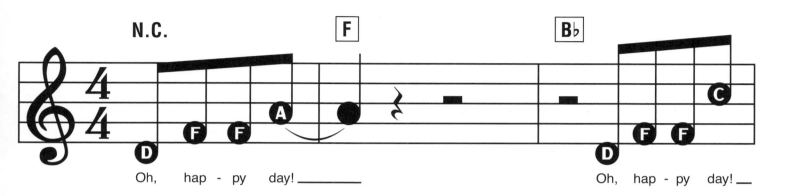

Oh, hap-py day! _____   Oh, hap-py day! __

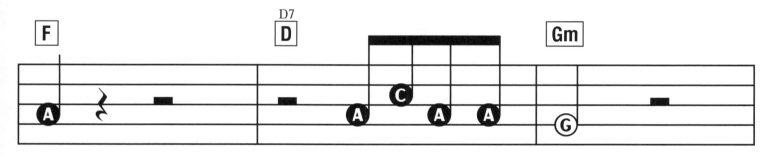

__   When Je - sus washed, _____

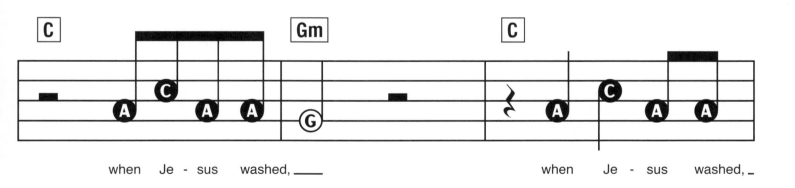

when Je - sus washed, ____   when Je - sus washed, _

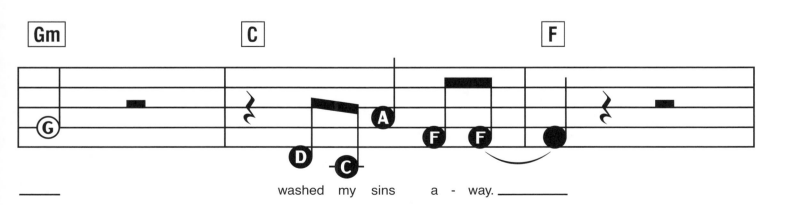

__   washed my sins a - way. _____

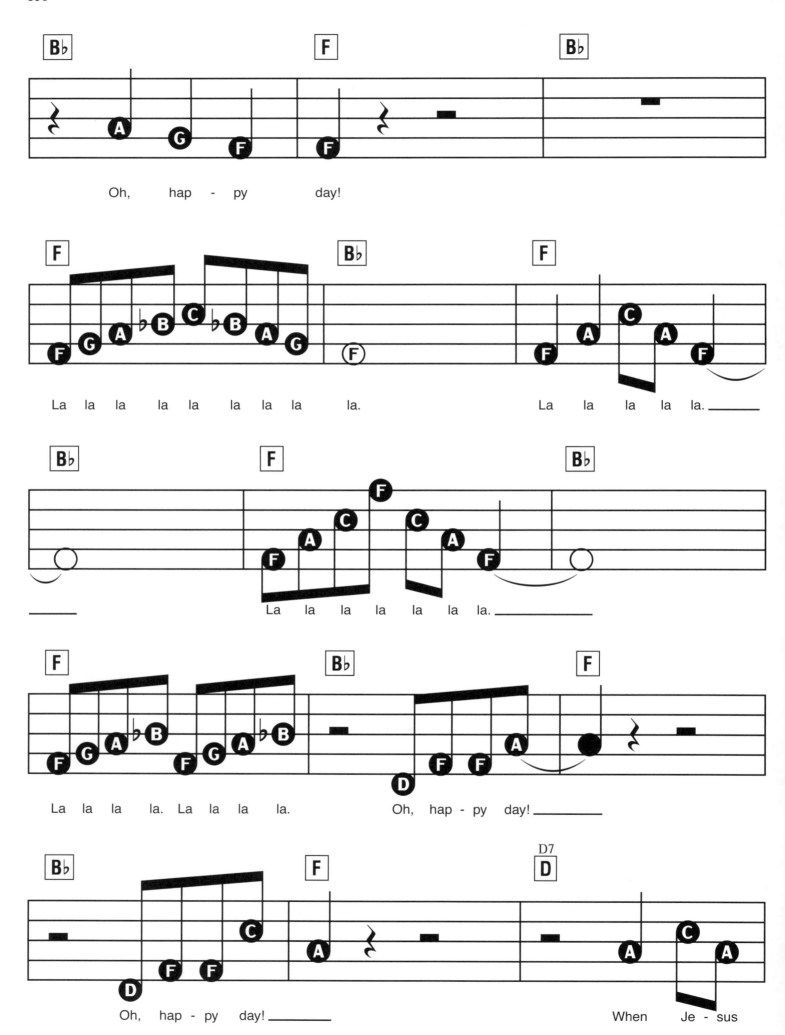

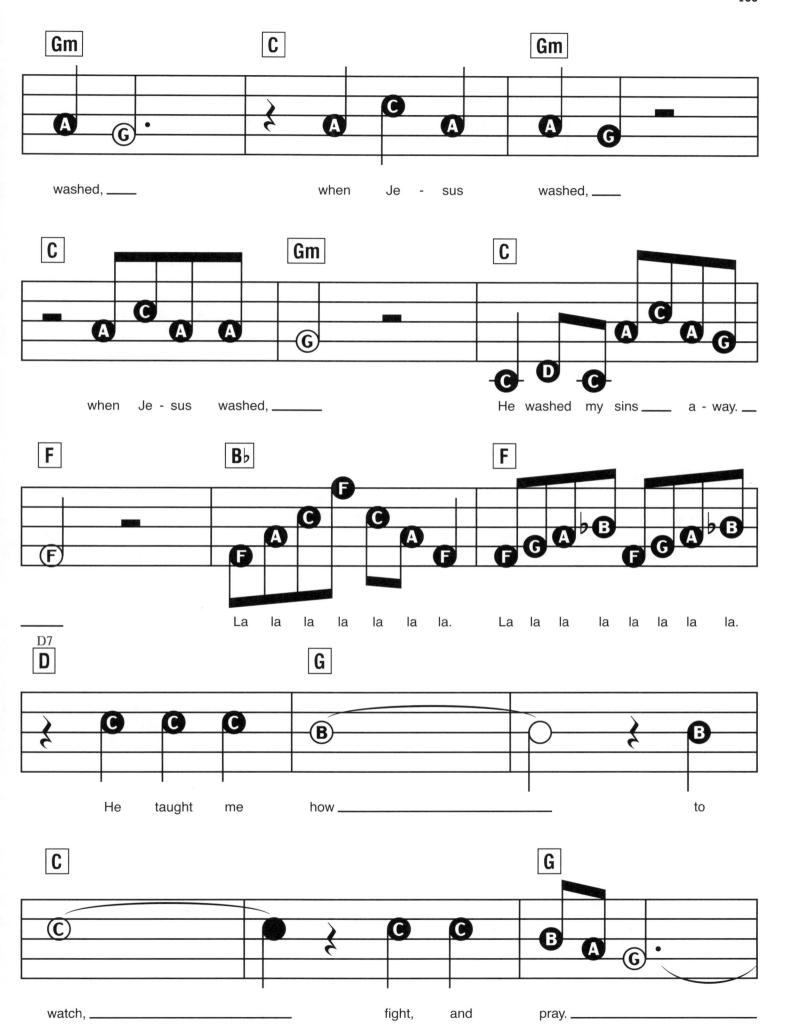

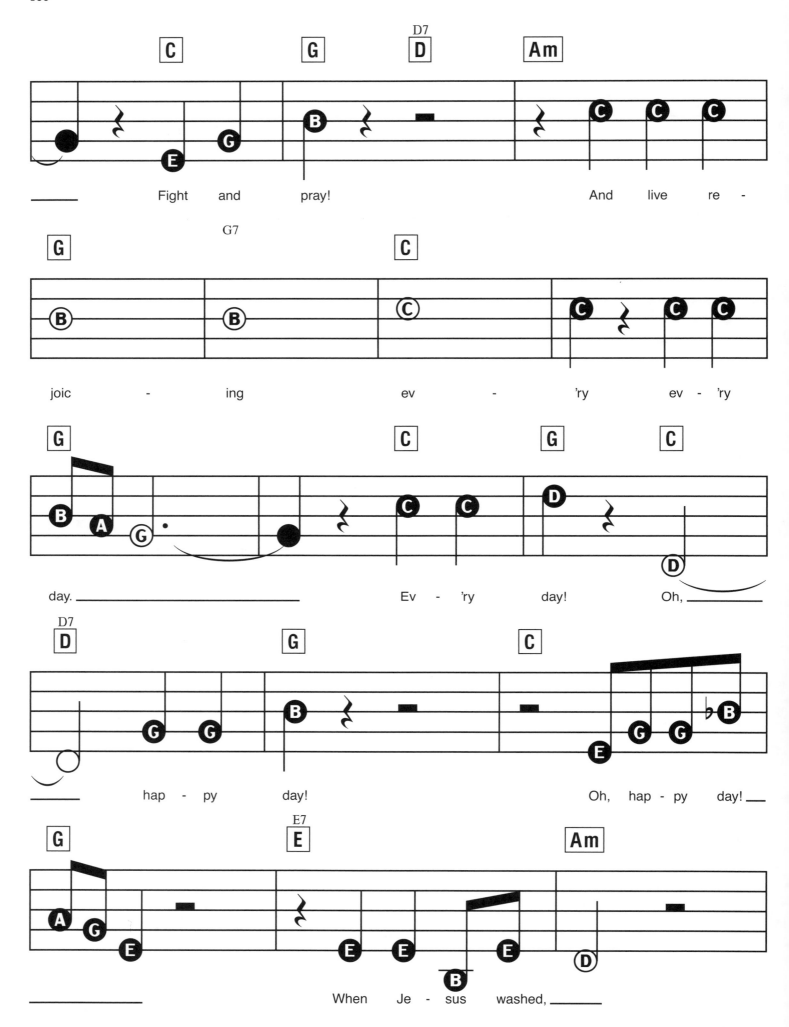

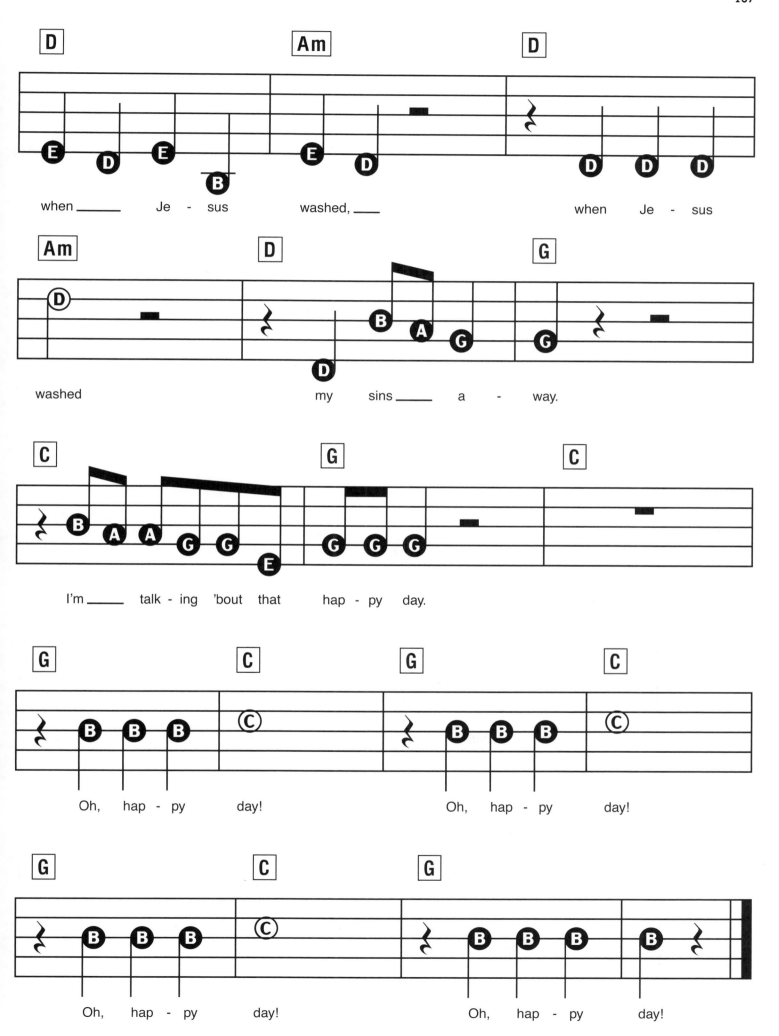

One Toke Over the Line

Registration 2
Rhythm: Rock or 8-Beat

Words and Music by Michael Brewer
and Thomas E. Shipley

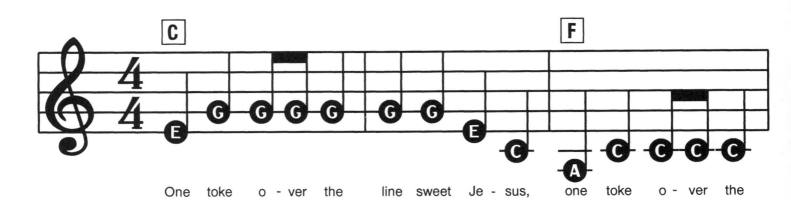

One toke o - ver the line sweet Je - sus, one toke o - ver the

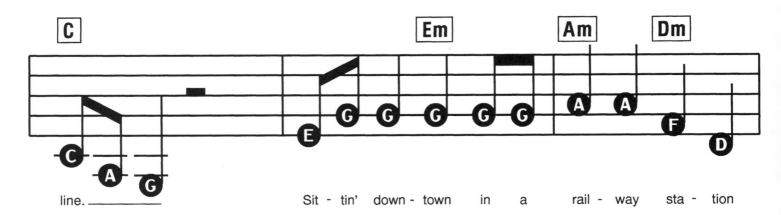

line. _____ Sit - tin' down - town in a rail - way sta - tion

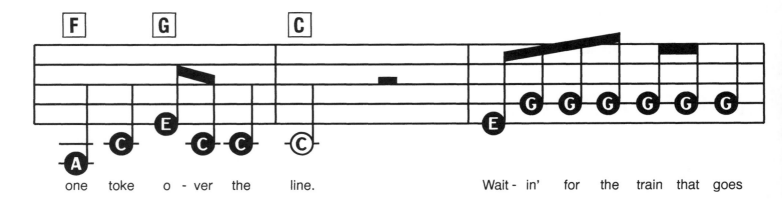

one toke o - ver the line. Wait - in' for the train that goes

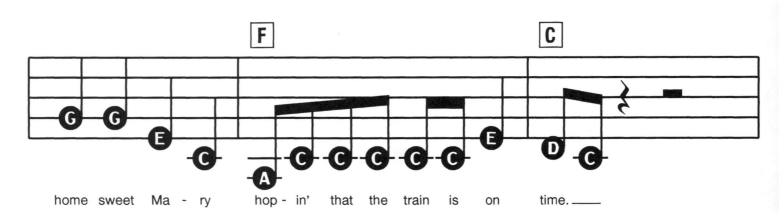

home sweet Ma - ry hop - in' that the train is on time. _____

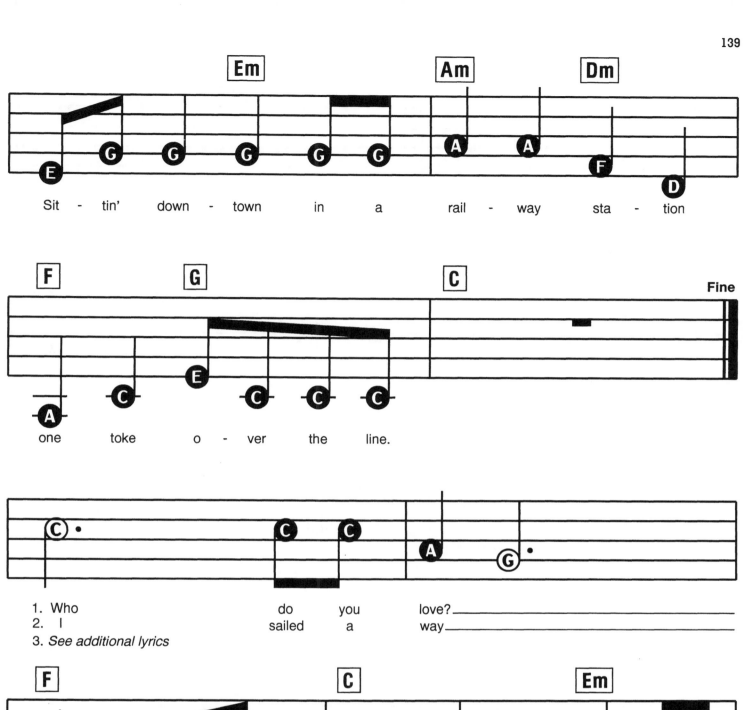

Sit - tin' down - town in a rail - way sta - tion

one toke o - ver the line.

1. Who do you love?_____
2. I sailed a way_____
3. *See additional lyrics*

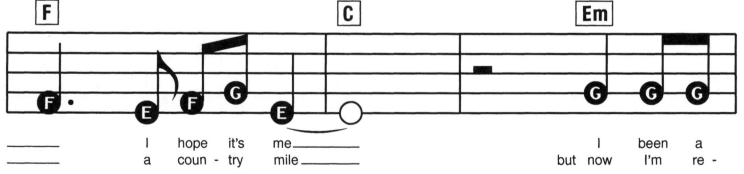

_____ I hope it's me_____ I been a
_____ a coun - try mile_____ but now I'm re -

chang - in' as you can plain - ly see
turn - in' show - in' off my smile

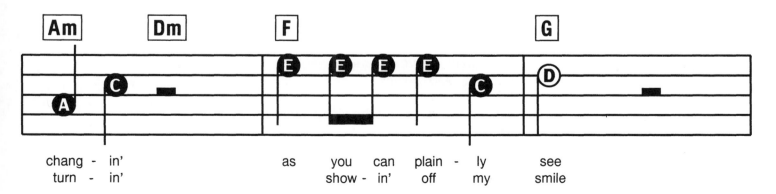

Additional Lyrics

3. I was born to give and take
   But as I keep growin'
   I'm gonna make some mistakes.
   Sun is gonna set and the bird is gonna wing
   They do not lie.
   My last wish will be just one thing
   I'm smilin' when I die.

(Sittin' on)
The Dock of the Bay

Registration 5
Rhythm: Rock

Words and Music by Steve Cropper
and Otis Redding

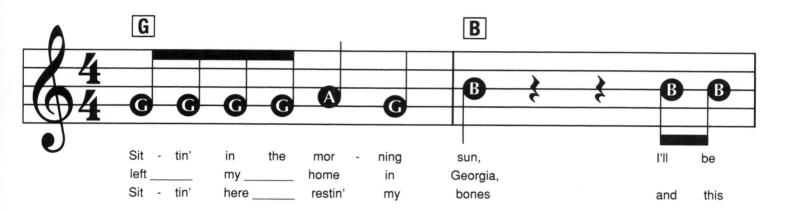

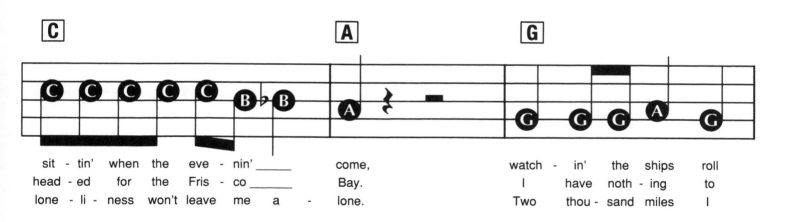

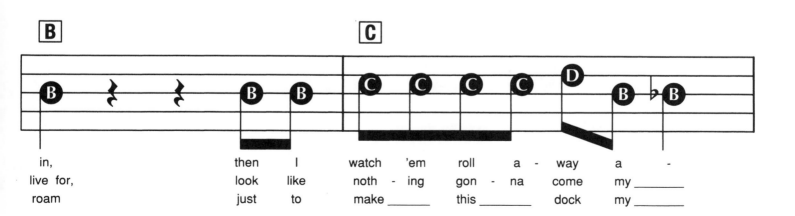

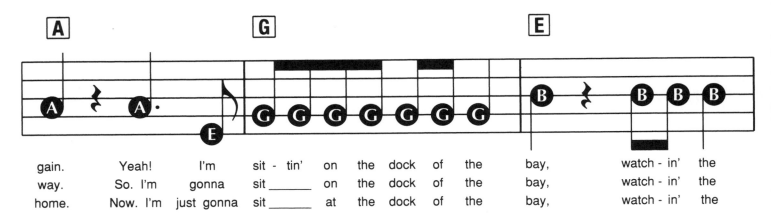

gain.   Yeah!   I'm   sit - tin'   on   the   dock   of   the   bay,   watch - in'   the
way.   So. I'm   gonna   sit _____ on   the   dock   of   the   bay,   watch - in'   the
home.   Now. I'm just gonna   sit _____ at   the   dock   of   the   bay,   watch - in'   the

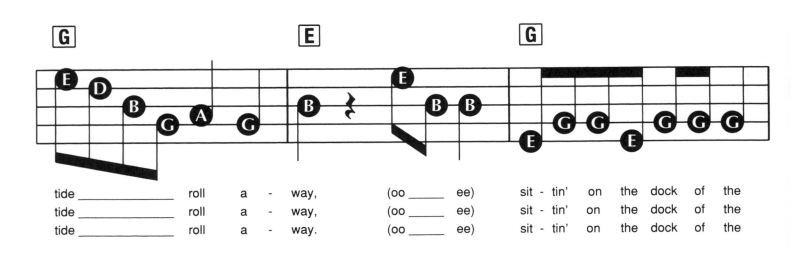

tide _____ roll   a - way,   (oo _____ ee)   sit - tin'   on   the   dock   of   the
tide _____ roll   a - way,   (oo _____ ee)   sit - tin'   on   the   dock   of   the
tide _____ roll   a - way.   (oo _____ ee)   sit - tin'   on   the   dock   of   the

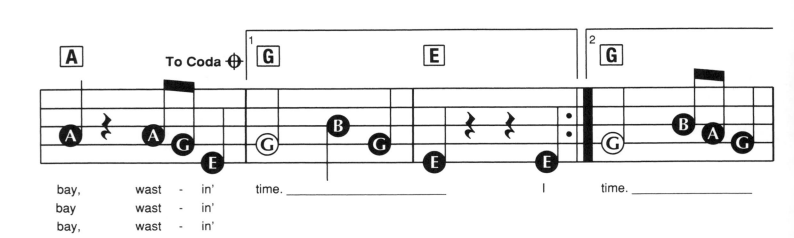

bay,   wast - in'   time. _____   I   time. _____
bay   wast - in'
bay,   wast - in'

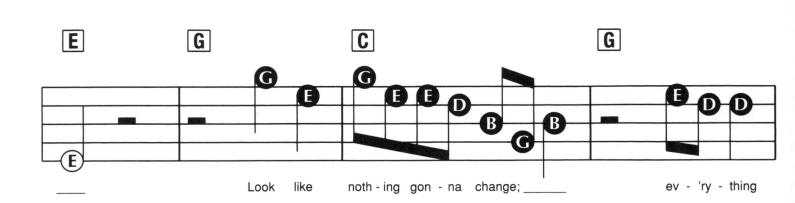

____   Look   like   noth - ing gon - na   change; _____   ev - 'ry - thing

143

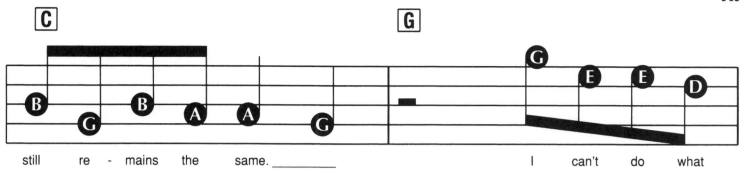

still re - mains the same. _____ I can't do what

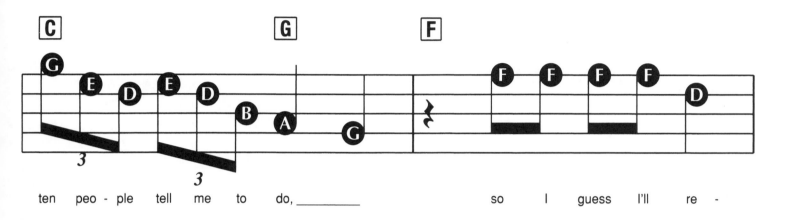

ten peo - ple tell me to do, _____ so I guess I'll re -

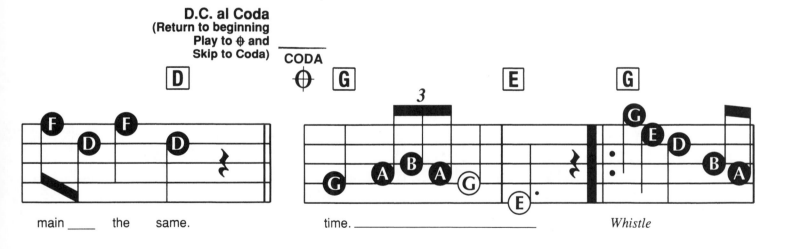

main ____ the same. time. _____ *Whistle*

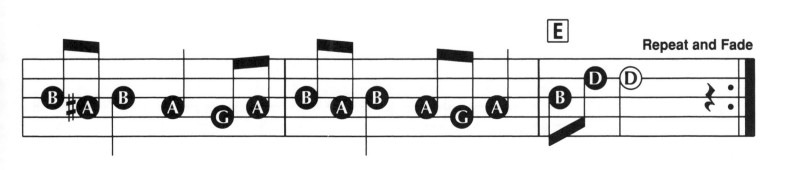

People Got to Be Free

Registration 4
Rhythm: Rock or 8-Beat

Words and Music by Felix Cavaliere
and Edward Brigati, Jr.

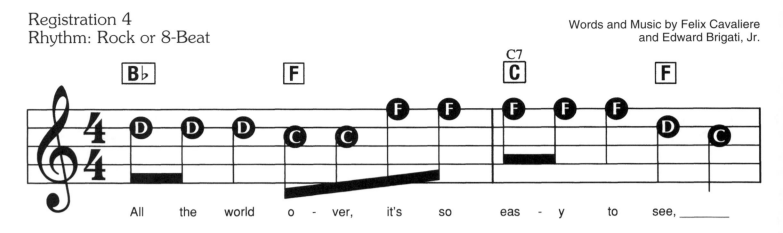

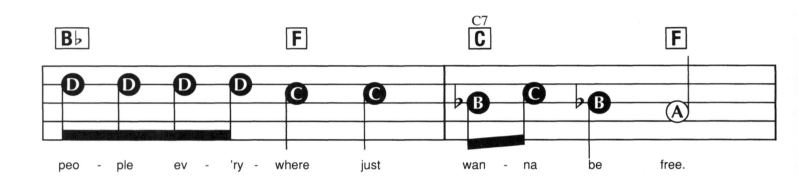

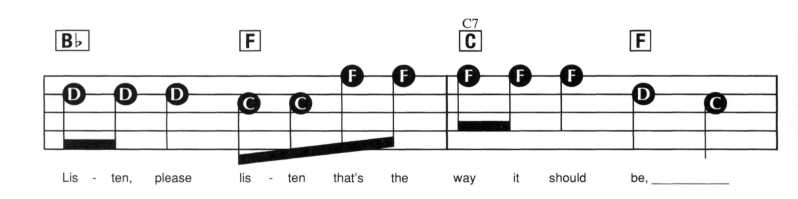

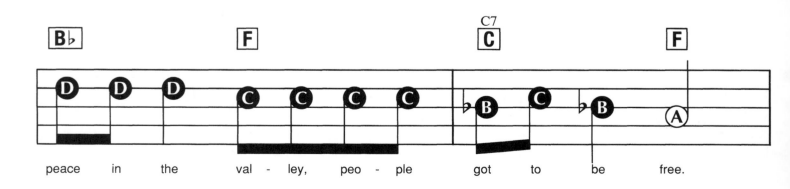

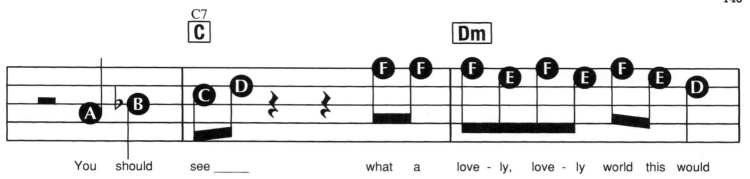

You should see _____ what a love - ly, love - ly world this would

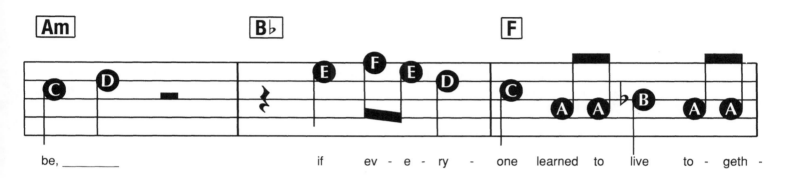

be, _____ if ev - e - ry - one learned to live to - geth -

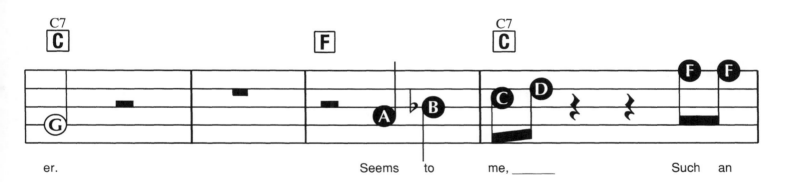

er. Seems to me, _____ Such an

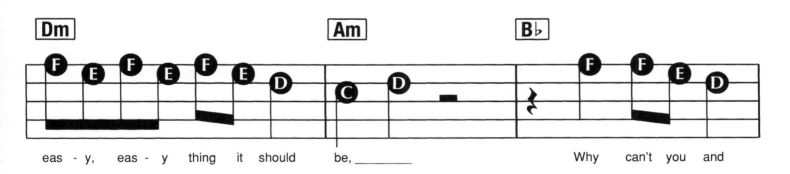

eas - y, eas - y thing it should be, _____ Why can't you and

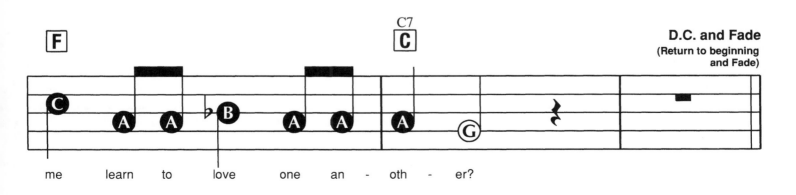

D.C. and Fade
(Return to beginning
and Fade)

me learn to love one an - oth - er?

Pleasant Valley Sunday

Registration 4
Rhythm: 8-Beat or Rock

Words and Music by Gerry Goffin
and Carole King

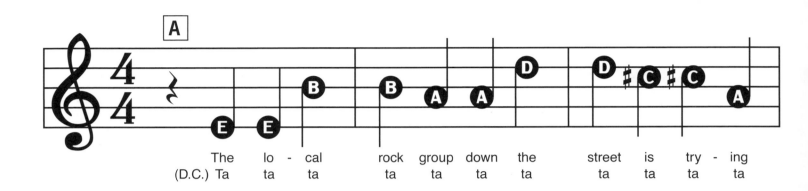

The lo - cal rock group down the street is try - ing
(D.C.) Ta ta ta ta ta ta ta ta ta ta ta

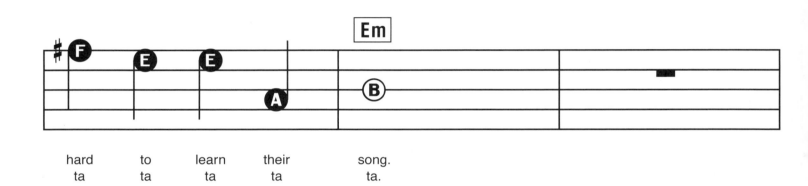

hard to learn their song.
ta ta ta ta ta.

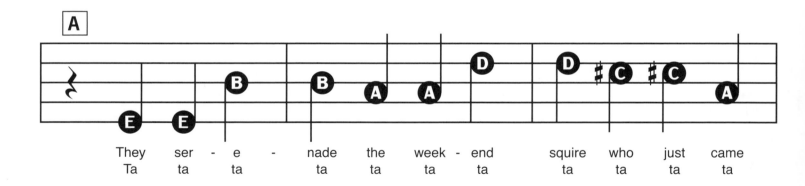

They ser - e - nade the week - end squire who just came
Ta ta ta ta ta ta ta ta ta ta ta

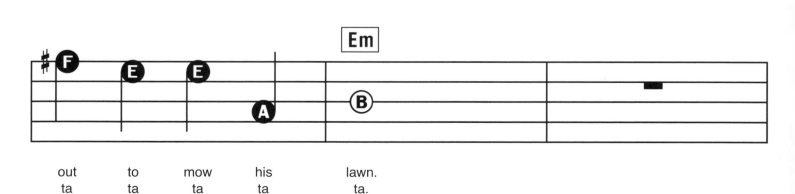

out to mow his lawn.
ta ta ta ta ta.

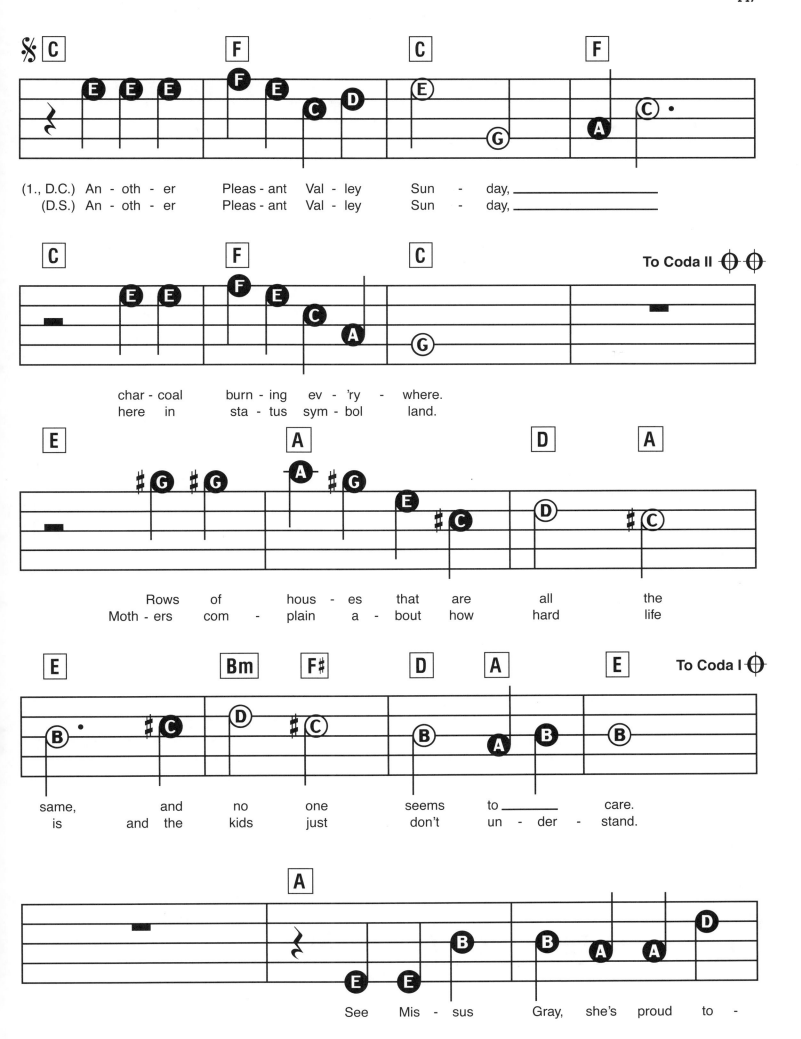

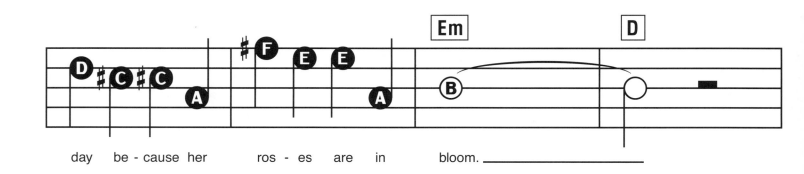

day be - cause her ros - es are in bloom. _____

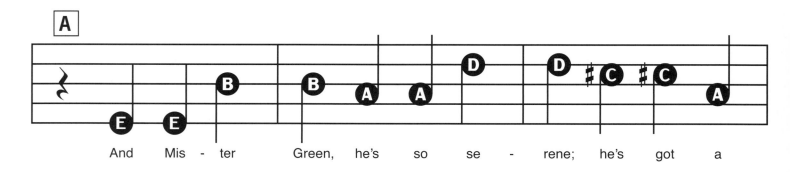

And Mis - ter Green, he's so se - rene; he's got a

D.S. al Coda I
(Return to 𝄋
Play to ⊕ and
Skip to Coda I)

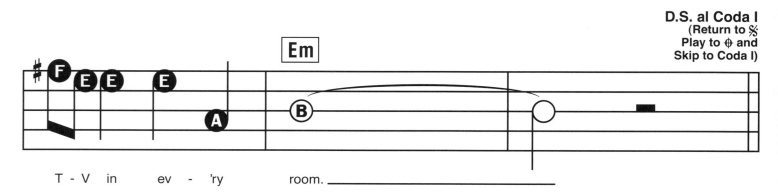

T - V in ev - 'ry room. _____

CODA I
⊕

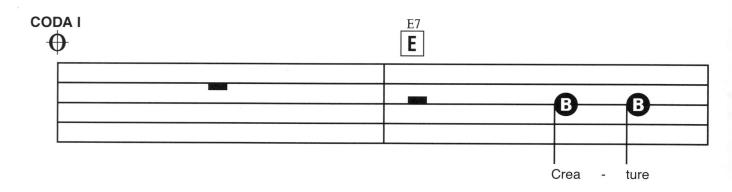

Crea - ture

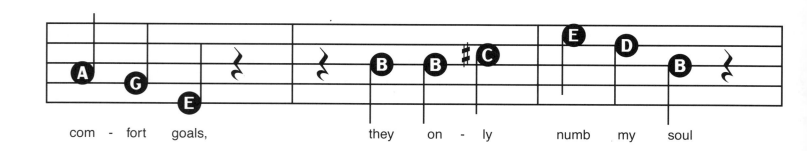

com - fort goals, they on - ly numb my soul

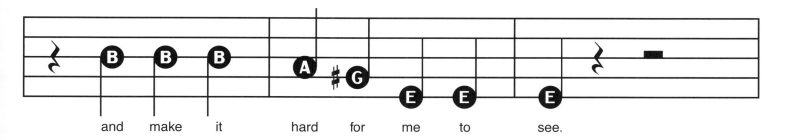

and make it hard for me to see.

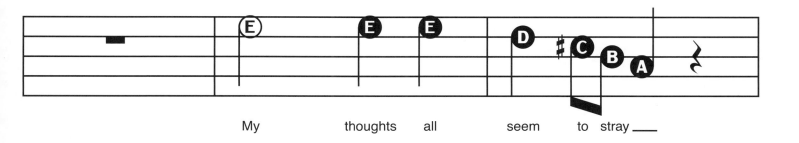

My thoughts all seem to stray ___

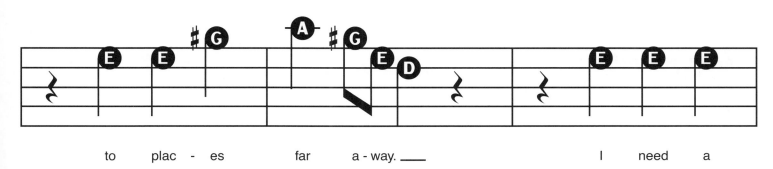

to plac - es far a - way. ___ I need a

D.C. al Coda II
(Return to beginning
Play to ⊕⊕ and
Skip to Coda II)

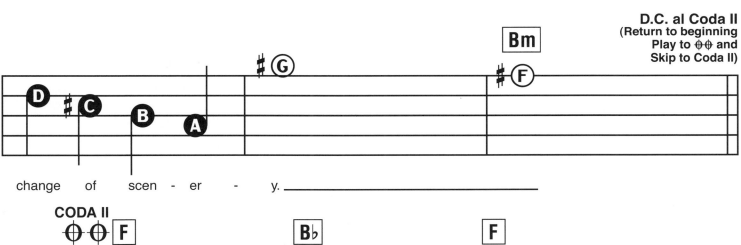

change of scen - er - y. _____

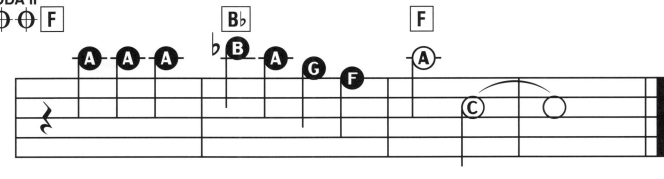

An - oth - er Pleas - ant Val - ley Sun - day. _____

San Francisco
(Be Sure to Wear Some Flowers in Your Hair)

Registration 2
Rhythm: Rock

Words and Music by
John Phillips

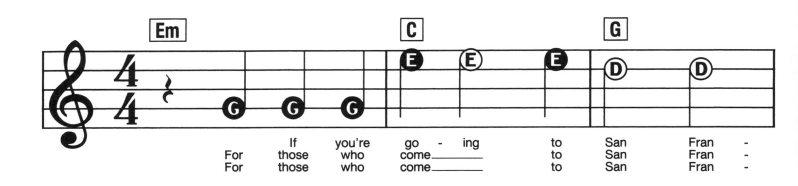

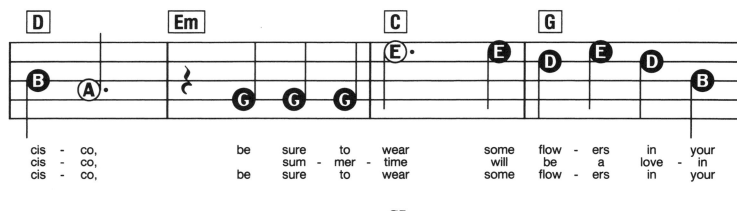

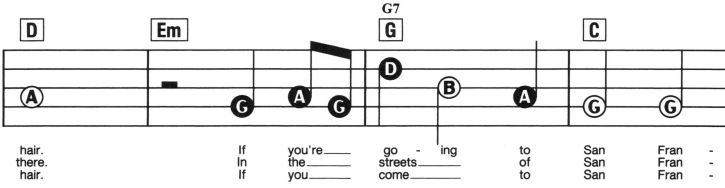

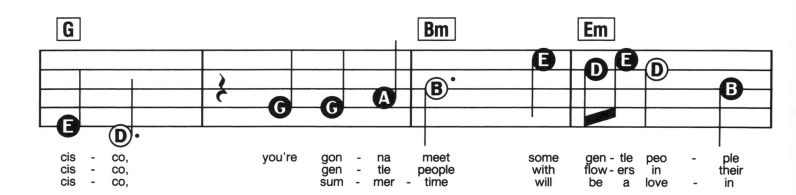

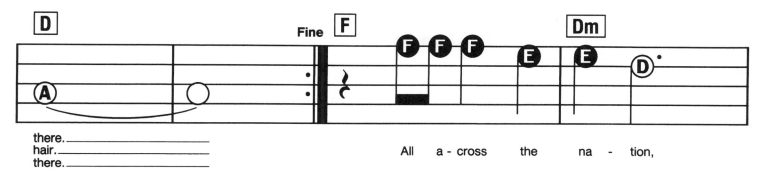

there.
hair.
there.

All a-cross the na - tion,

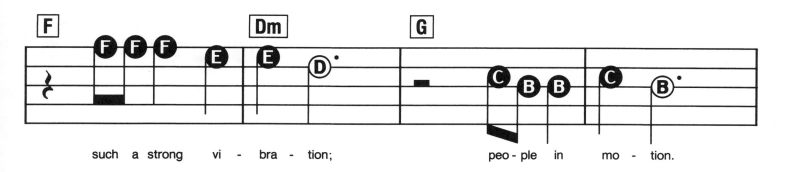

such a strong vi - bra - tion;

peo - ple in mo - tion.

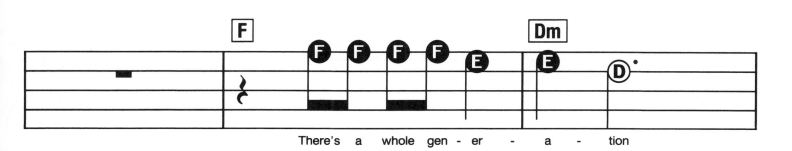

There's a whole gen - er - a - tion

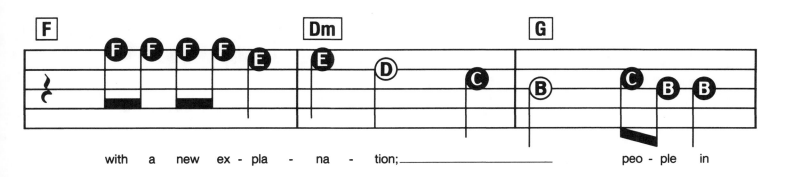

with a new ex - pla - na - tion;

peo - ple in

D.C. al Fine
(Return to beginning
Play to Fine)

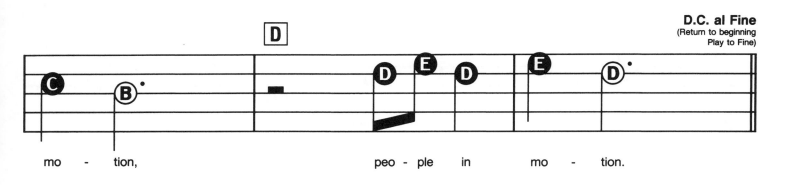

mo - tion,

peo - ple in mo - tion.

Stoned Soul Picnic
(Picnic, a Green City)

Registration 8
Rhythm: Rock

Words and Music by
Laura Nyro

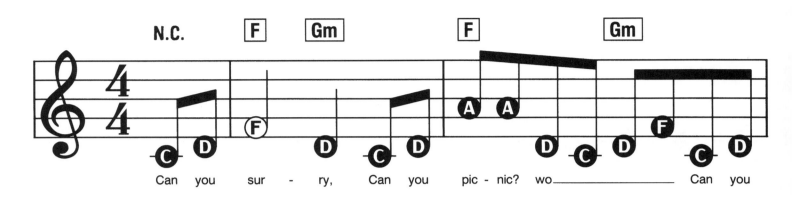

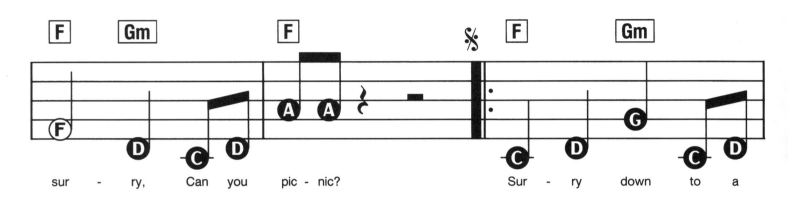

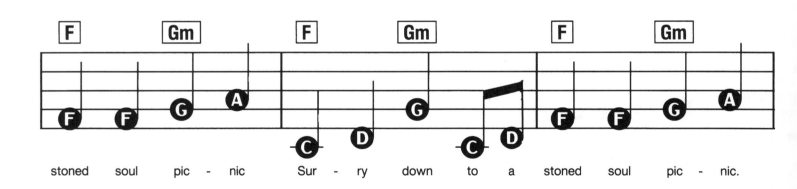

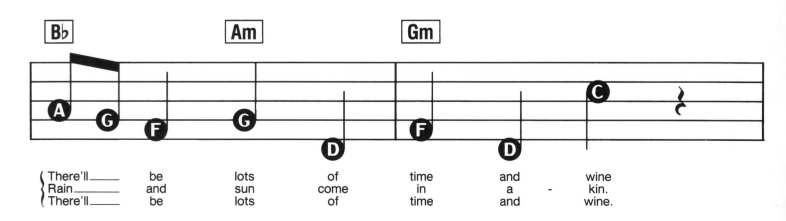

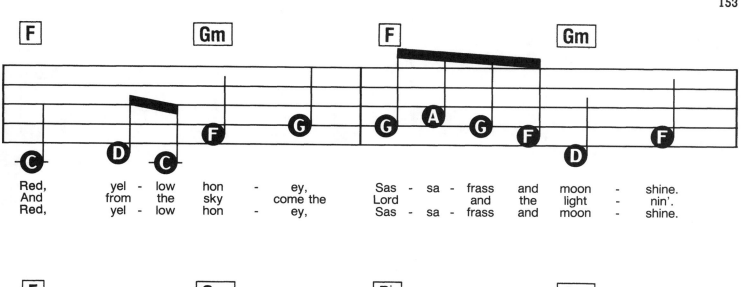

Red,   yel - low hon - ey,   Sas - sa - frass and   moon - shine.
And   from   the   sky   come the   Lord   and   the   light - nin'.
Red,   yel - low hon - ey,   Sas - sa - frass and   moon - shine.

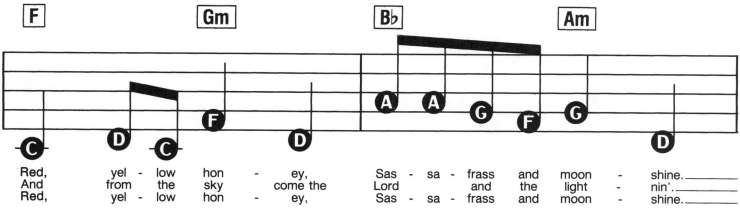

Red,   yel - low hon - ey,   Sas - sa - frass and   moon - shine._____
And   from   the   sky   come the   Lord   and   the   light - nin'._____
Red,   yel - low hon - ey,   Sas - sa - frass and   moon - shine._____

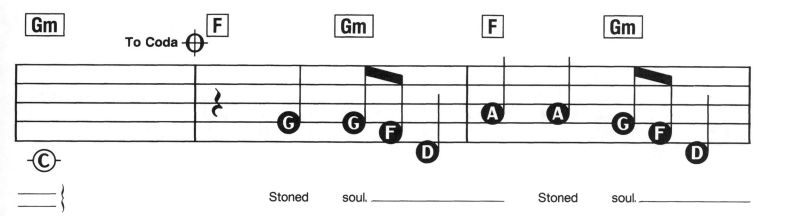

Stoned   soul,_____ Stoned   soul._____

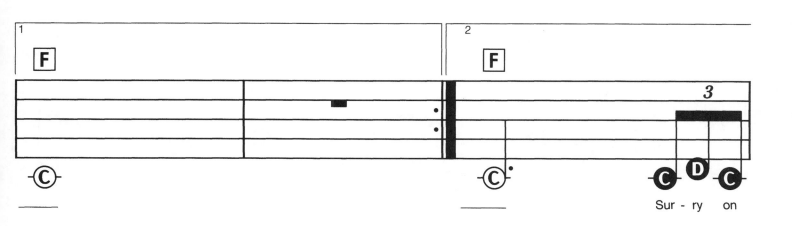

Sur - ry   on

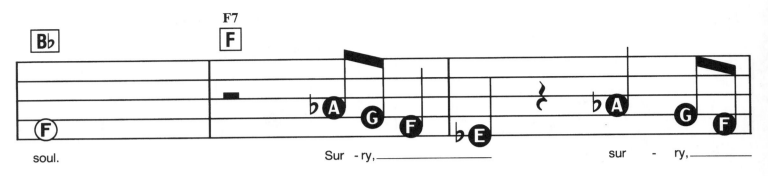

soul. Sur - ry, _____ sur - ry, _____

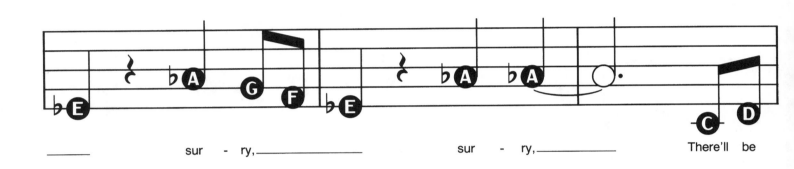

_____ sur - ry, _____ sur - ry, _____ There'll be

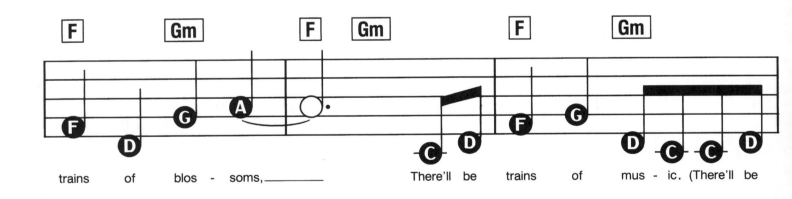

trains of blos - soms, _____ There'll be trains of mus - ic. (There'll be

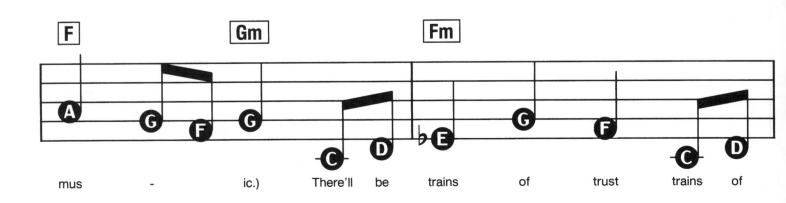

mus - ic.) There'll be trains of trust trains of

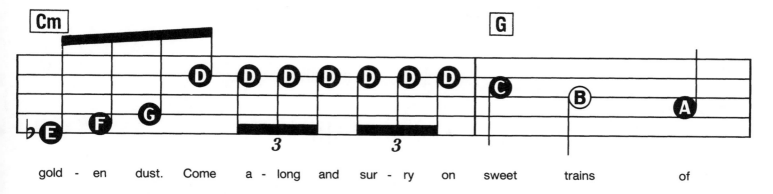

gold - en dust. Come a - long and sur - ry on sweet trains of

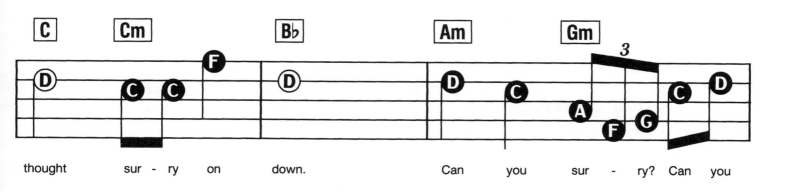

thought sur - ry on down. Can you sur - ry? Can you

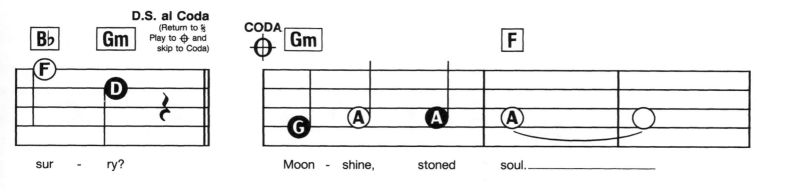

sur - ry?

Moon - shine, stoned soul._____

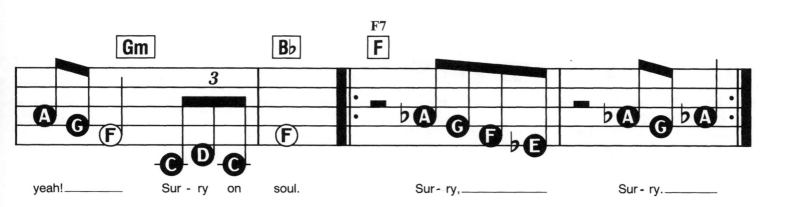

yeah!_____ Sur - ry on soul. Sur - ry,_____ Sur - ry._____

Summer Breeze

Registration 7
Rhythm: Rock or Ballad

Words and Music by James Seals
and Dash Crofts

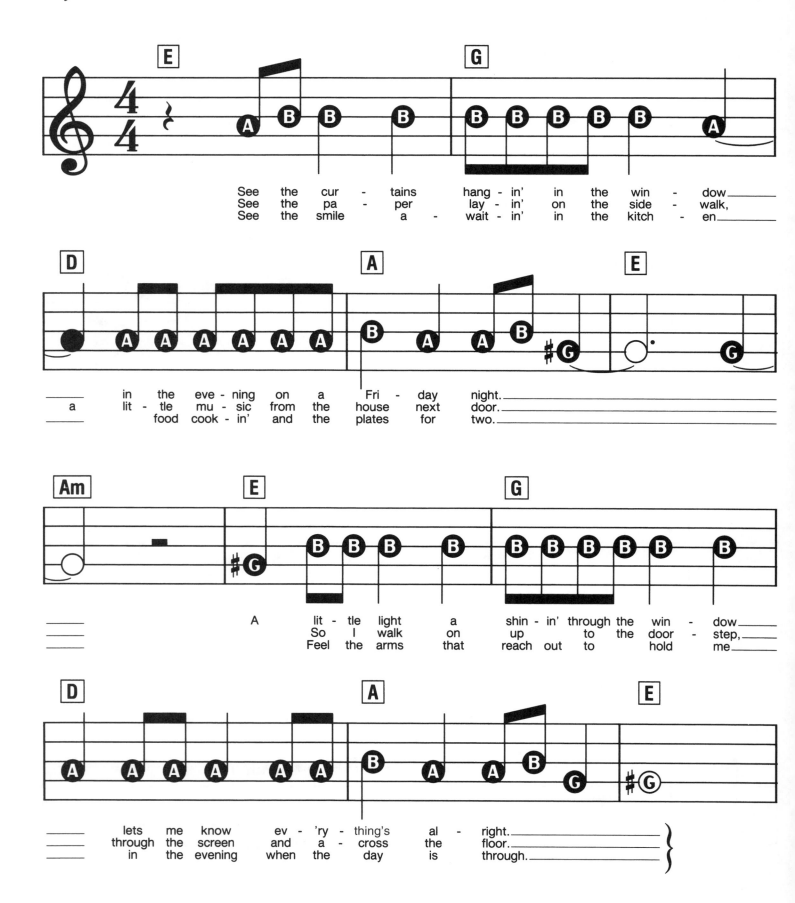

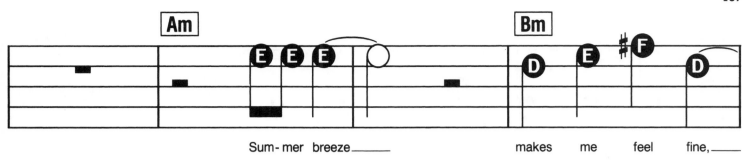

Sum-mer breeze_____ makes me feel fine,_____

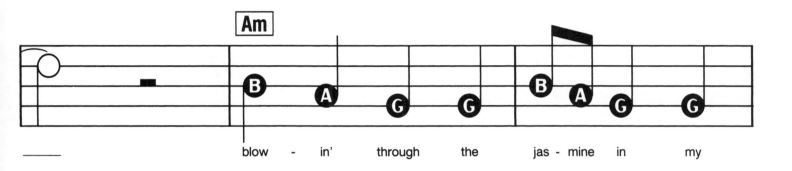

_____ blow - in' through the jas - mine in my

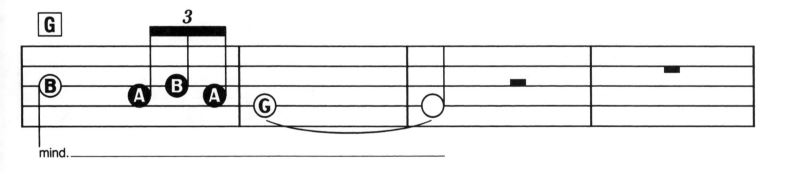

mind._____

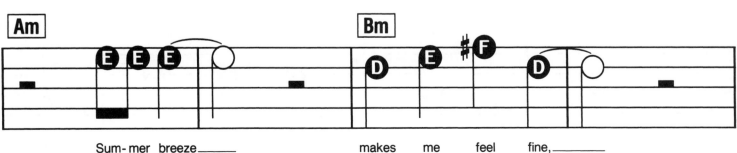

Sum-mer breeze_____ makes me feel fine,_____

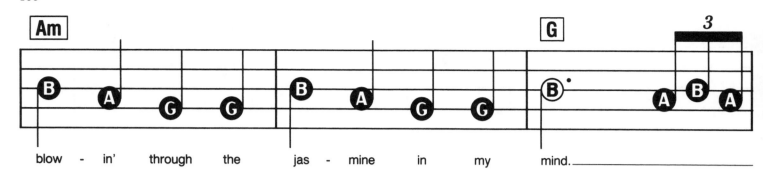

blow - in' through the jas - mine in my mind.

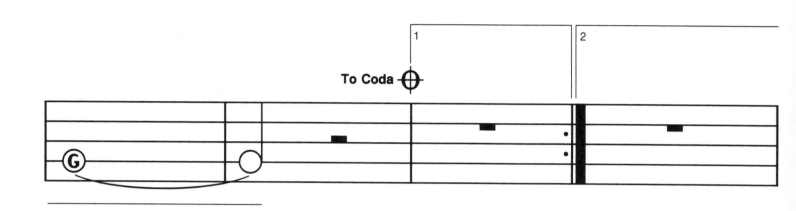

To Coda

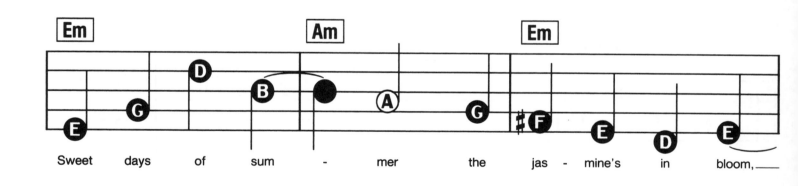

Sweet days of sum - mer the jas - mine's in bloom,

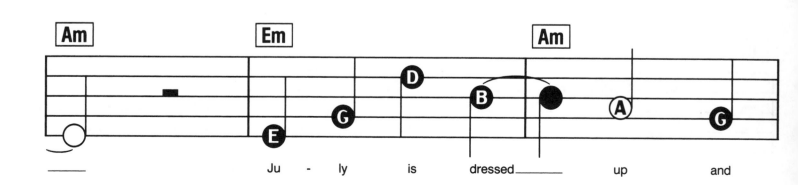

Ju - ly is dressed up and

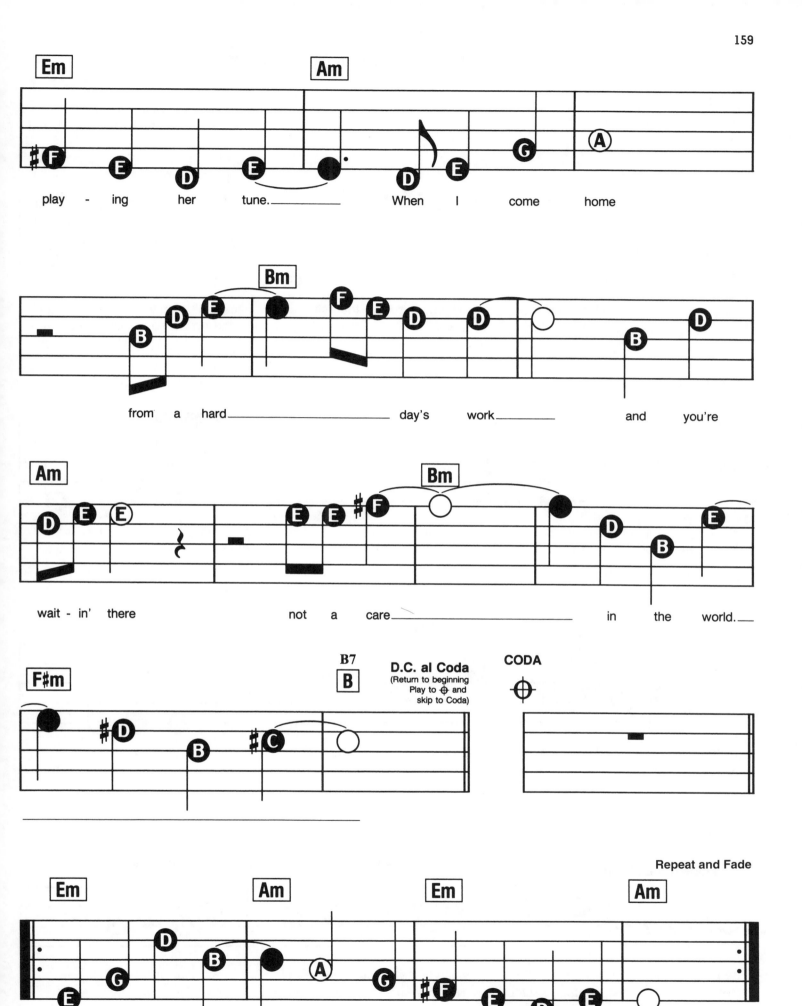

Summer in the City

Registration 9
Rhythm: Rock or 8-Beat

Words and Music by John Sebastian,
Steve Boone and Mark Sebastian

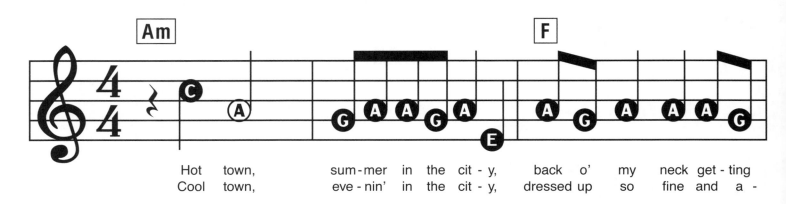

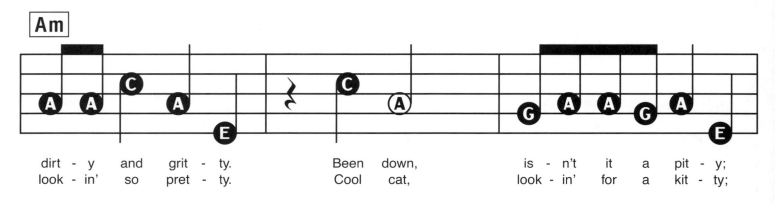

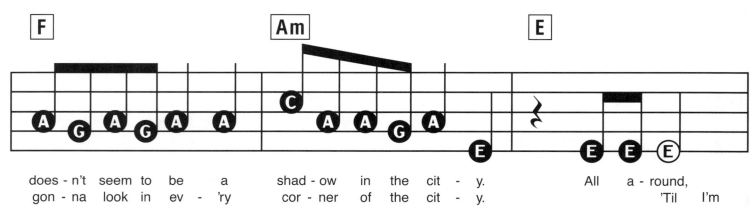

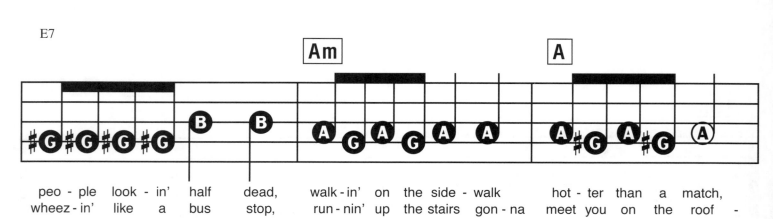

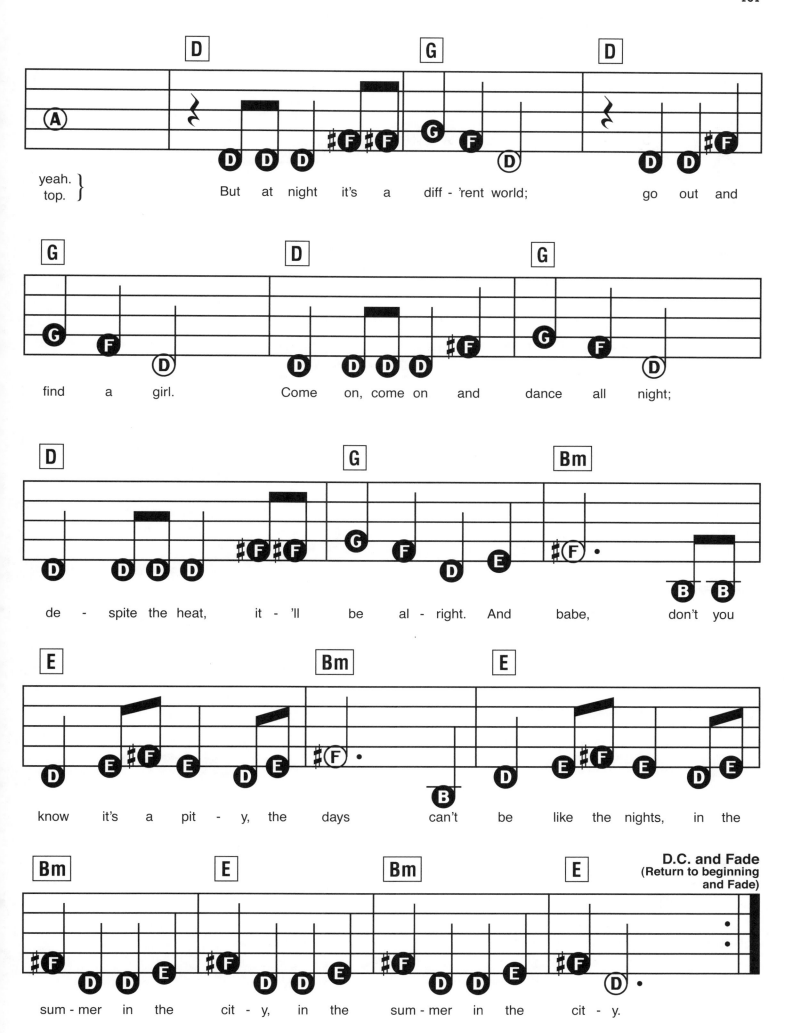

Sunshine Superman

Registration 4
Rhythm: Country Rock or Rock

Words and Music by
Donovan Leitch

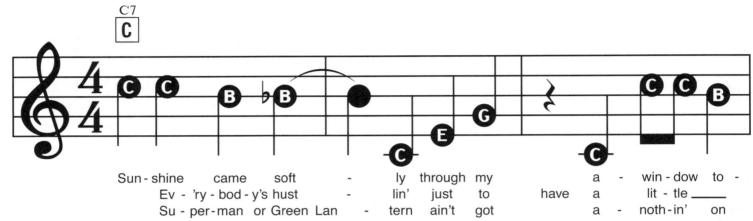

Sun - shine came soft - ly through my a a - win - dow to -
Ev - 'ry - bod - y's hust - lin' just to have a a lit - tle _____
Su - per - man or Green Lan - tern ain't got a - noth - in' on

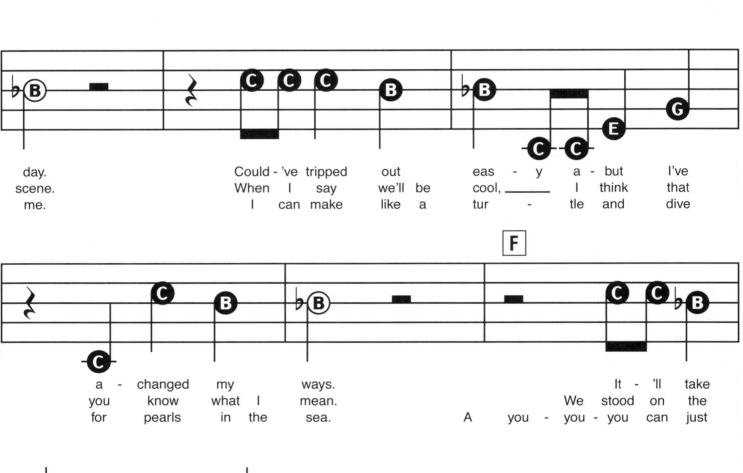

day. Could - 've tripped out eas - y a - but I've
scene. When I say we'll be cool, _____ I think that
me. I can make like a tur - tle and dive

a - changed my ways. It - 'll take
you know what I mean. We stood on the
for pearls in the sea. A you - you - you can just

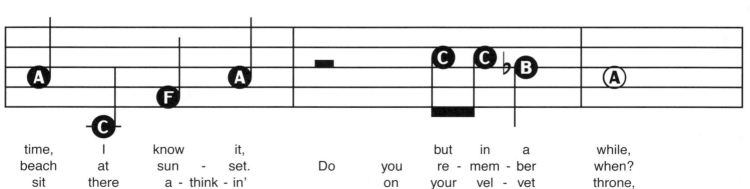

time, I know it, but in a while,
beach at sun - set. Do you re - mem - ber when?
sit there a - think - in' on your vel - vet throne,

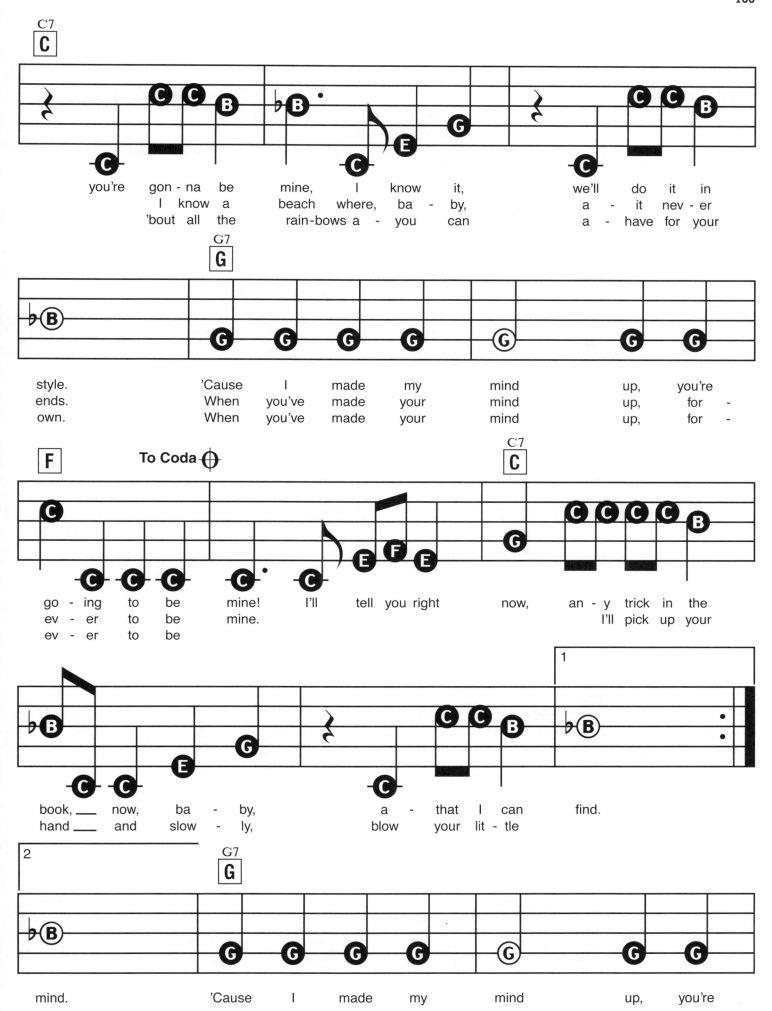

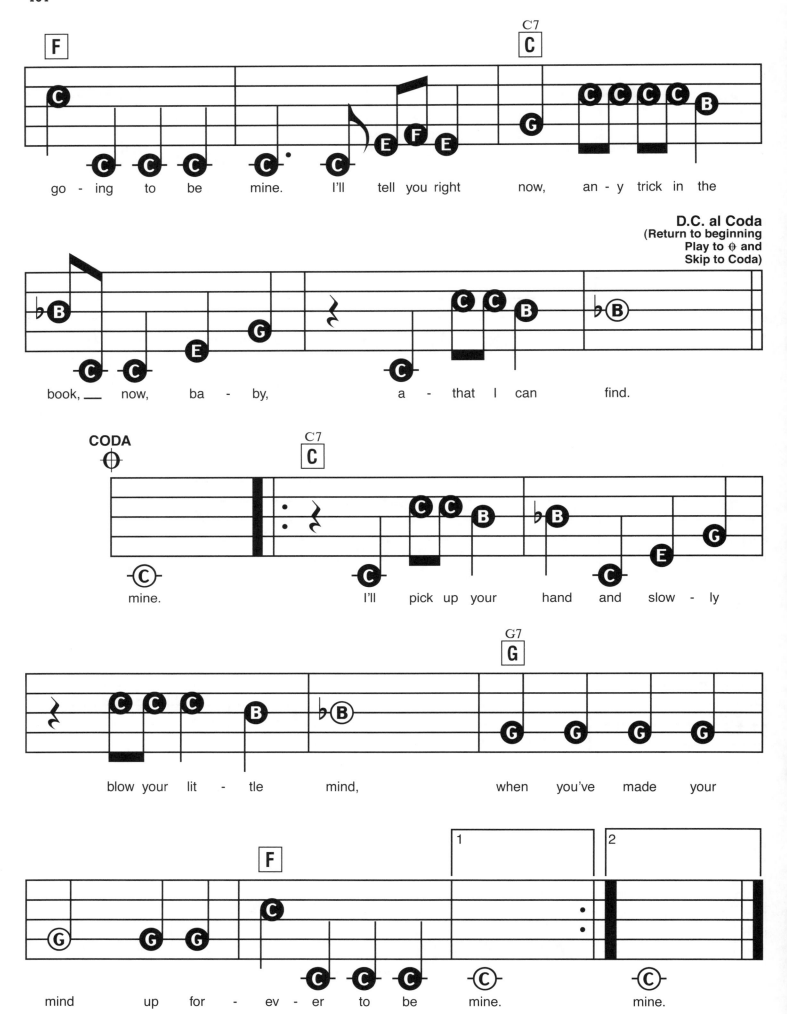

Teach Your Children

Registration 8
Rhythm: 4/4 Ballad

Words and Music by
Graham Nash

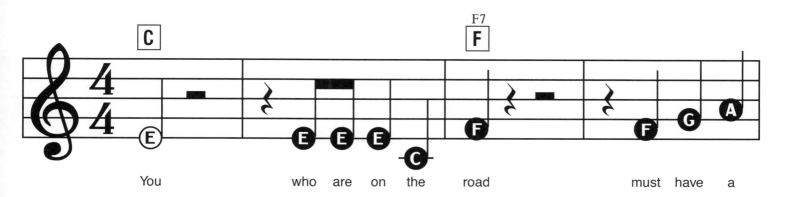

You who are on the road must have a

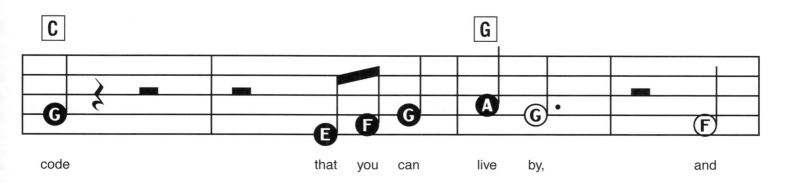

code that you can live by, and

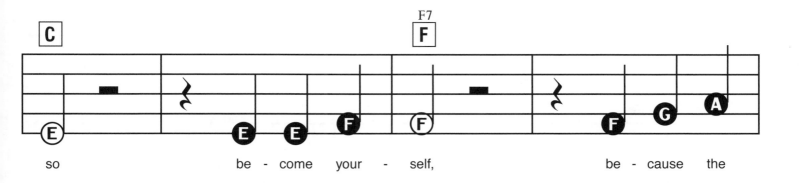

so be - come your - self, be - cause the

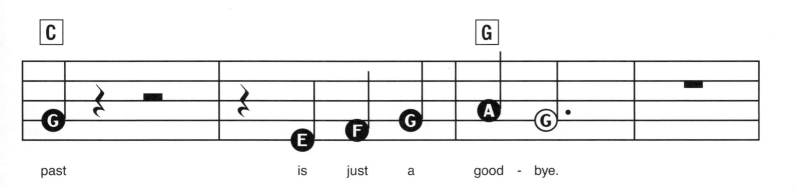

past is just a good - bye.

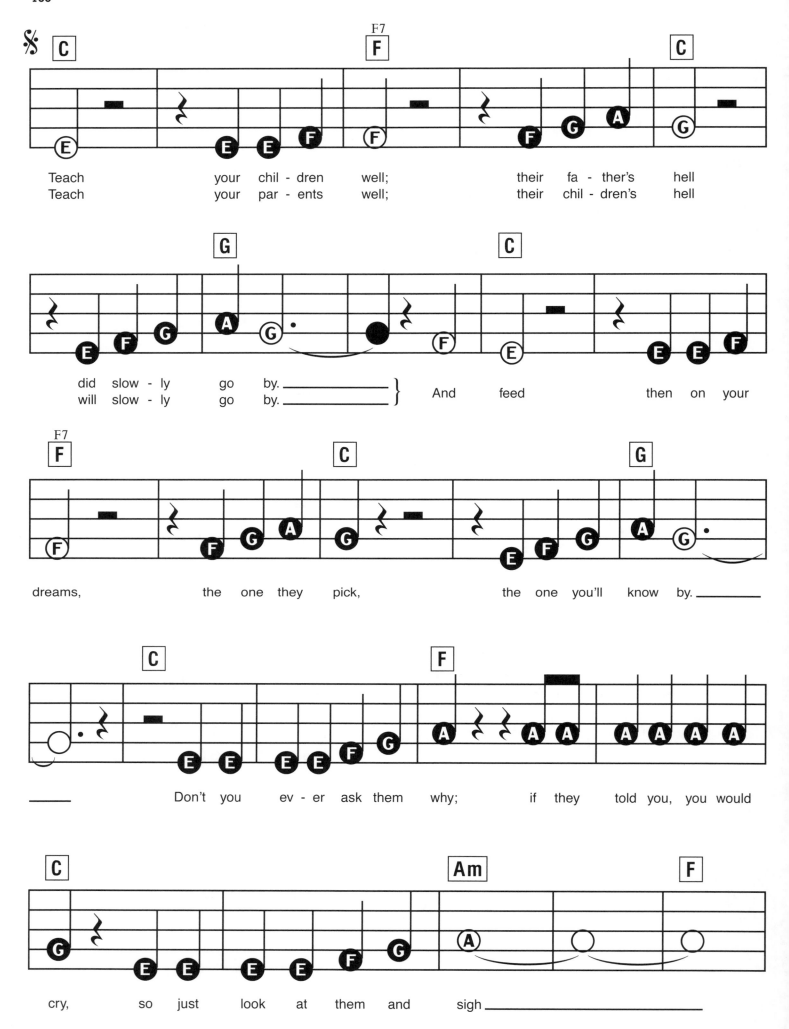

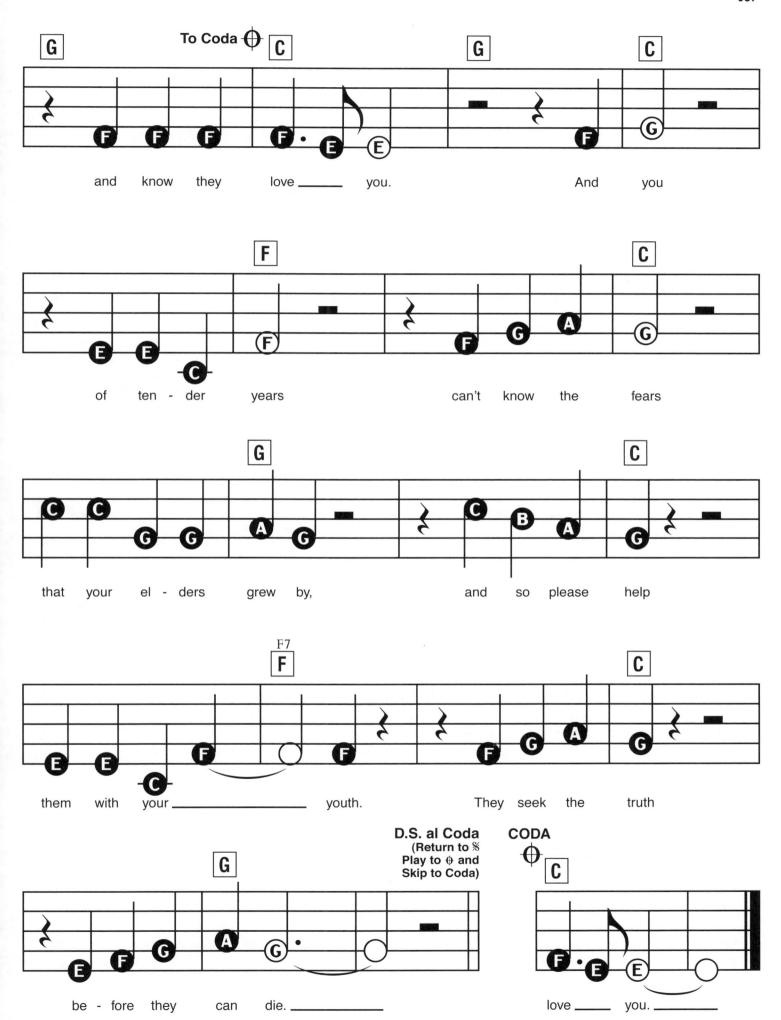

Those Were the Days

Registration 3
Rhythm: Fox Trot or March

Words and Music by
Gene Raskin

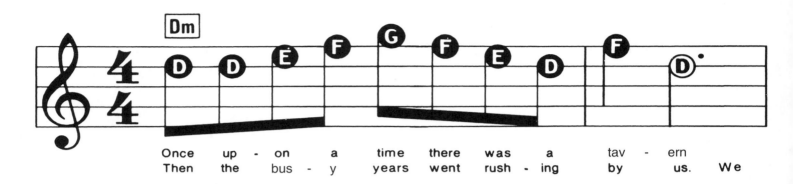

Once up-on a time there was a tav-ern
Then the bus-y years went rush-ing by us. We

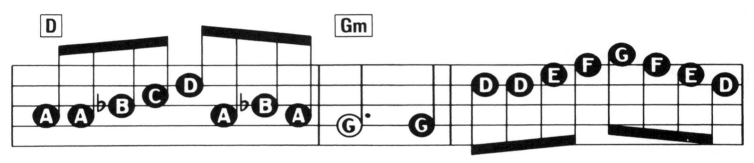

Where we used to raise a glass or two. Re-mem-ber how we laughed a-way the
lost our star-ry no-tions on the way. If by chance I'd see you in the

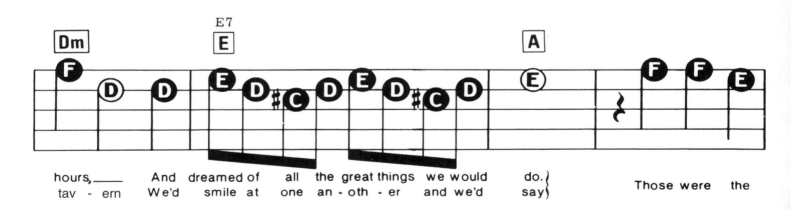

hours,_____ And dreamed of all the great things we would do.
tav-ern We'd smile at one an-oth-er and we'd say

Those were the

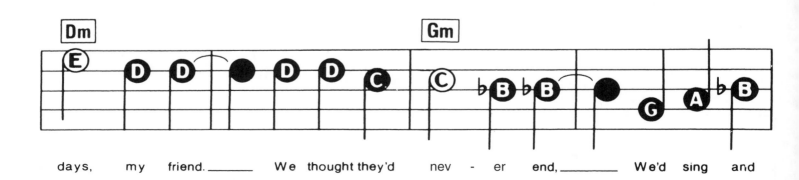

days, my friend._____ We thought they'd nev-er end,_____ We'd sing and

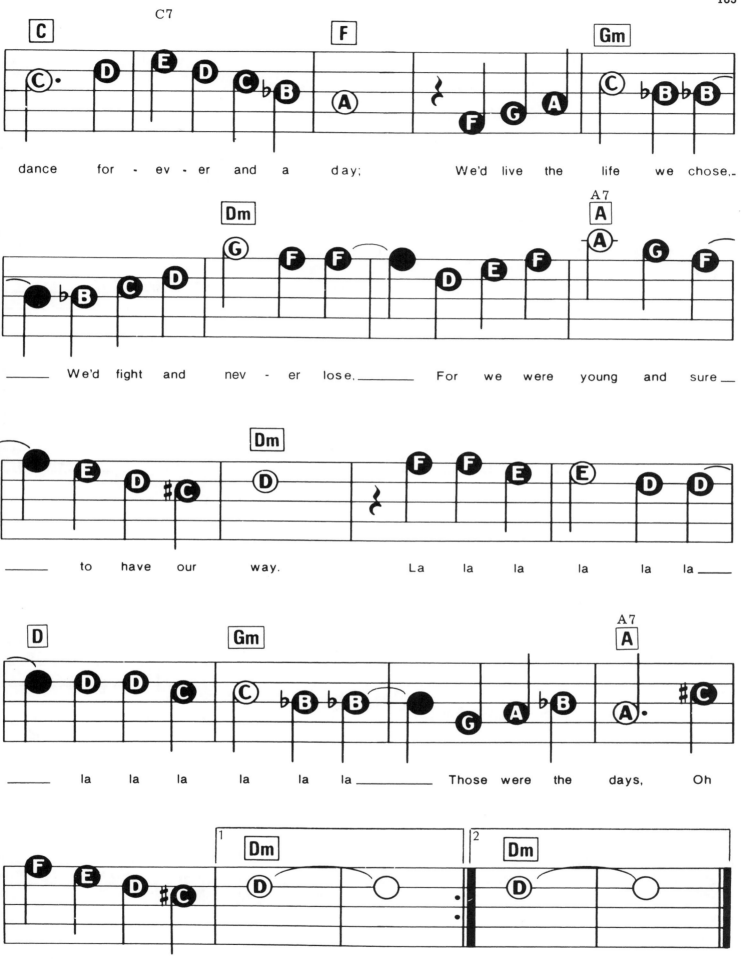

Time in a Bottle

Registration 8
Rhythm: Waltz

Words and Music by
Jim Croce

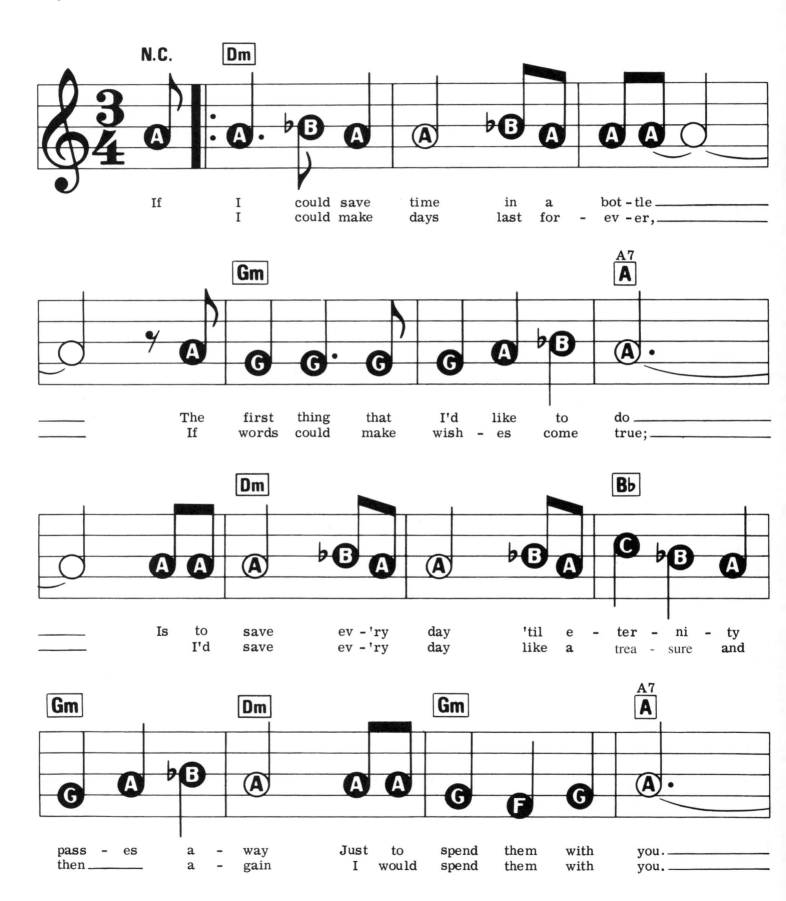

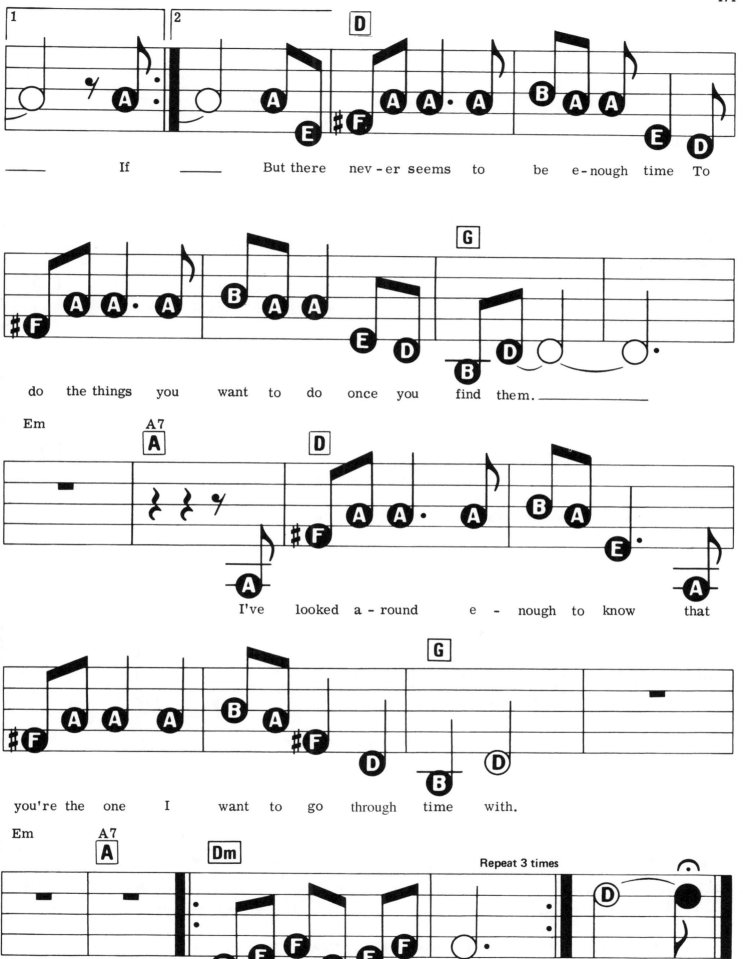

If _____ But there nev-er seems to be e-nough time To

do the things you want to do once you find them. _____

I've looked a-round e-nough to know that

you're the one I want to go through time with.

(Instrumental)

Turn! Turn! Turn!
(To Everything There Is a Season)

Registration 2
Rhythm: Ballad or Fox Trot

Words from the Book of Ecclesiastes
Adaptation and Music by Pete Seeger

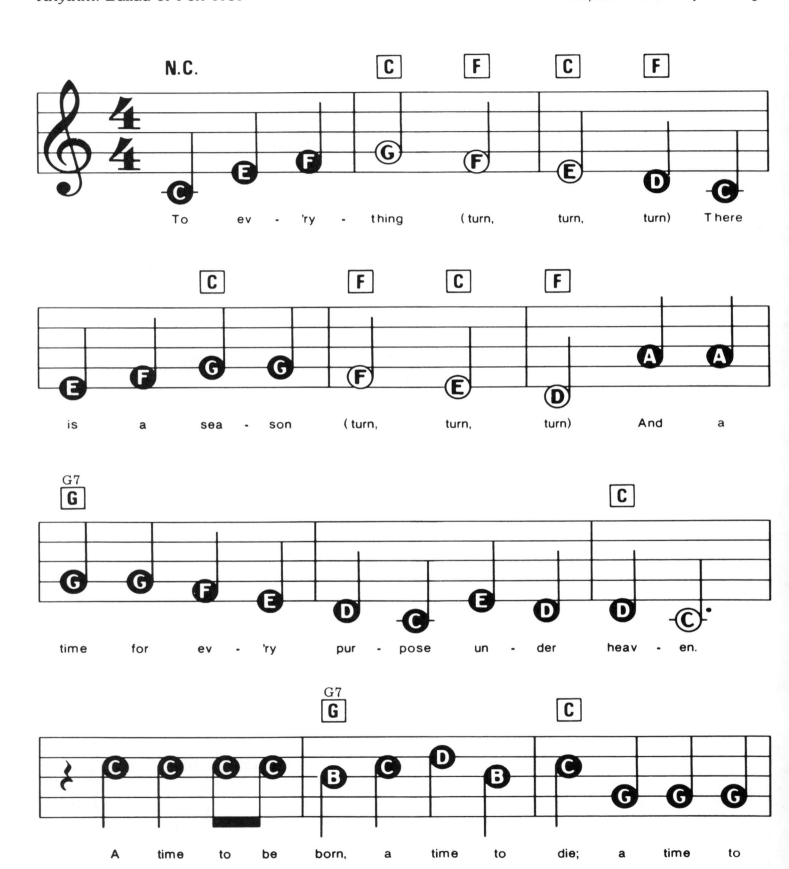

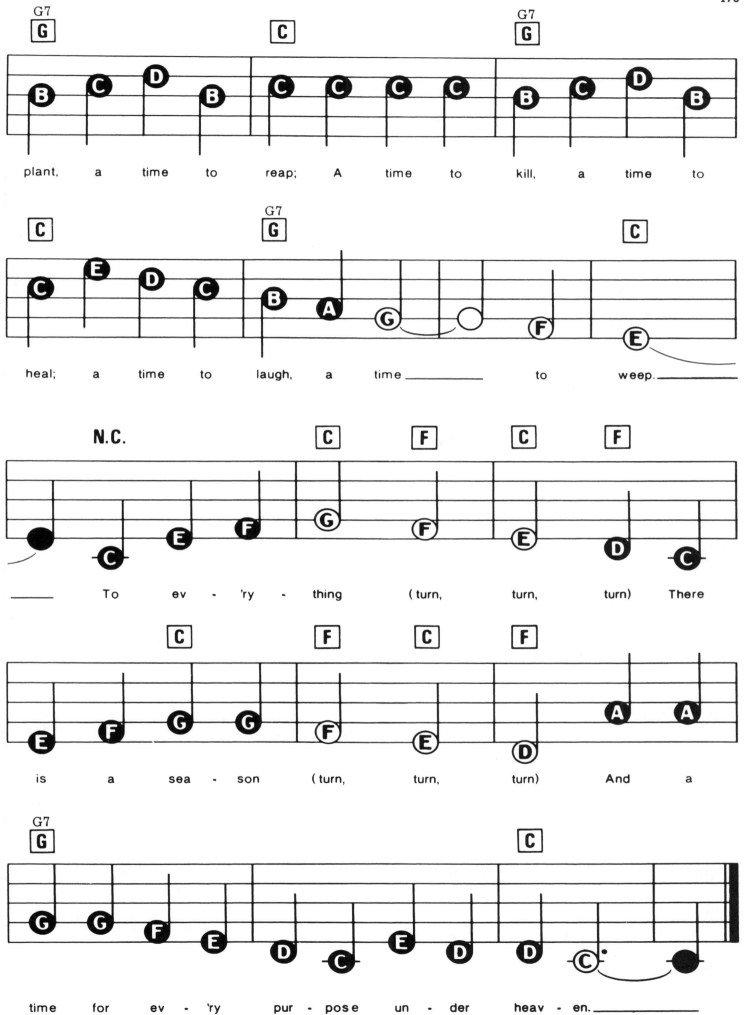

Up, Up and Away

Registration 2
Rhythm: Rock or Jazz Rock

Words and Music by
Jimmy Webb

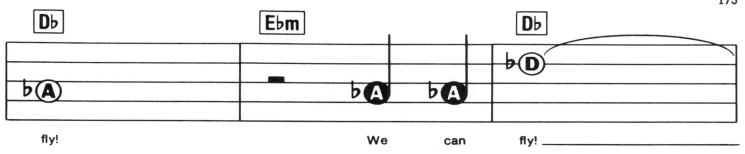

fly! We can fly! _____

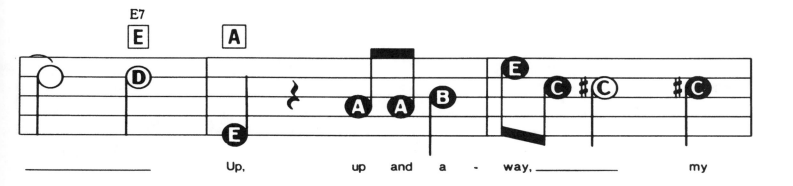

_____ Up, up and a - way, _____ my

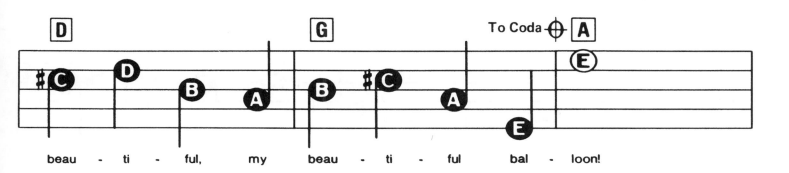

beau - ti - ful, my beau - ti - ful bal - loon!

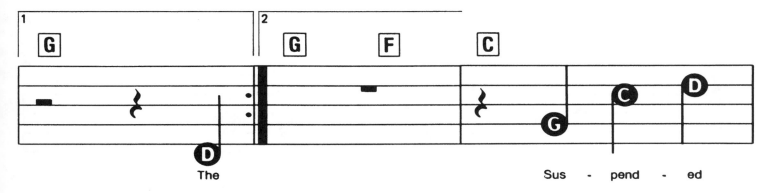

The Sus - pend - ed

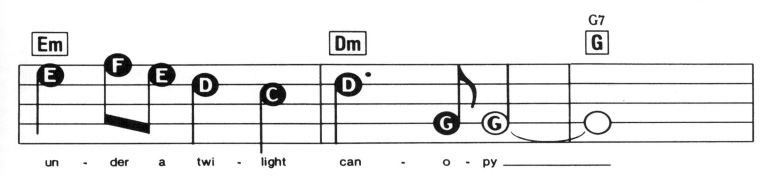

un - der a twi - light can - o - py _____

176

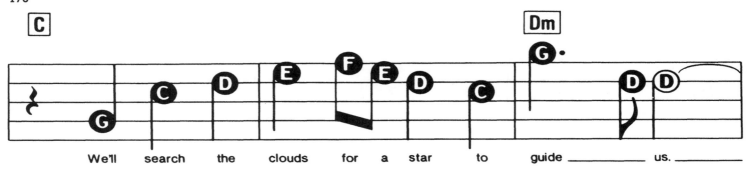

We'll search the clouds for a star to guide _____ us. _____

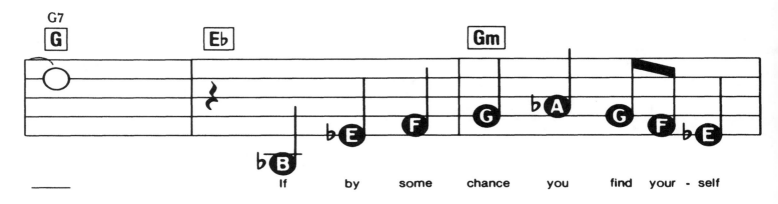

_____ If by some chance you find your - self

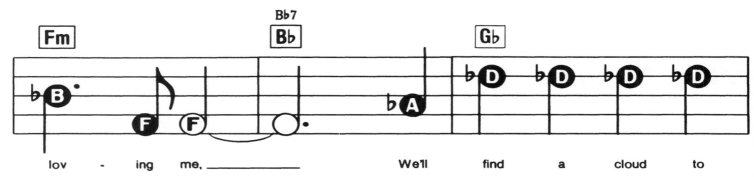

lov - ing me, _____ We'll find a cloud to

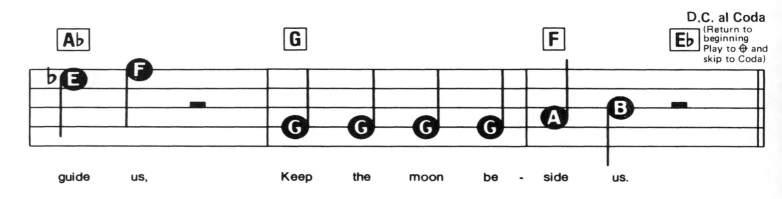

guide us, Keep the moon be - side us.

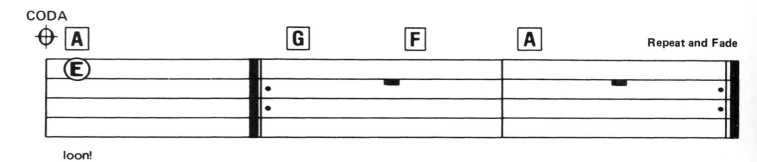

loon!

A Whiter Shade of Pale

Registration 6
Rhythm: Rock

Words and Music by Keith Reid,
Gary Brooker and Matthew Fisher

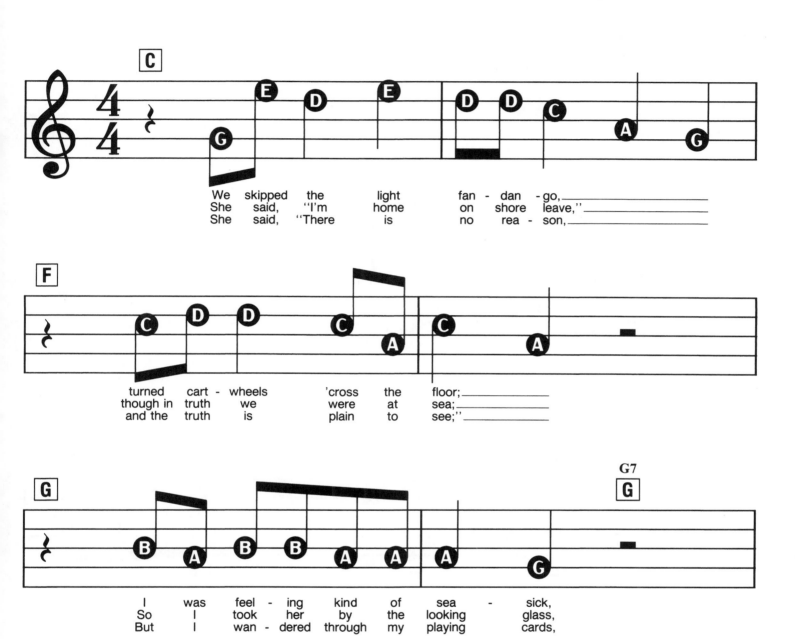

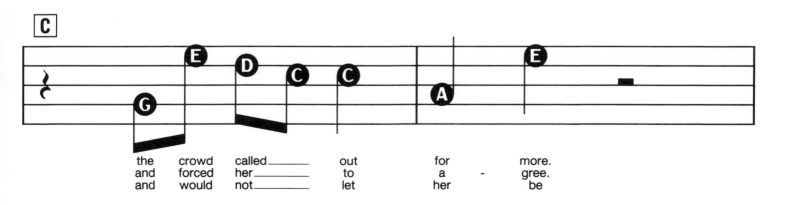

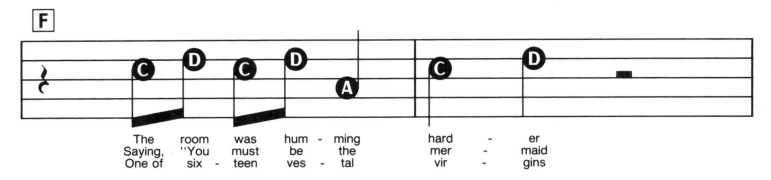

The room was hum - ming hard - er
Saying, "You must be the mer - maid
One of six - teen ves - tal vir - gins

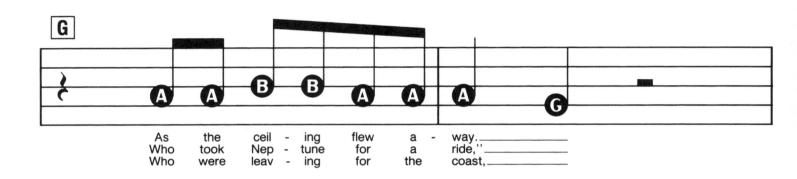

As the ceil - ing flew a - way._____
Who took Nep - tune for a ride,"_____
Who were leav - ing for the coast,_____

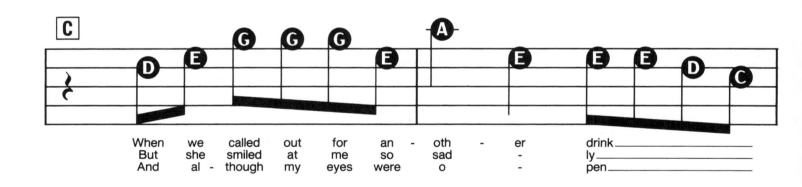

When we called out for an - oth - er drink_____
But she smiled at me so sad - ly_____
And al - though my eyes were o - pen_____

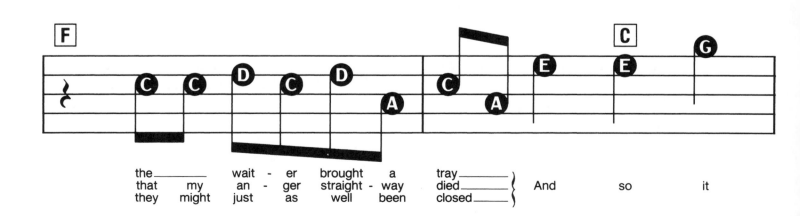

the_____ wait - er brought a tray_____ } And so it
that my an - ger straight - way died_____ }
they might just as well been closed_____ }

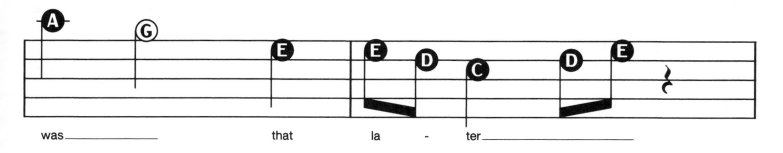

was _____ that la - ter _____

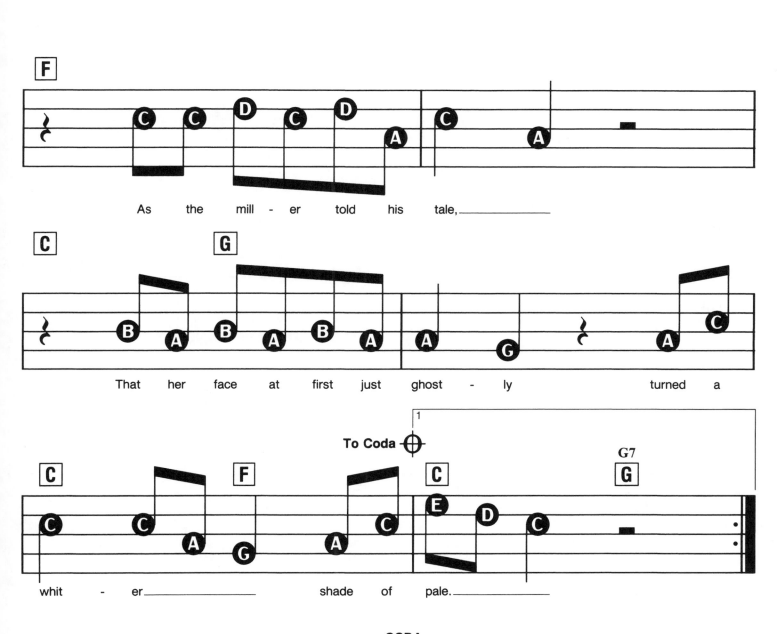

As the mill - er told his tale, _____

That her face at first just ghost - ly turned a

whit - er _____ shade of pale. _____

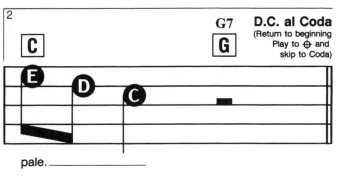

pale. _____

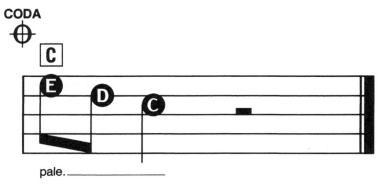

pale. _____

Where Have All the Flowers Gone?

Registration 10
Rhythm: Ballad

Words and Music by
Pete Seeger

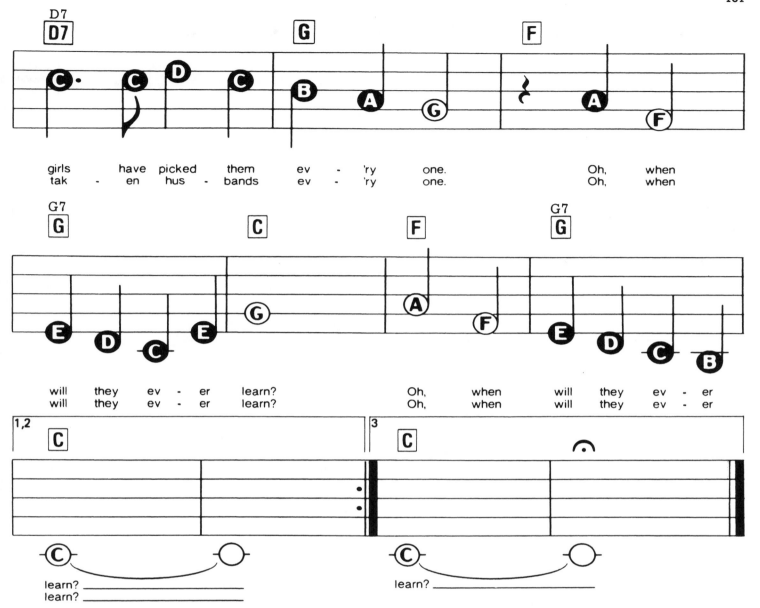

girls have picked them ev - 'ry one. Oh, when
tak - en hus - bands ev - 'ry one. Oh, when

will they ev - er learn? Oh, when will they ev - er
will they ev - er learn? Oh, when will they ev - er

learn? _____
learn? _____

learn? _____

Additional Lyrics

3. Where have all the young men gone?
   Long time passing.
   Where have all the young men gone?
   Long time ago.
   Where have all the young men gone?
   They're all in uniform.
   Oh, when will they ever learn?
   Oh, when will they ever learn?

Wild Thing

Registration 7
Rhythm: Rock

Words and Music by
Chip Taylor

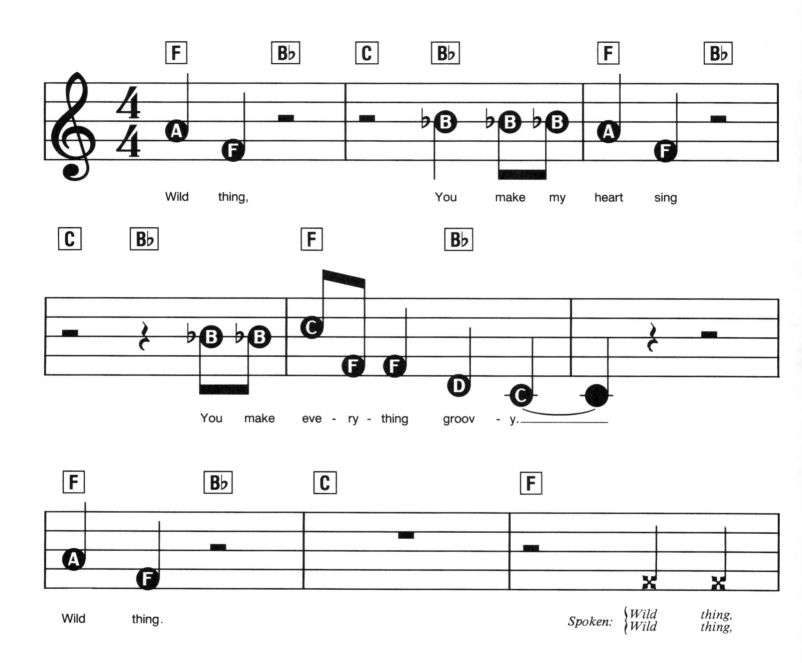

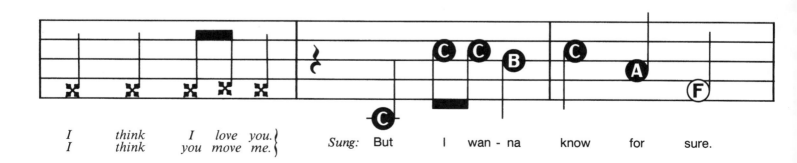

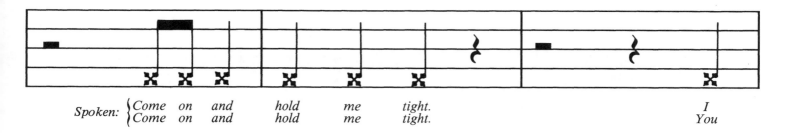

Spoken: { *Come on and hold me tight.* *Come on and hold me tight.* *I* *You*

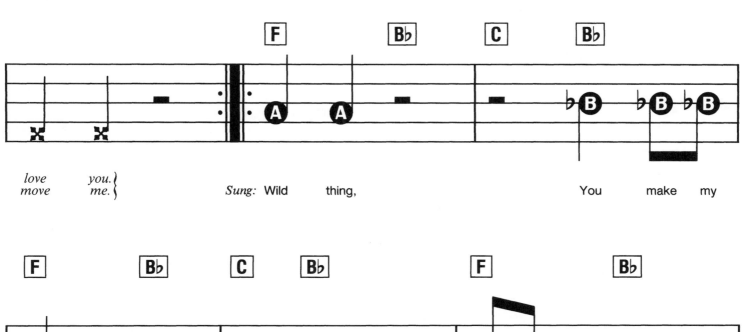

love you. *move me.* } *Sung:* Wild thing, You make my

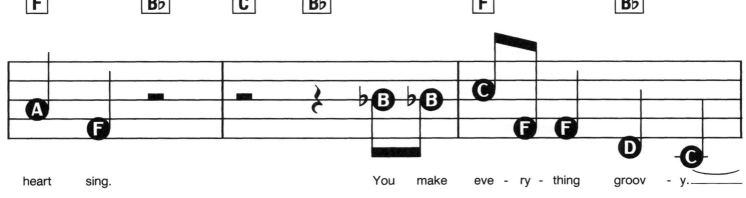

heart sing. You make eve - ry - thing groov - y.

Repeat and Fade

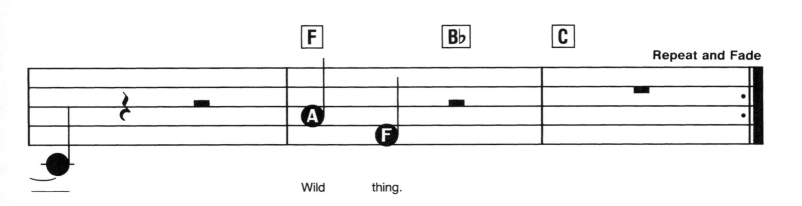

Wild thing.

 **Registration Guide**

- Match the Registration number on the song to the corresponding numbered category below. Select and activate an instrumental sound available on your instrument.

- Choose an automatic rhythm appropriate to the mood and style of the song. (Consult your Owner's Guide for proper operation of automatic rhythm features.)

- Adjust the tempo and volume controls to comfortable settings.

Registration

1	Mellow	Flutes, Clarinet, Oboe, Flugel Horn, Trombone, French Horn, Organ Flutes
2	Ensemble	Brass Section, Sax Section, Wind Ensemble, Full Organ, Theater Organ
3	Strings	Violin, Viola, Cello, Fiddle, String Ensemble, Pizzicato, Organ Strings
4	Guitars	Acoustic/Electric Guitars, Banjo, Mandolin, Dulcimer, Ukulele, Hawaiian Guitar
5	Mallets	Vibraphone, Marimba, Xylophone, Steel Drums, Bells, Celesta, Chimes
6	Liturgical	Pipe Organ, Hand Bells, Vocal Ensemble, Choir, Organ Flutes
7	Bright	Saxophones, Trumpet, Mute Trumpet, Synth Leads, Jazz/Gospel Organs
8	Piano	Piano, Electric Piano, Honky Tonk Piano, Harpsichord, Clavi
9	Novelty	Melodic Percussion, Wah Trumpet, Synth, Whistle, Kazoo, Perc. Organ
10	Bellows	Accordion, French Accordion, Mussette, Harmonica, Pump Organ, Bagpipes